Those Great
COWBOY SIDEKICKS

By
DAVID ROTHEL

McCOOK COMMUNITY COLLEGE
Learning Resource Center

Scarecrow Press, Inc.
Metuchen, N.J., & London 1984

Library of Congress Cataloging in Publication Data

Rothel, David, 1936–
    Those great cowboy sidekicks.

    Bibliography: p.
    Includes index.
    1. Western films––History and criticism.
2. Comedy films––History and criticism. I. Title.
PN1995.9.W4R673 1984   791.43'028'0922   84-10513
ISBN 0-8108-1707-1

In memory of

my brother Bob

I don't think he knew anything about cowboy
sidekicks, but he knew a lot about little brothers.

CONTENTS

Acknowledgments

When I started researching this book, I quickly discovered that very little had been written about the cowboy sidekicks when they were actively pursuing their craft. It was, therefore, necessary for me to contact many people who knew and/or worked with the sidekicks—actors, screenwriters, directors, relatives, friends—to see if they would be gracious enough to share with me their memories of these fine character actors. I am deeply indebted to the ladies and gentlemen listed below who literally spent hours with me discussing the sidekicks. Their firsthand knowledge of the cowboy sidekicks has made this history of their work possible.

As in any research project of this sort, the quest for the stories of the sidekicks took me to the works of my fellow writers in the Western genre. You fine writers who scattered information here and there about the sidekicks while pursuing other Western subjects, unknowingly dropped nuggets of informational gold which I have mined to help flesh out the profiles which follow. In many instances you invited me to utilize articles for my research which you had written about the sidekicks. For this I am deeply grateful. I have attempted to acknowledge each and every source of information, and I have also endeavored in good faith to never overstep the bounds of fair use. I have acknowledged your printed sources of information either in the text or in the bibliography of the book.

Equally important for mention here are those people who cheerfully provided obscure bits of information during late-night phone calls, who loaned me books, who made phone calls for me, who provided me with phone numbers and addresses when an informational source seemed to vanish from the face of the earth, and those who simply offered encouragement during the two years of researching and writing. I couldn't have done it without you!

I would like to express my sincere thanks and appreciation to the following persons who provided interviews, information, and/or assistance in the preparation of this book. And to the one person whom I may have inadvertently overlooked, I offer an especially heartfelt "thank you" for your anonymous contribution.

Slim Andrews

Jim Bannon

Don Barry

Rand Brooks

Ewing M. Brown

James Brown

Pat Buttram

Yakima Canutt

Buster Crabbe

Al Daub

Eddie Dean

Linda and Ron Downey

Oliver Drake

Tommy Farrell

Carolyn and Kirby Grant

Clark Hayes

Don Key

Pee Wee King

Lash LaRue

Gordon MacDonnell

Petria MacDonnell

Jock Mahoney

Richard Martin

Frank Mitchell

Eric Moon, Jr.

Ray Neilsen

Nell O'Day

Michael Pitts

Laura Rothel

John A. Rutherford

Jim Ryan

Fred Scott

Wayne Short

Richard B. Smith, III

Lillian Spencer

Charles Starrett

Greg Stewart

Ken Taylor

Merle Travis

Jimmy Wakely

Pat Watkowski

Nick Williams

Michael Wolff

Rob Word

and Rex Allen, Gene Autry, and Roy Rogers for their interviews for **The Singing Cowboys,** which provided additional input for this book,

and my wife Nancy for everything!

A Few Words Before Saddling Up...

I think perhaps a few words regarding the nature and format of this book are in order before we go galloping off into the chapters which lie ahead. The title of the book tells much about what you can expect to find as you turn the pages—profiles of the great cowboy sidekicks who rode alongside our cowboy heroes of the silver screen.

But a writer of this type of book runs into problems as he starts his research. He must be selective in his choice of performers, or he will find himself lost in a cloud of trail dust kicked up by the profusion of character actors, leading men, juveniles, and Indian actors who, for a few films or even dozens of films, rode beside the cowboy as a sidekick. If all the actors who ever played sidekicks were included in this book, the publisher would have to include a cart in which to haul around the hefty volume.

I have, therefore, limited the scope of the book to include only the *comic* sidekicks of the B Western series. The young romantic sidekicks such as Russell Hayden, Rand Brooks, and James Ellison are left for another time, as are the Indians (Tonto and Little Beaver) and the singing sidekicks such as Bob Nolan, Ray Whitley, and Foy Willing.

The B Western series produced from the mid-1930s through the early 1950s represent the heyday of the cowboy hero and his comic sidekick. It seems an appropriate trail to follow through these pages.

The filmographies include only the series films in which the sidekick appeared. In most instances these films cover the performer's most memorable appearances and, since some of the actors appeared in literally hundreds of films—Westerns and otherwise—during their careers, it was the only way to keep the filmographies from overpowering the book.

I have included notes within many filmographies regarding appearances of sidekicks in character or bit parts. It is always enjoyable to unexpectedly discover a familiar comic face peaking out from the screen. My notes may help the reader to be on the lookout for such appearances.

A cowboy-and-Indians childhood friend of mine once commented that he never felt that he could successfully play the cowboy hero in our Western games. My friend was at a rather gawky and clumsy age, and pretending to be the cowboy hero such as Gene Autry, Roy Rogers, or The Durango Kid made him feel uncomfortable. He always wanted to play the sidekick of the hero. He maintained that they were a little bit more "human." They didn't have to be perfect like the hero. If they stumbled and fell down, it was all right. The cowboy hero couldn't do that sort of thing. My friend thought the sidekicks probably had a lot more fun, too.

Let's saddle up and hit the trail.

I.

Out Where a Friend is a Friend

The Sidekick Superstars

SMILEY BURNETTE

"Hey, you kids know ol' Frog."

Lester Alvin (Smiley) Burnette was certainly not the first comic sidekick in Western films, but there is little disagreement that when he joined Gene Autry in their Republic Pictures' series in 1934, the cowboy comic sidekick was truly born and most of those who would follow him presented only a variation of the comic capers Smiley had created—each successor adding his own particular quirk to the sagebrush shenanigans.

Smiley was a far more complex person in real life than the cactus court jester, Frog Millhouse, he limned in the Autry and later films. Bending an ear to the cowboy stars who worked with Smiley, one gets a varied capsule perspective of this Western funnyman.

Gene Autry: *(On Smiley Burnette) In that part of the Southwest where I was born, on the Texas-Oklahoma line, they had a saying to describe a man who was loyal: "He'll do to ride the river with."*

Sunset Carson: *I wound up with second billing next to Smiley Burnette on our four films because I was smaller then he was. (laugh) You couldn't see a 165 pound kid, seventeen years old, whipping a 289 pound man. I didn't give him no argument. (laugh) But Smiley was a great guy to work with. The only thing we had to watch was his milk shakes and ice cream. He was always eating.*

Charles "Durango Kid" Starrett: *We had a lot of fun together. I sometimes think that a lot of people didn't understand Smiley. We got along fine. In many ways Smiley was sometimes his worst enemy, but he was a very wonderful guy. Smiley sometimes wanted to take the bit, you might say, and run with the scene, but I*

liked working with Smiley.

Jock "Range Rider" Mahoney: *Smiley was a hell of a businessman. He was a tough guy with a buck. When he would go out on tour, he would have a guy there with a camera. Smiley would have his picture taken with any kid in the audience. The kid would get a stub with the number of his picture, and Smiley would get a buck. When the picture was developed, it would be sent to the kid. This was back in the late 1940s when a buck was a buck.*

Kirby "Sky King" Grant: *He was one of the greediest persons I have ever known. You know that shirt that he wore, that black check shirt? He bought bolts of seconds of that material at Penney's. He cut off little inch squares and fastened them to a card with his autograph on it and sold them for two bits apiece. He would, of course, make a lot of friends around the country on his tours and he would never, never stay in a hotel or motel; he would always go to these acquaintances and stay and live off them. If he could have figured out a way to have sold his toenail parings, he probably would have.*

Merle Travis: *He was the reason I went to Hollywood. I'd just got out of the Marine Corps and went back to Cincinnati, Ohio, where I was working on a radio station. It was right in the dead of winter and the streets were covered with ice and everything. Smiley was playing a theater there, so I went backstage to talk with him. He was playing with old Bojangles Robinson, the Black dancer. On the way* *to eat, Smiley's feet liked to slipped out from under him and he stopped and said, "I'd rather live in California and eat lettuce than live in Cincinnati and eat caviar." I said to him, "It's really that good, huh?" He said, "Yeah." The next morning I was on a troop train, sleeping on the floor and everything. That's the reason I went to Hollywood—because of Smiley Burnette. Later I worked some pictures with Mr. Starrett and Smiley, and sung some of his songs. He was a good friend.*

Pat Buttram: *I knew Smiley when Autry found him in Tuscola, Illinois, at a radio station. Gene was working at the WLS "Barn Dance" and I was on the show. Smiley did more to help sidekicks in movies than anyone else because he established it as part of the series. In that first series when he and Autry hit, it was really big for both of them. He did go his own way a lot. He was an enterprising guy; he had all kinds of gimmicks going, but he helped a lot of people. He always said, "You know, when the elevator gets up near the top floor, send it down to bring up somebody else." He was always working with young kids. I think he was an inspiration to a lot of kids, and I loved the guy. I really understood him—maybe because I didn't have to ride alongside of him. He was always a friend of mine and a wonderful memory.*

★   ★   ★

Bev Barnett, a publicity writer for Gene Autry, Smiley, John Wayne, and others, wrote a short biography on Smiley in the mid-1940s for a small publication called "Cowboy Music World." Despite the show biz puffery of the forties that it evokes, the piece adequately capsulizes Smiley's early years. My thanks to Gene Autry collector and historian, Lillian Spencer, for making it available.

Life Story of Smiley Burnette
by
Bev Barnett

Smiley Burnette climbed the ladder of success the hard way. He was born in the town of Summum, Illinois. His parents, Mr. and Mrs. G.W. Burnette, were ordained ministers, who worked at the task of maintaining a small town pastorate. Smiley was brought up in a modest and frugal household, but was always surrounded with love and affection.

As a boy, his family moved to Astoria, Illinois, and it was there that he first manifested an interest in music that was to have a profound effect on his future career. A sympathetic musician living in Astoria kindled Smiley's enthusiasm for music by loaning him his instruments, of which he owned a score. At the ripe age of nine, Smiley earned his first money as an entertainer by playing the musical saw at a Y.M.C.A. banquet in Carthage, Illinois, for which he received three dollars.

Young Smiley's musical avidity ripened intensively in high school. He formed a band of his own, played in the school orchestra, took part in student operettas and musicals, and was an omnipresent figure at any and all functions involving music.

When Smiley graduated from Astoria, Illinois High School, he went to work in a canning factory. Then he was a motorcycle delivery boy for a department store in Astoria. Next he sold hot dogs on the campus of the University of Illinois during football games. For a while he drove a taxi in Urbana, Illinois, and later a concrete truck for the state. His last job before starting in radio work was as a snow-shoveller.

About this time radio came into its own and a new 100-watt station began operating in the nearby town of Tuscola. An enterprising Champaign furniture merchant offered Smiley a job as the entertainer and announcer for his sponsored program; Smiley leaped at the opportunity. Within two months, youthful Burnette had become the station's chief announcer, entertainer, manager and engineer rolled into one. He opened the station in the morning and closed it at night. While there he learned the words and music to more than two thousand songs, memorizing them from the phonograph records which were the musical programs of the station. Here also he taught himself to play many more instruments.

It was during his tenure at WDZ that a

young but ambitious entertainer named Gene Autry came down to Champaign one day for a personal appearance. He was seeking an accordian player for his stage unit. Someone mentioned the versatile musician working at WDZ. An appointment was made. Smiley played one number for Autry and was hired on the spot.

That was the beginning of the Autry-Burnette friendship. Smiley joined Autry forty-eight hours later in Chicago as a member of the "National Barn Dance" show airing over WLS. The two became fast friends. In 1934 they left Chicago for Hollywood where they made their first picture debut in a Western called **The Phantom Empire.** Immediately afterwards, believing themselves to be the world's worst actors, the two boys went to Louisville, Kentucky and worked on a radio program there.

A short time later the same studio that had made **The Phantom Empire** wired Autry and Burnette that a long term contract awaited them in Hollywood. Back they came. Originally Smiley had been brought out because of his music versatility, but in that first picture, he displayed such a natural flair for comedy that the producer immediately laid plans to feature him as a comedian. That decision proved eventful for Smiley. As Gene's comedy partner he rose rapidly as a favorite with movie fans and has been an essential factor in making the Autry-Burnette team an Ace-high draw from coast to coast.

Smiley portrays the part of Frog Millhouse, the comedy lead of all Autry starring pictures and will again work with him when Gene gets out of the Army. Right now he is working with Charles Starrett in Columbia Western pictures and doing camp shows for the service men.

Smiley Burnette is married to the former Dallas MacDonnell, author of the widely read column, "Roamin' Around Hollywood." They live in a lovely one-story ranch home in the San Fernando Valley with their adopted children: Linda, Stephen and Carolyn. His favorite sport is swimming; his hobby is cooking new and tasty dishes. After the war he plans to travel again in his car trailer.

★   ★   ★

Few people outside the range of that 100 watt station in Tuscola had ever heard of Smiley Burnette until Gene Autry came riding out of the canyons of Chicago on a personal appearance tour. Gene recounts the events this way in his autobiography:

Gene Autry: It happened that we were short a musician on a tour of the Midwest. We were playing at Champaign-Urbana, in a theater near the University of Illinois, and I asked the manager if he knew where I could find an accordian player. He said, "Why, yes, there is a young feller down the road at Tuscola, about twenty-five miles south of here. Works for the radio station. Plays the piano, gittar, sings. Has lots of talent."

He gave me the name, Smiley Burnette, and the number of the station. I got him on the phone, told him who I was, and said, brightly, "I hear you play the accordian."

He said, "Yep, sure do."

I asked him how much he was making at the station.

"Eighteen dollars a week," he said.

"I'll pay you fifty," I told him, "plus your expenses on the road. You think about it and if you want to come with us let me know."

He said, "I just thought about it. You done hired yourself an accordian player."

And so Smiley joined Gene on his personal appearance tours, the "National Barn Dance" radio show on WLS in Chicago, and also played backup on many of the popular Autry recordings of the day. Gene and Smiley became close friends on and off stage, and as Smiley's natural comic procliities crept to the fore, Autry incorporated them into the shows. The two performer discovered that they played off each other very well in front of an audience.

During this incubation period, another of Smiley's abilities came to Autry's attention—composing. Autry has said, "He [Smiley] couldn't read a note of music. He wrote three hundred and fifty songs, some of them with me, and I never saw him take longer than an hour to compose one."

During those early years of the 1930s the livin' may not have been easy for these two cowboy troubadours, but it was good. The routine called for performing on the popular "National Barn Dance"

Smiley Burnette and Gene Autry began their association in 1933. Smiley was Gene's main sidekick during his film career.

radio program, long sessions in the recording studio, and, interspersed, the grueling ordeal of the personal appearance tours. The tours, of course, were the exhausting part of it all; but for Autry, in particular, they were the most satisfying. He liked the live audience out there in front of him; he also liked Smiley there beside him.

Early in 1934 a long-time Autry dreammaterialized—a call from Hollywood. Autry recalled the events to me for my book, *The Singing Cowboys.*

> *Gene Autry: Nat Levine was an independent producer that owned Mascot Pictures. He was famous for his serials; he had made several of them. He was in New York talking about financing with Herbert Yates, who owned Consolidated Film Laboratories, which developed, I would*

say, seventy-five to ninety percent of the movies that were made here in Hollywood. Yates also financed them.

Levine was talking about making a feature with Ken Maynard and also a serial. Moe Siegel, who at that time was president of American Record Corporation, was sitting in with Levine and Yates when Nat was talking about financing this Western. Siegel said to Levine, "Instead of doing a regular formula Western, why don't you try a musical-type Western? Everybody is making movies of regular program Westerns—Hoot Gibson, Buck Jones, Ken Maynard. Why don't you try something musical? We have a young man out in Chicago on WLS that's selling a hell of a lot of records and is very popular on the radio. Why, I think you

The WLS National Barn Dance radio stars (1934). Shown are Gene Autry-#1, Patsy Montana-#3, Smiley Burnette-#4, and to left of Smiley is Max Terhune.

ought to talk to him." So Nat said he would.

I got a call from Moe Siegel and Art Satherley, who told me that Nat Levine would be in Chicago on a certain day, I forget when it was, and that he wanted to talk to me. So I met with Levine; I had a talk with him. He said, "I'm thinking about making a Western feature with some music in it and you were recommended to me. Siegel and Yates told me how big your records are going and of your popularity on the 'National Barn Dance.' I want to give it a lot of consideration. I'll be in touch with you." I said, "Fine."

So time rocked along and I got another offer—from Monogram Pictures. I wrote Levine a letter and told him [about the Monogram offer] and asked him if he'd given up on his idea. Because if he had, I was going to talk to these other people. He wrote me back and said, "We are making a picture with Ken Maynard called In Old Santa Fe and I will give you a part in the picture and a chance to do some songs. It can be a screen test." So I took it; I came out in June.

Gene, ever the shrewd businessman, signed Smiley to a personal contract and insisted that he be included in the Hollywood tryout deal. So in the summer of 1934 Gene, his wife Ina, and Smiley left Chicago by car and headed West. As Gene later wrote, "We drove through in five days and on the way, rolling through Arizona, Smiley and I wrote a song called 'Ridin' Down the Canyon.' Smiley scored the music in the back seat. Later, he would tell people, jokingly, it took him three miles to finish it, and I paid him $5.00 for the rights to the song, so he made $1.67 a mile."

In Old Santa Fe was a routine Ken Maynard Western with George Hayes playing his sidekick, Cactus. An interesting sidelight is that the film begins (as so many later Autry films would) with the star and his sidekick, Ken and George Hayes, riding across the desert as Ken strums a guitar and sings a song—not well, it should be added.

But back to Smiley and Gene. Their roles in this modern-day 1930s Western were as entertainers at a dude ranch. Otherwise, they were totally superfluous to the plot. Their scene—consisting of Gene calling a square dance, a solo number for each, and a duet of the title song—seems an intrusion in the film. It is somewhat surprising that

Maynard, who was never known to be charitable or easy to work with, would tolerate the two interlopers—especially since he sang a couple of songs in the film with much less success than Gene and Smiley.

Before the public had a chance to assess the performances of Gene and Smiley in **In Old Santa Fe,** the two were rushed into a Maynard serial entitled **Mystery Mountain** in which neither of them sang a note. Their small roles would have gone unnoticed if **In Old Santa Fe** had not been released, resulting in a small flood of mail regarding the musical interlude at the dude ranch and its two pleasing performers.

Ken Maynard had been a big Western star for years, but a violent temperamental nature supplemented generously by bottled spirits were causing him to become unmanageable by the studio. His temper tantrums and alcoholic hangovers delayed production, running the limited budgets into the red. The **Mystery Mountain** serial, for example, was budgeted at sixty-five thousand dollars; it, reportedly, ended up costing ninety thousand due to Maynard's behavior. A little production company like Mascot Pictures could not afford the luxury of a temperamental star.

It was for these very practical reasons that producer Nat Levine dropped Maynard from his next serial, **The Phantom Empire,** and decided to risk assigning the starring role to that young singing cowboy who had made such a good impression on the fans in **In Old Santa Fe**—Gene Autry. Oh, yes, the comic singer who was with Autry in **Santa Fe**—they wanted him, too.

Thus Gene and Smiley got their big chance in the twelve-chapter science fiction/Western serial. Budgeted at only $79,000, **The Phantom Empire** went on to great financial success and established Gene and Smiley in the minds of film audiences throughout the country. Smiley shared the comic chores in the serial with a now long-forgotten performer named William Moore. Jon Tuska in his book, **Filming of the West,** writes that their "comedy was singularly confined to slapstick antics and simply incompetent and stupid behavior." Tuska is right, as a viewing of the film will somewhat painfully verify. But from those humble, almost embarrassing, beginnings Smiley began to develop his Frog Millhouse character, a bumbling, lovable comic foil who, according to writer Tuska, "placed more impediments in the hero's path than the villains could." Frog Millhouse would serve Smiley throughout the long Autry series of Westerns—a series that was born out of the success of **The Phantom Empire** and would continue for fifty features,

Oliver Drake wrote the screenplays and songs for some early Autry pictures.

until Autry entered the service in 1942. From **Tumbling Tumbleweeds** in 1935 through **Bells of Capistrano** in 1942, they would appear together in all but two Gene Autry films: a Twentieth Century-Fox picture with Jane Withers entitled **Shooting High** and a big-budget Republic entry with Ann Miller and Jimmy Durante called **Melody Ranch.**

Oliver Drake, who was a songwriter/screenwriter/producer/director for hundreds of Western films over a forty-plus year career, joined the Autry series with the third feature, **The Singing Vagabond** (1936), as co-writer of the screenplay. Oliver continued to work on the Autry screenplays and to help compose songs for the pictures for the next couple of years. His Autry credits include such films as **Comin' Round the Mountain** (1936, story and screenplay), **Guns and Guitars** (1936, wrote the title song), **Oh, Susanna** (1936, screenplay), **Round-up Time in Texas** (1937, screenplay), **Public Cowboy Number 1** (1937, screenplay), and **Boots and Saddles** (1937, screenplay). I talked with Oliver about working with Smiley and Gene on those early pictures.

Oliver Drake: *Smiley Burnette was one of the funniest men in the picture business and a nice guy. I got to know Smiley better than most people because we wrote music together. Smiley was a very clever song writer. He wrote some big hits: "It's My Lazy Day," "Song of the Range," "Call of the Canyon"—it is still a classic. We wrote a lot of them together. I saw one of the pictures the other night on television which had a lot of our songs in it—**Oh, Susanna.***

I worked with Smiley not only on the stories which we set together from a comedy standpoint, but the studio found out that I was also a music writer, so they would put me with Smiley—sometimes with Gene—and we'd write songs together. Gene and I have a song, "Guns and Guitars," and some others. But Smiley and I must have twenty or thirty songs together. He was as crazy as I was, and we'd come up with these crazy songs. We wrote such comedy songs as "The Defective Detective from Brooklyn" and "Don't Trust a Bicycle Racer," which

Smiley's song book contained many of his comic cowboy ditties.

*Smiley did hilariously with Earle Hodgins in **Oh, Susanna**. Smiley and I would get together and have a ball writing songs.*

Some of the "crazy songs" Smiley wrote were published in the **Smiley Burnette Cowboy Song Book** published in 1940. One can glean an idea of the zany quality of these tumbleweed tunes just from their titles: "Elmer the Absent Minded Cowboy," "In a Cabin on a Cliff in Cleveland," "Minnehaha (She Gave Them All the Ha Ha)," "You Can Keep Me in the Saddle (If You Keep Me in Your Heart)," and "The Stills in the Hills are Still Tonight."

During the late 1930s the Gene Autry films had a phenomenal success record at theatres all over the country. As part of the Autry team, Smiley's popularity rose right along with Gene's. In early 1940 **Boxoffice** magazine, a leading trade publication, completed its yearly poll among theatre managers and owners to determine the nation's foremost Western stars. Gene Autry topped the poll followed by Smiley Burnette. Smiley was the only sidekick selected among the first ten Western stars.

This composite of scenes from Gene Autry-Smiley Burnette films was included in the *Smiley Burnette Cowboy Song Book.*

A duded-up young Smiley Burnette is revealed here in this close-up of a photo composite.

Smiley's high ranking in Western films was duly noted in "The Westerner," the official publication of the newly organized Smiley Burnette Fan Club—a club initiated by Smiley and his busines associates. Petria MacDonnell, Smiley's niece, was kind enough to share a rare existing copy of the first edition of "The Westerner," an eight-page newsletter published in early 1940.

Public interest and loyalty are key factors in the continued success of any performer, and Smiley in his fan club publication was working that mine for every stray nugget. Excerpts from "The Westerner" provide a fascinating forty-plus-years-later view of this enterprising comedian. The only direct message from Smiley is "A Greeting" on the cover page under the official fan club picture of Smiley and his horse Black Eyed Nellie. (The horse was just as often called Ringeye. Sunset Carson told me, "A lot of people ask what they used to put the ring around the eye of Frog's horse. Well, at that time I think it was about five-cents-a-bottle shoe polish. It was just regular shoe polish that you get with the little brush on the handle of it. They just painted a circle around

Vol. 1, No. 1   OFFICIAL PUBLICATION OF THE SMILEY BURNETTE FAN CLUB   Hollywood, Calif.

'THE WESTERNER' MAKES ITS BOW

'RANCHO GRANDE' NEW TRIUMPH FOR GENE AND SMILEY

Here is news that will interest every one of you!

We saw a private preview the other night in Pomona, California, of Smiley's newest Republic western, "El Rancho Grande," and as Jimmy Fidler would say, Smiley rings the bell with what we sincerely believe is just about the best picture he's made. And in saying that, we're not overlooking his fine work in "South of the Border" and "In Old Monterey."

"Rancho Grande" is definitely a winner and if it doesn't smash all kinds of boxoffice records we're going to stop prophesying for good. As the one and only "Frog Millhouse," Smiley has never been better. He has a rich comedy part and from beginning to end he had the preview audience laughing uproariously. There are comedy scenes in "Rancho Grande" that rank as good as any Smiley has ever done.

Like "South of the Border" this latest picture of Smiley and Gene has been given an excellent production by Republic studio and it is certain to win plaudits as a top notch western in every respect. It has everything you want in a western—magnificent scenery, fine music, excellent acting, comedy and plenty of rousing action.

The currently popular tune "Rancho Grande" is the musical theme in this new western and you'll get a thrill when you see and hear Smiley, Gene, and members of the cast sing "Rancho Grande." This particular sequence is done against an outdoor background with the beauty of the open range photographed in all its breathtaking splendor. It's a scene you won't forget.

As a song "Rancho Grande" has a very catchy melody and you'll prob-

Smiley 'Frog' Burnette and 'Black Eyed Nellie'

A Greeting

It has been a dream of mine for several years to have a medium which would furnish my friends with the information they request in their letters. "The Westerner" is the realization of that dream. I hope, therefore, that you will consider this magazine a personal message to each and every one of you who belong to my club and who enjoy my portrayal of "Frog" in the Gene Autry pictures.
—Smiley

Smiley Voted No. 2 Box Office Western Favorite In Poll

If any reminder is necessary of Smiley's popularity at the box office, it was impressively provided by no less an authority than BOX OFFICE Magazine, a leading trade publication whose annual polls carry tremendous weight in Hollywood. Just recently the magazine completed its yearly poll among theatre managers and owners to determine the nation's foremost Western stars and the final vote disclosed our own "Frog Millhouse" as

the No. 2 favorite.

In receiving the No. 2 honor, Smiley finished only a fraction of a point behind his own screen pal, Gene Autry. It was a great tribute to Smiley and clearly shows what a universal favorite he is.

The fact that Smiley was the only comedian selected among the first ten Western stars speaks volumes and adds another lustrous page to his distinguished career.

NEW PUBLICATION SIGNALIZES RAPID RISE OF FAN CLUB

With this issue, "The Westerner" makes its bow as the official publication of the Smiley Burnette Fan Club, an organization of his fans of all ages and walks of life who have enjoyed his wholesome humor on the screen, stage and radio.

"The Westerner" is whole-heartedly dedicated to the interests and varied activities of the SBFC and in furthering, in every way it can, the popularity of "Frog" as America's No. 1 Western comedian. To each and every member of the Fan Club "The Westerner" is sent free.

The appearance of this initial issue of "The Westerner"—edited and published in Filmland's glamorous metropolis, Hollywood—signalizes the amazing growth the SBFC has enjoyed in the space of a few months. The club, in fact, is less than six months old. The first official announcement of its formation was made by Smiley personally in the City of Salisbury, Md., last November when he was beginning his long personal appearance tour.

In city after city on his personal appearance tour he personally distributed applications for membership. So spontaneous was the response that when Smiley returned to California late in January, he found his mailbox filled to overflowing with applications from every part of the country.

No time was lost getting the new membership cards and photos ready as had been promised, and in the following few days hundreds of envelopes from Hollywood carrying good tidings were on their way to the four corners of the United States. In order that applicants receive their membership cards and photos promptly, a large

"The Westerner" was the official publication of the Smiley Burnette Fan Club.

Smiley Burnette, the one-man band, is astride Ring-eyed Nellie. Fans have always been fascinated by the ring around the horse's eye and wondered if was real.

Sunset Carson: A lot of people ask what they used to put the ring around the eye of Frog's horse. Well, at that time I think it was about five-cents-a-bottle shoe polish. It was just regular shoe polish that you get with the little brush on the handle of it.

his eye and that was it. He sometimes called the horse Nellie, but it was the same horse whether it was called Ringeye or Nellie.")

In his greeting for "The Westerner" Smiley states:

It has been a dream of mine for several years to have a medium which would furnish my friends with information they request in their letters. "The Westerner" is the realization of that dream. I hope, therefore, that you will consider this magazine a personal message to each and every one of you who belong to my club and who enjoy my portrayal of "Frog" in the Gene Autry pictures.

Articles in "The Westerner" have such captions as "New Publication Signals Rapid Rise of Fan Club," "Every Section of U.S. Represented in Smiley's Club," and "Fans Hail Smiley on Recent Tour." Within the articles it is stated:

The appearance of this initial issue of "The Westerner"—edited and published in filmland's glamorous metropolis, Hollywood—signalizes the amazing growth the SBFC has enjoyed in the space of a few months. The club, in fact, is less than six months old. The first official announcement of its formation was made by Smiley personally in the city of Salisbury, Md., last November when he was beginning his long personal appearance tour.

In city after city on his personal appearance tour he personally distributed applications for membership. So spontaneous was the response that when Smiley returned to California in late January, he found his mailbag filled to overflowing with applications from every part of the country.

Another article mentions:

Although certain sections lead in membership totals, it is encouraging to note the response to the club from all parts of the country. That in itself is a tribute to Frog's popularity in all four corners of this great country of ours.

Smiley's latest Autry films are chronicled prominently, but as might be expected in the "Official Publication of the Smiley Burnette Fan Club," Gene is little noted:

Here is news that will interest every one of you!

We saw a private preview the other night in Pomona, California, of Smiley's newest Republic Western, "El Rancho Grande," and as Jimmy Fidler would say, Smiley rings the bell with what we sincerely believe is just about the best picture he's made. And in saying that, we're not overlooking his fine work in "South of the Border" and "In Old Monterey."

"Rancho Grande" is definitely a winner and if it doesn't smash all kinds of box-office records we're going to stop prophesying for good. As the one and only "Frog Millhouse," Smiley has never been better. He has a rich comedy part and from beginning to end he had the preview

audience laughing uproariously. There are comedy scenes in "Rancho Grande" that rank as good as any Smiley has ever done.

Like "South of the Border" this latest picture of Smiley and Gene has been given excellent production by Republic Studio and it is certain to win plaudits as a top notch Western in every respect.

Another headline proclaims, " 'South of the Border' Smash Hit!" The article goes on to state:

Toppling one boxoffice record after another, "South of the Border," Smiley and Gene's current smash hit, is making screen history as few Westerns have ever succeeded in doing. Even Hollywood, which doesn't startle easily, has been sitting up and taking notice at the enthusiasm and popularity "South of the Border" has kindled in all parts of the country.

All of which has added fresh laurels to the prestige of Smiley and Gene and established them more firmly than ever as the screen's number one Western team. Hollywood old-timers have had to admit that never has any pair scored so sensationally in Westerns.

Again, one cannot help noticing Autry's billing in the article. "The Westerner" revealed personal and professional information about Smiley in a specially formatted column:

DO YOU KNOW THAT....

✓ Smiley's favorite musical instrument is the accordian?

✓ He is particularly fond of Mexican food and can prepare such dishes as enchiladas?

✓ He is descended from a long line of clergymen and that both his father and mother were preachers?

✓ He played on a Mississippi River showboat when he was fifteen years old?

✓ He earned his first money as an entertainer when he was nine? He performed on a musical saw at a banquet for

which he received $3.00.

✓ His wife, Dallas MacDonnell, was an ace Hollywood columnist prior to her marriage and that they first met at a picnic?

✓ One of his favorite tunes is "She's Nobody's Sweetheart Now"?

✓ He once wrote 11 songs in 8 hours?

✓ He and Gene played together on the WLS "National Barn Dance" program before they came to Hollywood?

And what would a fan club publication be without a fan club pledge?

THE FAN CLUB PLEDGE

Listed below are the cardinal pledges of the Smiley Burnette Fan Club. We hope every one of you will read them and remember their importance, for they constitute the club's basic foundation.

I promise to make every effort to see Smiley "Frog" Burnette in every picture he is in.

I promise always to let my friends know where and when they can see "Frog" in pictures.

I promise to show my loyalty to "Frog" by writing him once each month faithfully and will offer constructive and helpful suggestions regarding his pictures.

I promise to show my interest in our club by doing everything I can to get new members.

I promise to carry my membership card with me at all times and to obey the pledges guiding our fan club.

It should be noted that the fan club membership was free and that a "handsome" photo, membership card, and copy of "The Westerner" were sent without charge to anyone joining the club. The only advertising in "The Westerner" was for "Genuine Indian relics" which were being made available "exclusively" to Smiley Burnette Fan Club members at a special price.

"The Westerner" staff extended their "greetings" to members in the initial issue. The staff was headed by W.R. Mattox, Smiley's business manager, and G.W. Burnette, Smiley's father ("a former clergyman, he now enjoys the distinction of supervising certain phases of his famous son's fan club activities").

In the eyes of the fans Gene and Smiley (Frog) were a team just as much as Abbott and Costello or the later Martin and Lewis. A show business team is much like a marriage, of course, and like most marriages the teams go through periods of tension which threaten their continuation. It is no secret that Abbott and Costello did not speak to each other during many of the years they worked so successfully together. Dean Martin and Jerry Lewis felt their real talents were being smothered working as a team, and, so, split up. With both of these teams there were friends and hangers-on who sided with one or the other as frictions developed which eventually brought about the demise of the duos.

Certainly Autry and Burnette never thought of themselves as a team in such a way as the other two teams mentioned, but they did make fifty movies together and countless personal appearances and radio shows between the early 1930s and 1942. It was inevitable, therefore, that over time rumors should spread that the two cowboys were not on the best of terms and might get on their horses and ride off in separate directions.

I asked Oliver Drake what he could tell me about these stories which went around during the Republic Pictures years that Gene and Smiley worked together.

Oliver Drake: *You know a star like Autry picks up a lot of driftwood, friends, and they can't leave well enough alone. They kept trying and trying to breakup Smiley Burnette and Autry. They'd tell Gene, "Smiley Burnette has too much to do in this picture." Now these were Gene's friends; they worked with him; some of them were the heavies; some his musicians; some were from back home—these were his pals. Smiley Burnette was Gene's pal, too. But they kept nagging and nagging and talking that Smiley Burnette had too much to do in this or that picture. Gene would say, "Look, they sell Gene Autry if we make good pictures. I trust Mandy Schaefer [who was Gene's production supervisor]. If Mandy thought Smiley has too much to do in the pictures he wouldn't let the picture go out." Well, this nagging of these people went on and on.*

There might be two sides to it, but I never heard the Smiley Burnette side. All I heard was the Autry side. I was writing some of the stories and music for the films, and we were pals when he first started. Gene'd say, "What do you think about it?" I'd say, "Well, it's a good script; Smiley doesn't have too much to do. You're got your number of songs, the Lightcrust Doughboys, the Tennessee Ramblers, and the Sons of the Pioneers for your music—you've got good musical things. If you just leave Mandy alone, he'll make good pictures with you," which he would. I heard friends of Gene's, who were probably jealous of Smiley and who would have liked to take Smiley's place, trying to cause problems.

A rare Lobby Card from Smiley and Gene's first film appearance.

16

In this rare photo Smiley is in the control room of his home recording studio. Pee Wee King is performing in the main studio.

Every performer needs to feel his worth, his value to the overall job that is being done. It is acknowledged by Smiley's contemporaries that he was extremely proud of his popularity in the Autry series and he he doubtless felt that the series' success was in no small part due to his participation. Smiley's publication of "The Westerner" would certainly attest to that. Some fellow performers felt that Smiley over-estimated his contribution and was led astray by those who encouraged this type of thinking.

Fellow singing cowboy and Autry friend, Jimmy Wakely, told me he placed the blame for friction in the Autry-Burnette camp upon the film distributors, a powerful force in filmmaking during the thirties and forties.

Jimmy Wakely: You had to watch the distributors. Sometimes the distributors would tell Smiley Burnette, for instance, that Gene couldn't make it without him; that he was making the movies a hit and so forth. Whether Smiley believed it or not, God will only ever know. Smiley was strong in the Autry pictures. But the point is, the distributors kept saying to Smiley that Gene couldn't make it without him, and they were wrong. Gene Autry was so strong at the box office that he'd make it with any comic; it didn't matter. Even though Smiley was very strong and a very big part of the pictures, he wasn't thirty percent. You could take Smiley out of the series and you still had the best series of Westerns. You could get a Gabby Hayes or somebody, and as long as you had

Gene Autry and some laughs and some songs, who cares? Gene had "star quality" and was not dependent upon any one comic. That was demonstrated during the war when Gene went into the service and Smiley was starred with Sunset Carson and Eddie Dew, and it didn't happen; it didn't work.

★   ★   ★

When I was at the Memphis Film Festival in 1982, I came across a rare picture of Smiley in his home recording studio with composer, singer, and musician Pee Wee King. Pee Wee, you will remember, wrote such standards as "Slow Poke," "Bonaparte's Retreat," and "The Tennessee Waltz." A year later at the Charlotte Western Film Fair I had the chance to meet Pee Wee King and to ask him about the picture and Smiley.

Pee Wee King: *The picture was taken around 1952, I think. We had gone out to California to do a Charles Starrett picture. In fact, Smiley had a cookout at the house the day this picture was taken, a barbecue for all of us. I remember that the Sons of the Pioneers joined us. Bob Nolan, Tim Spencer, and all the boys came out. Smiley also fixed a Caesar's salad. He prided himself on his mastery of cooking; he was a fine cook.*

What amazed me about Smiley's house was that he had one room in the back of the house that was sealed in and soundproofed. There were no windows in the room; you couldn't see out at all. There was just absolute silence. The stillness was almost scary. Smiley said, "There's where I go for an hour or two when I come back from a trip. Dallas doesn't bother me; the kids can't bother me; and I sit

Smiley is seen here greeting his guests at his home recording studio.

Singer, composer, and musician Pee Wee King was a close friend of Smiley Burnette.

there and meditate." He said, "It gives me a lift so that I can go on to other things." Of course, Smiley was a very religious guy. His father was a minister.

I know when Gene Autry first hired Smiley he had to go meet his mother and dad. His dad said, "If you'll sign this paper, Lester can go with you." The paper was a release stating that Gene would see to it that Smiley went to church. Gene was surprised, of course. He wondered why he should have to become Smiley's nursemaid, but he signed it. Of course, he and Smiley hit it off and the rest is history.

Smiley was an individual; he was a loner in some ways. He made friends, millions and millions of friends, but he also knew how to seclude himself and to get away from the hubbub of activities.

I think when Smiley went to work with Autry, he proved himself to be one of the finest sidekicks any cowboy could have. Because Smiley was a musician and a fine composer, he could also write songs for the Autry pictures. Smiley had the

spirit of the West in him; that came out in the wonderful Western music he wrote.

Gene Autry always used to say, "We make movies out West, but we make our living out East." The popularity of the pictures made it possible for them to do personal appearances in the East and, really, throughout the country. Gene Autry went out on the road with his entourage, his stage show. Smiley went out and did his thing; he played the littler theaters, and he played the shopping centers, which were just breaking into business at that time. They became a big thing. He'd park his trailer in a shopping center and soon he was the center of attention. Shortly the radio stations would find out he was there and they'd come out to interview him, giving him free publicity for his show.

In the theatres he'd always have to have a way to empty out the house so that he could bring another crowd in. Smiley'd say, "Okay, little boys and girls, right after the stage show old Frog will be out behind the theater. If you come out there, you can have your picture taken with me." Well, naturally, every kid wanted to have his picture taken with Frog. It was the old one-on-one relationship with your fans. You can't beat it.

★   ★   ★

Doing research for a book such as this is a little like playing detective. You make dozens of phone calls trying to locate people who worked with or were friends or relatives of your subject in hopes that they will share remembrances with you. Sometimes you travel to out-of-the-way places to follow-up a lead someone has given you, only to find that the lead died in 1967.

Then there are times when a goldmine of information arrives unexpectedly in the morning mail. Such was the case in one aspect of my research on Smiley Burnette. I wanted to talk with someone who could shed light on the personal side of Smiley; who knew about his home life and family. In February of 1982 I received a letter from a lady named Petria MacDonnell who complimented me on my book **The Singing Cowboys**, which she had just read. She wrote that she found my chapter on Gene Autry particularly interesting because her uncle had been Smiley Burnette. She mentioned that if I should ever plan a book on the sidekicks, she and her father,

Smiley and Dallas are seen here in their back yard with their four adopted children. Seated left to right are Brian, Steven and Linda. Caroline is standing next to Smiley.

Dallas' younger half-brother, would be happy to share family remembrances, since they both had lived with Smiley and Dallas during a portion of their youth.

I was on the phone immediately to Petria and, later, her father, Gordon MacDonnell, to get their close-up insights of Smiley, his wife Dallas, and their adopted children.

Petria, who lived with Smiley and Dallas while her father was in the service during World War II, remembers Smiley as a substitute father and the complete family man. "My main memory," Petria told me, "is of his deep, just absolutely beautiful voice—that gorgeous voice he had. I remember he would spend a lot of time alone with me, just talking. He always had these very gentle, calming, wise, comforting things to say. And he was a wonderful listener. He holds a very precious place in my heart because of it. I remember he always listened to me

and he really took time out for me—we would just sit and talk in their back yard. They had a home in Studio City—a beautiful place, I remember very well, with a big yard. His greatest joy was cooking; he just loved it. And he just loved to take care of people— a gentle sweetness in the man."

I asked Petria about the adopted children. "Linda is the oldest of Smiley and Dallas' four adopted children; the others, in order of age are Steven, Caroline, and Brian. I always used to wear Caroline's hand-me-downs, pink frou-frou organdy things that were too tight."

After years of lost contact with Linda, Petria finally located her in 1980 through an ad in the Camarillo, California, paper. The ad said, "Linda Burnette: your cousin Petria would like to find you." Linda responded to the ad by phoning Petria and talking with her for over two hours. Linda currently owns a beauty shop and operates a family search service, hunting down the natural parents of adopted people. According to Petria, "Linda laughs a lot, has a wicked sense of humor, and is as earthy, irreverent, and trouble-making as I am."

Neither Petria nor, later, Petria's father could say much about the other three children of Smiley and Dallas. Petria described Steven, the older boy, as "bright, precocious, good-looking, and always Dallas' favorite." Caroline was described as "a little blond, spoiled beauty; she was a handful." Petria informed me that Brian, the youngest, was "small for his age and somewhat hyperactive." Linda was described by Petria as "so much like Smiley and Dallas that it was amazing. She was very sweet-tempered and loving."

Gordon MacDonnell, Petria's father, commented about the children, "When they were little, they were an incredible group of children. The first three in particular were such beautiful children; it was just unbelievable, unreal. Linda was just a breathtakingly beautiful girl.

Petria, moved and delighted by her 1980 reunion with Linda, commented, "I was absolutely thrilled that my long lost favorite cousin Linda turned out to be an honest, funny, witty, earthy, goodhearted person. Just as special as she was when a child. It's nice to know that there's some of Dallas and Smiley still around."

Gordon MacDonnell, Dallas' half-brother, lives in California and has fond memories of the times he spent with Smiley and Dallas at their home in Studio City. In a long, far-ranging phone conversation in mid-1982, he discussed with me his remembrances of the sidekick and his lady.

Gordon MacDonnell on early memories of Smiley and Dallas: *My half-sister Dallas was a columnist for a couple of Hollywood newspapers. She wrote a column called "Roamin' Round Hollywood"*

This earlier family photo from the late '30s was taken when they had only the three children. (left to right) Smiley, Linda, Steven, Caroline, and Dallas.

that was in the **Hollywood Reporter,** and also a column in the **Hollywood Citizen News**. She interviewed Smiley at one point when he first came out to Hollywood and that's how they met.

I didn't even know I had an older half-sister until I was thirteen. That was the year that my father died, and that's when I first met Dallas. As a teen-ager I used to spend summers and most of my school vacations with Smiley and Dallas. I used to sleep in their den where they had a Hammond Novachord. Smiley would get up early in the morning—he was always an early-rising country boy until the very end—and before anybody else was up, he'd come into the den and unplug the speakers and play the Hammond Novachord. He'd be sitting there with headphones on playing for hours before anybody else got up. If I'd wake up hearing the footpetal thumping, he would unplug the earphones and I could listen to it on the speakers. That's the part of him that I wish the rest of the world could have heard. His music was just so beautiful. It didn't fit his image of the cowboy simpleton, and, as a result, most of it was never published.

On tour with Smiley: I traveled with Smiley occasionally during relatively short tours, particularly within California. Mostly it was as a teen-ager when I was staying at the house.

When I joined him on tour, I was a go-for. I hauled the instruments more than anything else. When I was older, I drove. He would usually take a small group on the road with him—anywhere from three to five people would travel with him. A lot of his work was county fairs and theaters in small towns. When it was theaters, he pretty much worked alone. One of Smiley's pictures would be shown at the theater and then he would come out. It was sort of "Smiley Burnette Day" at the theater. His show was really aimed at the children. He could put on a pretty thorough show by himself because he played so many instruments. At most he needed one or two sidemen to help make music for the children. He would sing songs that he had written for the kids.

On the songs that Smiley wrote: Many of the songs, I guess, were never even published or recorded. He liked to write songs on the spur of the moment about particular kids or people he'd meet on the road. I guess half of the songs he ever wrote were written on toilet paper rolls.

Most of the songs I knew about were used in movies. Many of the songs that he wrote I don't think were ever published because the output was so enormous for those days and so many of them were written just to please individual people. But songs that did get into the movies, many of those that he wrote not only with Autry, but with any of the other people he worked with in movies, whoever sang them was usually the person who was indicated as the author. I know that at one point he told me that most of the songs that he'd written had gotten published in other people's names and that he got fifty dollars a piece for them.

(As a side note to Gordon's comment on Smiley's song royalties—writer Jon Tuska, while participating on a 1979 Western Author's Panel, of which I was a member, commented on an alleged Autry-Burnette dispute over song royalties.

Jon Tuska: When he [Smiley] started at Republic with Autry, Gene put him under a personal contract. It meant all of Smiley's songs belonged to Gene, and Gene started a music publishing company. Then Gene went into the Air Force and Smiley's contract ran out, and he could go to Columbia. By 1950 Smiley was darned near destitute except for the money he got for the Starrett Westerns. He went to Gene and he said, "Listen, can I have some royalties from my songs?" Gene said, "No, they belong to me. But I will do this for you. I'll let you star in my last series for Columbia." With him it was a business and the Autry films were primarily a means of income and not his greatest income.

It should be noted that writer Tuska has little use for Gene Autry [see his book, **The Filming of the West,** for evidence] and seems to delight in reciting a litany of real or imagined Autry shortcomings. But back to Gordon MacDonnell.)

On Smiley's home recording studio: Smiley had two lots side by side on Hortense Street on the edge of Studio City. His house was located on one of the lots. He lived in the same house during all these years. On the back of the second lot he had a little shop for himself and a little recording studio as well. It was a professional quality studio. He had a brick wall that went all around the entire property for privacy. This was during the mid to late '40s after World War II, after I got out of the service. I was going to audio engineering school in Hollywood and was planning to go to work at Columbia Pictures as a sound mixer, so I was running the equipment while Smiley was recording things in his studio. Most of what he was recording was pre-recording material for the pictures [Charles Starrett films]. The recordings would be used down at the [film] studio to do the arrangements for some of those little cowboy ditties—some of them had a full orchestra in the background when they finally were in the movie.

He did a lot of multiple-track recordings in his little studio, and no one was doing that professionally in those days. Les Paul and Mary Ford were the first ones to do records that way, I think, and I didn't hear of them until some years later. This was around 1946 or '47 when Smiley had the studio and I was still in school. 1946 to '48 was when I was going to audio engineering school.

Smiley would record his voice and one instrument and then I would play it back and record it again with him doing a second voice and a second instrument. Gradually, he would record four-part harmony with his voice and four instruments, and maybe even add other instruments afterwards. We could go on like this for days—we were just playing—like kids playing with a very sophisticated toy. There wasn't audio tape yet, of course, so everything Smiley did was on disk.

In many cases Smiley was simply recording for his own fun and for friends or acquaintances. For example, we would take a soundtrack background for a movie that, say, Gene Autry was going to sing a song—one that had been pre-recorded with a full orchestra. Smiley would write four or five different new lyrics for it about different people he had met. Then we would record Smiley singing with this record, but with each of these new lyrics. He'd give these records to people, particularly when he traveled. If he stayed with people or met people that he liked when he was traveling, he would generally write a song with words about these people and record it in his studio, and send them the master on it. As a result, unless any of those people have kept their records, they were one-of-a-kind, the records no longer exist. There were never any duplicates made of them. That was his form of thank you—to either write poetry and leave it or to write a song and send it, recorded, back to people he had met and liked while on tour.

The character he played in pictures was a very sympathetic character, but it wasn't exactly a brilliant one—something of a buffoon. So the songs he published under his own name were mostly the little comic songs—very rarely anything serious. I think he felt he couldn't get his serious music published under his own name, or he didn't want to; I'm not sure which.

On Smiley's personality: In his private life I would say that he was a far more serious man than you could ever imagine from his screen role—particularly in his music and his recreation. I mean when he went fishing he was very serious about his fishing and he would travel a lot of miles to go to the right fishing spot. If he was off on tour where he would be working, say, Friday, Saturday, and Sunday nights at a county fair, he might fish four or five days of that same week and drive a hundred miles each day to do it.

His personality, of course, may have been slightly different for me because I was young and family. Most of the time, though, he was very serious about things that we were working on in the recording studio. All that was very serious. I have seen him get extremely hotheaded at people who would do stupid things. I remember one fellow that worked for him that wasn't too bright. Smiley kept him around for years. Most of the time Smiley put up with him without incident, but

Smiley makes his point to Gene in this scene from one of the pre-war Autry pictures for Republic Pictures.

once in a while it got to be too much, and I would see the flash of temper. I didn't see it often, but when I wasn't around there were probably more of those incidents. I found him pretty easy to be around, very forgiving; he certainly was of me.

I first met Smiley just as my father died—for a thirteen-year-old boy that's a crucial moment between a boy and his father. I guess Smiley was really a substitute father for me from then on. I don't know any other way to describe it. To me Smiley was a very warm and caring person.

On Gene Autry and Smiley: On occasion Smiley would go out to Gene's place and I would go with him. When Smiley would have parties, Gene generally came. In the

later years when television was showing so many movies and Gene bought up ownership of all his movies and would never allow them on, I know Smiley was unhappy about that. I don't know whether I could say bitter or not, but I know he was pretty unhappy that other people who'd made movies were getting a crack at some later-in-life earnings out of them and he never could because Gene had them frozen.

On Smiley's money matters: I remember two very important financial events in Smiley's life. One was the day that he came home and realized that his business manager had run him to the edge of bankruptcy. It was particularly sensitive because the business manager was married to my father's first wife, Dallas' mother. Smiley had a separate business office over in Studio City where all the bills were to be sent. Suddenly bills began coming to the house. The first few times this happened Smiley just forwarded them to the office. Then he began getting dunning and phone calls at home. I went with him over to the office, and that's where he found out, suddenly, that all the money he'd been making hadn't been going to pay anything, and that he was on the edge of ending up in court as a bankrupt. I remember this as being some time around the early 1940s.

Smiley immediately started working one-night stands everywhere he could drive in a day. I know we went up to Bakersfield and Fresno. We drove an awful lot of miles in that big old car in the next few months. He really had to work hard to accumulate money in a hurry to pay off all those debts that had accumulated. Smiley got back in good financial shape very quickly.

The other financial event I remember took place about the time he was getting out of debt. He got a new contract at Republic and came home very happily to announce that he'd gotten what he'd asked for, which was a thousand dollars a day. That was a thousand dollars a day while he was making a picture. Of course, they'd make a whole movie in about seven days, so, per picture, it wasn't a lot of money. But he was so tickled to be able to say, "I'm making a thousand dollars a day." I'm pretty sure this was during the Roy Rogers and Sunset Carson period of his career with Republic [which would be 1942-1944].

On why Smiley left Republic Pictures: I understand it was because he was going to get more money with Starrett at Columbia. He was particularly happy with the people at Columbia apparently. I don't remember Republic as being a particularly happy time at work, but Columbia I do. He was very determined that I should become an audio engineer after the war and go to work at Columbia. I don't remember anything especially negative about Republic; just the positive attitude about Columbia—probably one or two people at Columbia who treated him well.

On Smiley and Dallas' parties: Smiley was a gourmet cook; constantly experimenting. His backyard barbecue was a very elaborate affair because that was his pleasure when he wasn't working. He and Dallas entertained very often and, generally, it was outdoors entertainment. They had a huge backyard because of buying the two lots. I think their friends were quite a mixture of people in and out of show business. I would say that more of them were from the music business than were from the movies.

On Dallas' accident: She fell, of all things, on a bicycle. She was built like Smiley and had no business on a bicycle, but she was riding and went over the handlebars and landed on her elbows. As a result, her elbows became completely useless; she couldn't bend them. So to put a bite of food in her mouth, it took a special utensil a little over a foot long for her to reach her mouth. So this was when, to a very large extent, Smiley took over the cooking when he was home. She had household help, but he just preferred doing it; he loved that part of it. Her accident occurred sometime during the mid to late forties, but that's just a guess— we're talking about something that happened about forty years ago. The only time her difficulty really showed much was when they'd eat out in a restaurant and she had to eat with these strange tools. They had a pretty smooth act where he would get her food prepared to the point where nobody really noticed her problem.

On Smiley's horse and hat: Smiley didn't actually own the horse, Ringeye, that he used in the movies. It was a studio horse and the ring around the eye was painted on every one of them that I knew about. The hat that he wore in the films was a very precious thing to him. That old hat, I think, made every movie he ever made. As far as I know, it was the same one all the way through.

On Smiley and Dallas' practical jokes: He and Dallas were both practical jokers to a dangerous extent. As an example, they had an outhouse in the backyard when

To my friend David Rothel - from one who rode the Hollywood Range for the brand - Columbia Pictures 1935-1952. Charles "Durango" Starrett

Charles Starrett was under contract to Columbia from 1935 until 1952, one of the longest running studio contracts in Hollywood.

they had big parties. If they had some first-time visitors at the party, they would lock the doors to the main house so that people who had to go to the bathroom had to use the outhouse. Just about the time the unsuspecting person would get comfortably seated in the outhouse, the walls would automatically fall down, revealing the embarrassed first-timers for all to see.

This isn't a practical joke, but it gives you an idea of some of the crazy kinds of parties they sometimes had. They had a giant lazy Susan table that was about twelve feet in diameter. One party was a birthday party for Smiley's horse, Ringeye. Smiley had the other movie cowboys bring their horses with them to the party. They put hay and oats on the lazy Susan in the middle of this huge table and tied all of the horses around it.

Puns were a big part of their life. They had a couple of cows that they kept on a ranch about two or three blocks away. It was a ranch that normally just stabled horses for cowboy people. One of the cows was called Carolina for "Carolina **Moo**'n." The other cow was named Magnesia. We used to drink milk of Magnesia.

When I brought my new wife home from Washington, D.C., we stopped at Smiley's house to visit and spend the night before continuing to our home. As it turned out, Smiley was away, and they had just finished building a wing of the house—let's see, this was late 1943. They had a new master bedroom and bathroom that they built onto the house. So Dallas turned over this new master suite to us, the newlyweds. She showed us into the room, and I remember thinking that the carpeting felt like it was a foot deep as I walked on it. My wife walked around the bed to the other side and there on the floor was a big pile of dog do—on this brand new carpeting in this brand new bedroom. It took my wife, who was a pretty naive country girl from North Carolina at the time, to get around to telling Dallas about her discovery on the new carpeting. When she finally did, Dallas said, "Oh, they do that all the time," and reached down with her hand and put it in the smock she always wore.

My wife almost fainted. Well, the dog do was rubber and was Dallas' little joke. That was Dallas' idea of how you met people; how you broke the ice in a hurry.

I remember once Dallas greased the toilet seat with butter and Smiley slipped down off the toilet seat a little too fast. That was the last practical joke she pulled on him for a long time because he really wounded himself. But this was the way Smiley and Dallas were; they did these things to each other and to everybody around them all of the time.

★   ★   ★

In 1946 Smiley moved from Republic over to Columbia Pictures where he was to co-star with Charles Starrett in fifty-six films in the popular Durango Kid series. Smiley's role in the Durango pictures was much the same as it had been in the Autry series and other Western films he had made when Autry was on studio strike or in the service. The one difference was that he was now called Smiley in the pictures since Frog Millhouse was a character owned by Republic Pictures.

Smiley's job with Starrett was to supply the buffoonery, be the comic foil for the hero, and provide comic musical interludes while the hero let his guns cool down. It was the stock stuff that Smiley had cut his teeth on a dozen years before and could do in his sleep. And by the late 1940s it more and more appeared to this viewer that Smiley was doing just that—sleepwalking through the series. When one observes Smiley in the pre-war Autry series, he finds the comic exuding an inner zest for the zany shenanigans he is up to in the films; he genuinely appears to be having fun. Autry has said that Smiley was a "human sunbeam" around the movie sets.

In the later Starrett pictures, say from 1949 to 1952, Smiley looks tired, even distracted. The "inner zest" seems to be missing, and the sidekick just seems to be going through the motions. It is no secret that the Starrett films were produced on a shoestring budget compared with the Autry's and utilized much stock footage from other films (many of them earlier Starrett pictures.) The scripts were comic book paste-ups with little inventiveness. (I know there are B Western critics who would say this about the scripts for the entire genre, but be that as it may.) Then, too, Smiley and Starrett did not always get along too well. Starrett had little appreciation for Smiley's type of clowning or music. It is possible that all of these factors (and others) led Smiley to become somewhat bored/disen-

Charles Starrett is seen here reminiscing about his long film career at the Memphis Film Festival in August of 1982.

chanted with the Durango Kid series. Whatever the reasons, this viewer felt that there was a definite let-down in Smiley's performances during this time.

In the summer of 1982 I talked with Charles Starrett, who retired from films in 1952 when the Durango Kid series ended. Ever the gracious gentleman, Charlie, now in his seventies and nearly blind, still leads a fairly active life and is certainly hale and hearty when reminiscing about his film career. It soon becomes apparent when talking with him that the early years of his career are remembered as the golden times, even though he acknowledges that the later Durango Kid series is the most fondly remembered by his fans. Charlie is far more willing to acknowledge the shortcomings of the Durango Kid series than are most of his many fans.

Charles Starrett worked with Smiley longer than anyone except Gene Autry. Smiley made fifty-six pictures with Starrett, compared with fifty-seven with Autry. Though it is not in Charlie Starrett's nature to say anything bad about anyone, he gradually revealed to me in our conversation that the relationship he had with Smiley was not always a comfortable one.

Charles Starrett on working with Smiley: *I got along very well with Smiley, but we didn't start off that way during the first few pictures after he came over from Republic. He was pretty well established at Republic, starting with Gene Autry. Smiley had good material there; he really did. Armand Schaefer was Gene's producer, you know. They had money, and they spent it on the pictures. Gene was going along by leaps and bounds and doing great. So Smiley did very well with Gene. Gene was a very broad-minded guy and I think he saw in Smiley what I saw, and being the loyal guy that Gene is, he got along with Smiley. But I know there was a little friction there.*

When Smiley came over to Columbia, he—I don't think he came over with a chip on his shoulder, but to some people he seemed to be self-defensive. Now, I'm going to tell you this story about Smiley because I think that I understand him like a lot of people didn't. Actors are actors, and somebody once said, "We're a great big family of barracudas." Well, one day I was sitting on the set by myself and Smiley came over and sat down side of me. We were getting along, you know, but

we were just starting to work together. As we sat there, Smiley proceeded to enlighten me as to why he was at Columbia. He said, "Well, you know, Charlie, I'm over here at Columbia as a shot in the arm."

As you can imagine, I didn't like his remark too much. You know, I'd been at Columbia for ten years and Harry Cohn, the head of the studio, wasn't hiring me to sweep out the soundstage.

But as time went on Smiley and I got better acquainted, and I began to understand him better. He had a good sense of humor. If he muffed a line when I'd give him a cue, I'd say, "Smiley, come on; get going, man. You're supposed to be a shot in the arm!" He'd laugh and we'd do the scene again.

I think I got along with Smiley Burnette as well as any actor who worked with him because I was honest with him, and I could kid with him, and he would kid back with me. We both had the attitude that we were not competitive on the set. We were both trying to make a good picture and do the best we could with the material we had. I really think Smiley liked me and I liked Smiley. I had a lot of respect for him.

*I think Smiley was misunderstood in a lot of ways. David, he was his own worst enemy. Smiley was on the defensive a lot of the time with people. And he wasn't really like that if you really knew him. It wasn't an inferiority complex, because he didn't act **that** way. He just felt: "I'm as good as you are, and maybe I'm better, and I want you to know that. I'm a shot in the arm"; you know what I mean? He was pretty aggressive to work with. Smiley worked too hard for Smiley. He could be a "take charge" person.*

On Smiley's music and comedy: *Well, his big asset was his music, and I wasn't too crazy about his music. I'd had the Sons of the Pioneers to begin with when I went to Columbia. I won't say that they were number one or anything, but I've known nobody that's been any better than Bob Nolan and the boys. Smiley was allowed free rein on his music in the films. I would usually leave the set and wait until I got a call to come back. Smiley understood, I think. I saw and appreciated what it add-*

29

ed to the pictures, but I didn't put him in a class with the Sons of the Pioneers. His music added comedy to the pictures. He worked well with our producer, Colbert Clark.

The comedy routines were generally written into the scripts, but if we didn't like them, or if I didn't like something, I'd say, "Smiley, let's try it this way." He was most cooperative after a while; he was very cooperative, and we worked well together—with the material we had, of course.

I liked comedy if it was what I consider good comedy. Smiley had to be held down lots of times with his broad comedy, but we finally got along great because I'd say, "Hey, let's try this again Smiley; what do you say?" I didn't think our comedy in the Durango series was so good as in the earlier pictures that I did. It wasn't Smiley's fault, that was Smiley, and that's the way he was, but I didn't think our comedy was as good in those pictures. Anyway, as an action person, I would have preferred to have gone along with a person like Bob Nolan as a sidekick or co-star, but that's nothing against Smiley. Smiley was in there for his value and he worked hard. That's all I can tell you.

★　　★　　★

In early 1951 when Pat Buttram was injured during the filming of a Gene Autry TV film, Smiley was reunited with Autry for a feature film entitled **Whirlwind**. Autry commented about the reunion, "Events and timing had caused us to split, and the same conditions brought us back. But Smiley and I had come

Smiley and Gene Autry are seen here in one of their last pictures, *Winning of the West* (1953).

During the time Smiley was appearing in "Petticoat Junction" he posed for this picture with Elvis Presley.

to Hollywood together and there was always that bond between us."

When the Charles Starrett series ended in 1952, Gene brought Smiley back as his sidekick for the final six Western features that either of them would ever make. As Autry said, "We had gone in together and we would go out together. Fair is fair."

After the B Western films succumbed to the onslaught of television, it was back on the road for Smiley. With his films no longer playing in neighborhood theaters, the touring business was less lucrative. Finally, Smiley went into semi-retirement, spending less time on the road and more time on his first love, composing.

In 1963 he was offered the featured role of Charlie Pratt on the CBS television series, "Petticoat Junction." Smiley, along with another former sidekick, Rufe Davis, played the two Hooterville train engineers on the popular series. Smiley continued in the series until his death on February 16, 1967, of leukemia.

Gene Autry commented in his autobiography: "It pleased me that he had a few good years on television, near the end, so he could relax and travel less." Gene and Smiley's last appearance together had been on a 1965 television revival of the old "Melody Ranch" radio show.

Dallas moved to Palm Desert after Smiley died. She survived him by ten years, dying in 1977. Gordon MacDonnell, her half brother, told me he was dismayed to find that she was almost penniless when she died, even though she had lived frugally during those last years. Dallas, like Smiley, was a soft touch when it came to certain people.

"He was a sweet and easygoing fellow," Gene Autry wrote, "with a talent not everyone noticed or appreciated behind that zany appearance. He could play more musical instruments than I knew existed; someone once said a hundred.... But best of all he could make children laugh."

SMILEY BURNETTE FILMOGRAPHY

Smiley Burnette made a few films outside the Western genre during his first couple of years in Hollywood. For the purpose of this filmography I have only included those films in which he played the comic sidekick in series B Westerns.

GENE AUTRY series: (Republic Pictures)

Tumbling Tumbleweeds (9/35) George Hayes is also in the cast.

Melody Trail (9/35)

The Sagebrush Troubador (11/35)

The Singing Vagabond (12/35).

Red River Valley (3/36)

Comin' Round the Mountain (3/36)

The Singing Cowboy (5/36)

Guns and Guitars (6/36)

Oh, Susanna (9/36)

Ride, Ranger, Ride (9/36) Future sidekick Max Terhune is making his film debut in this film.

The Big Show (11/36) This big-budget feature includes Max Terhune and the Sons of the Pioneers. Bob Nolan and Roy Rogers were members of the

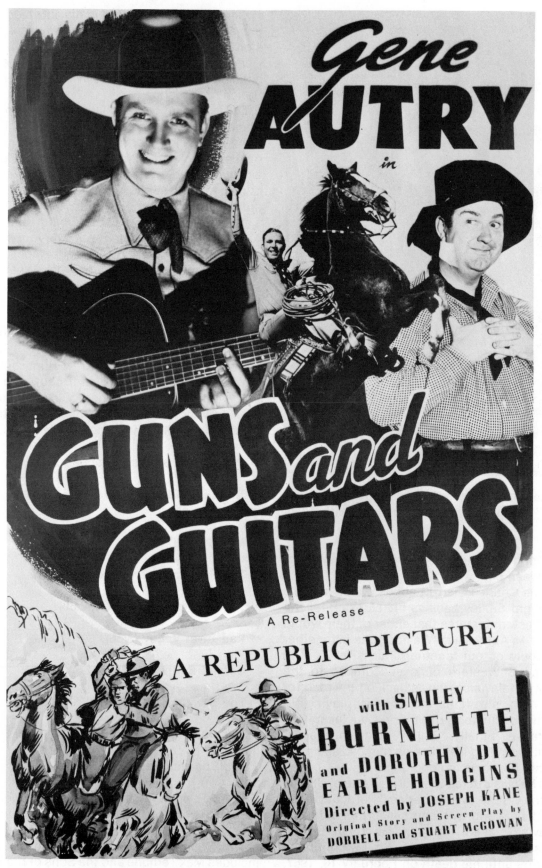

Smiley was usually featured prominently in the publicity (as here) for the Gene Autry films.

Smiley, Duncan Renaldo (later the Cisco Kid), Gene Autry, and Harold Huber practice their knife-throwing skills in this scene from *Down Mexico Way* (1941). Their target, of course, is a tongue-tied outlaw. He soon tells all!

Pioneers at this time.

The Old Corral (12/36) The Sons of the Pioneers appear again with Gene in this feature. Gene has a fight scene with Roy in the film. The star of the film wins, of course.

Round-up Time in Texas (2/37)

Git Along Little Dogies (3/37)

Rootin' Tootin' Rhythm (5/37)

Yodelin' Kid from Pine Ridge (6/37) Guy Wilkerson, a later comic sidekick in the Texas Rangers series, has a small role.

Public Cowboy Number 1 (8/37)

Boots and Saddles (10/37) Chris-Pin Martin, a later Pancho in the movie Cisco Kid series, has a small part in this picture.

Manhattan Merry-Go-Round (11/37) Although this wasn't one of the regular Autry series pictures, Gene, Smiley, and Max Terhune made guest appearances. The real star was Phil Regan.

Springtime in the Rockies (11/37)

The Old Barn Dance (1/38)

Gold Mine in the Sky (7/38)

Man from Music Mountain (8/38)

Prairie Moon (9/38)

Rhythm of the Saddle (11/38)

Western Jamboree (12/38) Later singing cowboy star, Eddie Dean, has a bit part.

Home on the Prairie (2/39)

Mexicali Rose (3/39)

Blue Montana Skies (5/39)

Mountain Rhythm (6/39)

Colorado Sunset (7/39)

In Old Monterey (8/39) George "Gabby" Hayes helps Smiley set some laughs in this episode.

Rovin' Tumbleweeds (11/39) Fellow sidekicks Lee "Lasses" White and Horace Murphy have featured roles.

South of the Border (12/39)

Rancho Grande (3/40) Eddie Dean's sidekick in later years, Roscoe Ates, has a featured role in this film.

Gaucho Serenade (5/40)

Carolina Moon (7/40) Eddy Waller, later to be Allan Lane's sidekick, has a featured role.

Ride, Tenderfoot, Ride (9/40)

Fay McKenzie, pictured here with Smiley and Gene, was a popular heroine in five straight Gene Autry films: *Down Mexico Way, Sierra Sue, Cowboy Serenade, Heart of the Rio Grande,* and *Home in Wyomin'.*

ROY **ROGERS**
SMILEY **BURNETTE**
IN
UNDER WESTERN STARS

A RE-RELEASE

WITH **CAROL HUGHES · MAPLE CITY FOUR**

A *REPUBLIC* PICTURE

Smiley Burnette helped Roy Rogers to get his starring series off to a good start. He co-starred with the singing cowboy in his first two features, *Under Western Stars* and *Billy the Kid Returns*.

Ridin' On a Rainbow (1/41)

Back in the Saddle (3/41)

The Singing Hill (4/41)

Sunset in Wyoming (7/41) Eddie Dew has a small part in this picture. In 1943 Smiley would co-star with Eddie in two episodes of the short-lived John Paul Revere series. Comic Syd Saylor has a small role, too.

Under Fiesta Stars (8/41)

Down Mexico Way (10/41)

Sierra Sue (11/41) Sidekick Syd Saylor has a small role.

Cowboy Serenade (1/42) This picture was loaded with once or future sidekicks: Rand Brooks from the Hoppy series; Slim Andrews from the Tex Ritter series; and Tom London who was also a Sunset Carson sidekick.

Heart of the Rio Grande (3/42) Future singing cowboy, Jimmy Wakely is in the cast with his musical trio.

Home in Wyomin' (4/42) Comic Olin Howlin has an important role in the film.

Stardust on the Sage (5/42)

Call of the Canyon (8/42) Bob Nolan and the Sons of the Pioneers are on hand for this one. Pat Brady, one of the Pioneers, was later to become Roy

Rogers' sidekick. Eddy Waller has a featured role.

Bells of Capistrano (9/42) Gene Autry went into the service upon completion of this film.

ROY ROGERS series: (Republic Pictures)

Under Western Stars (4/38) This feature and *Billy the Kid Returns* were made while Gene Autry was on strike from Republic.

Billy the Kid Returns (9/38) Tex Ritter's sometime sidekick, Horace Murphy, is featured in this film.

Heart of the Golden West (11/42) George "Gabby" Hayes and Bob Nolan and the Sons of the Pioneers are included in the cast.

Idaho (3/42) As usual, Bob Nolan and his Sons of the Pioneers are in the cast.

King of the Cowboys (4/43) Bob Nolan and the Pioneers.

Silver Spurs (8/43) Bob Nolan and the Pioneers.

Eddie Dew series: (Republic Pictures) Eddie had an extremely short-lived career as a cowboy star—just two features. He was to be the star of a John Paul Revere series of pictures. Eddie did not work out, and the role was recast with Robert Livingston. Livingston did two more pictures in the series and then it was dropped.

Beyond the Last Frontier (9/43) Robert Mitchum is featured in the cast.

Raiders of Sunset Pass (12/43)

Robert Livingston series: (Republic Pictures)

Pride of the Plains (1/44)

Beneath Western Skies (3/44)

Roy ROGERS Smiley BURNETTE in BILLY THE KID RETURNS A RE-RELEASE WITH LYNN ROBERTS DIRECTED BY JOE KANE A REPUBLIC PICTURE

Smiley seems to have a leg up on the problem in this scene with Sunset Carson, his co-star in four Republic features.

Laramie Trail (4/44) Comic Emmett Lynn has a featured role.

Sunset Carson series: (Smiley received star billing for the four features he made with Sunset. They were made by Republic.)

Call of the Rockies (7/44)

Bordertown Trail (8/44)

Code of the Prairie (10/44)

Firebrands of Arizona (12/44)

Charles "Durango Kid" Starrett series: (Columbia Pictures)

Roaring Rangers (2/46)

Gunning for Vengeance (3/46)

Galloping Thunder (4/46)

Two-Fisted Stranger (5/46)

Desert Horseman (8/46)

Heading West (8/46)

Landrush (10/46) Emmett Lynn is featured in the cast.

Terror Trail (11/46)

Fighting Frontiersman (12/46) Emmett Lynn is on hand again.

South of the Chisholm Trail (1/47)

Don't worry, Smiley, the Durango Kid has the situation under control. That's Charles Starrett behind the Durango mask.

South of Death Valley (8/49)	**Lightning Guns** (12/50)
Bandits of Eldorado (10/49)	**Frontier Outpost** (12/50)
Desert Vigilante (11/49)	**Prairie Roundup** (1/51)
Horseman of the Sierras (11/49)	**Ridin' the Outlaw Trail** (2/51)
Renegades of the Sage (11/49)	**Fort Savage Raiders** (3/51)
Trail of the Rustlers (2/50)	**Snake River Desperadoes** (5/51)
Outcasts of Black Mesa (4/50)	**Bonanza Town** (6/51)
Texas Dynamo (6/50)	**Cyclone Fury** (6/51)
Streets of Ghost Town (8/50)	**Kid from Amarillo** (10/51)
Across the Badlands (9/50)	**Pecos River** (12/51)
Riders of Tomahawk Creek (10/50)	**Smokey Canyon** (1/52)

Hawk of Wild River (2/52) Syd Saylor is featured in the cast.

Laramie Mountains (3/52)

Rough, Tough West (6/52)

Junction City (7/52)

Kid from Broken Gun (8/52)

Gene Autry series: (Columbia Pictures)

Whirlwind (4/51) This feature was filmed while Smiley was still in the Starrett films. He substituted for Pat Buttram who was injured in an accident while filming a Gene Autry TV episode.

Winning of the West (1/53)

On Top of Old Smokey (3/53)

Goldtown Ghost Raiders (5/53)

Pack Train (6/53)

Saginaw Trail (9/53)

Last of the Pony Riders (11/53)

★   ★   ★

GEORGE "GABBY" HAYES

Dale Evans: The first day I set foot inside Republic Studios I was walking over to the main office for my interview when a long, black Continental convertible came along with a man sitting in it driving straight as an arrow. He was wearing the most beat-up Western hat I had ever seen in my life—the most ancient looking hat—and he had a long beard; really, I'll never forget it. I thought, "Who can this man be? Who is that character sitting in that car?" It was Gabby Hayes.

Roy Rogers: Back in the late 1930s I was always after the studio to get me a sidekick that would be a good contrast and a good playback for me. Gabby had worked with William Boyd in the Hopalong Cassidy series as Windy, and, somehow, Republic got him under contract and they put him in my pictures. He was like my father, my buddy, my brother all wrapped up in one. I loved him.

Dale Evans: You know, a lot of people ask me about Gabby when I'm out doing concerts around the country. "Was he really like he was in pictures in real life?" I tell them, "You'd really be surprised. Gabby Hayes was one of the most cultured men, one of the most well-read men, one of the best-educated men I've ever met. He wore very natty tweeds and he would smoke a pipe. I tell you, he was a very distinguished-looking gentleman."

I loved working scenes with Gabby. He was such a good actor and such fun. He could steal the scene off a billy goat. You know, he taught me probably more than anyone did in the picture business.

Kirby Grant: Gabby Hayes was not genuinely a funny person at all. He was very serious minded. He was something of a raconteur and a gourmet. He was an extremely dapper dresser, beautiful clothes. His beard was beautifully trimmed and he kept his teeth in when he wasn't making a picture.

Charles Starrett: Did you know that Gabby and I did a picture years ago before he became Gabby? During the early 1930s we did a picture called **The Return of Casey Jones**. You know, the railroad person, Casey Jones, from the song. Gabby was a delightful guy. I would love to have had him for comedy in my pictures.

Lash LaRue: One time in San Francisco when I was just getting started, I saw some reporters and photographers hanging around Roy Rogers and Gabby. They told me later what Gabby had said. He told them, "You fellows have got all the information you need on Roy and me. If you want to get some information on somebody who's going to be big in this business, go over there and talk to that fellow, Lash LaRue. He's a young man and he's a comer." Gabby was the first one in the industry who paid me such a compliment.

Jimmy Wakely: Every time I was around Gabby he was a perfect gentleman and a fantastic guy. He was very serious; he was a very fine actor. I've got a picture of ol' Gabby that was taken one night when we went out to 20th Century-Fox for a

The disgruntled Gabby is probably thinking, "Durned persnickety females!"

cocktail party for Greg Peck's new picture—I forget the name of it now. Gabby, Gregory, and I are standing there in the picture. Gabby's got a glass of whiskey in one hand and a cigarette in the other, and I'm thinking, "If his fans could see him, they'd never recognize ol' Gabby. (laugh) He was a beautiful person; I liked him very much. He wasn't a drunk; don't get me wrong, but he'd have a cocktail like most people will. It just looked funny; him holding it there.

He was more of an actor than he was a cowboy. I had a feeling that he wasn't particularly hung up on Westerns, but he never said so. That's just a guess on my part.

Sunset Carson: *Gabby became the measuring stick with which to judge all other sidekicks. He wasn't just a comedian, but he had the ability to turn in some mighty fine acting when needed. Gabby could make you cry as well as make you laugh.*

George Hayes, the definitive cowboy sidekick, in a scene from one of his early Western films.

Gabby Hayes was, indeed, the measuring stick by which to judge all of the other cowboy sidekicks. He was the quintessential sidekick. He was, in fact, a cowboy sidekick before anyone got around to really understanding what a sidekick's role and function were to be in Western films.

Perhaps the point should be made here that George Hayes and several other character actors lay the groundwork for the comic cowboy sidekick, but Smiley Burnette was the first to popularize the sidekick as an integral part of the B Western film. After Smiley and Gene Autry became such a tremendously successful team in films, few producers would think of making a B Western without a comic sidekick. George Hayes took the ingredients for the cowboy sidekick and created "Gabby," the character that most Western film aficionados name as the definitive representation of the cowboy sidekick.

George Francis Hayes was born in Wellsville, New York, on May 7, 1885. When only a teen-ager, he left home to join a traveling show as a song and dance man. Burlesque and vaudeville performing followed as he gradually gained a reputation for pleasing audiences. As the years passed, he toured both the Orpheum and Keith vaudeville circuits.

In 1914 he married Olive Dorothy Ireland, a Ziegfeld Follies show girl. After the marriage, Olive retired from show business. The marriage was a

good one, lasting forty-two years until her death in 1956. They never had any children.

In the late 1920s Olive and George moved to Hollywood where he became active as a film actor just as silent films were about to give way to the coming of sound. George started with bit parts and gradually worked up to featured roles in a wide variety of films as his reputation grew. His first sound picture was **The Rainbow Man** in 1929. It wasn't until he was called upon to work in a Western picture that he got aboard his first horse and learned to ride. By this time he was in his forties.

In a burst of Western film acting starting in the early 1930s George Hayes began to shape the mold for what we would later call the cowboy sidekick. His work with such early cowboy stars as Bob Steele, Harry Carey, Rex Bell, Hoot Gibson, Randolph Scott, and John Wayne ran the gamut from outlaws to fatherly ranchers to garrulous, comic old-timers. Within this wide assortment of roles, he began to fashion the unique sidekick that would eventually become "Gabby."

Although one can locate generous traces of the Gabby character in some of his early Westerns, the definitive character evolved gradually in stages over

Hoppy pulls Windy up short in this scene from *Bar 20 Rides Again* (1935). This is the first Hopalong Cassidy film in which George Hayes plays the character of Windy.

a period of several years. Significant signs of the emerging Gabby character can be located in a few of his Lone Star pictures with John Wayne. In **West of the Divide** (1933), for example, George plays a character called Dusty. He's a tobacco-chewing old codger with a stubble of a beard. He's not really in the film for comedy relief; he's just John Wayne's old pal. Lurking just beneath the surface, however, are signs of the Gabby that is eventually to be.

In 1934 George is again with Wayne in a picture called **Blue Steel.** This time he wears a walrus mustache and a scraggly beard in his role as the town sheriff. He's called old-timer by Wayne. Again, the role is not specifically comic in nature, but there are touches of comedy throughout.

In late 1934 George made a quantum leap towards his Gabby character when he played Ken Maynard's sidekick Cactus in the landmark B Western, **In Old Santa Fe.** (I say landmark because the film introduced Gene Autry and Smiley Burnette to films and set the style, however primitively, for the majority of musical B Westerns that were to follow for the next twenty years.) The bearded, tobacco-spitting, old curmudgeon facets of the later Gabby come to the fore in the film ("My name is Cactus, mister, and don't you forget that I'm prickly!") and, to a degree, the deep warmth of personality which always permeated the definitive Gabby character is revealed.

George's scene with Ken after he has bet and lost Ken's horse Tarzan in a fixed race is particularly moving when he gradually breaks down and expresses his remorse. In the ranch party scene where Gene and Smiley sing, a light-hearted Cactus is carried away by the music and breaks into a vaudeville-type shuffle dance, which adds an additional humorous dimension to his character.

Even the later Gabby costume—tattered black hat pushed up in front, plaid shirt, worn leather vest, and loose-hanging trousers—is pretty much evident in his Cactus role. Throughout the film Cactus, an old desert rat, looks to be in dire need of a bath. His clothes are worn and dirty, and he looks as if he is wearing several months of trail dust and sweat. It's small wonder that the dudes and society ladies at the ranch avoid him. The latter Gabby character might be frayed around the edges, but he was always meticulously clean.

The Gabby persona became even more clearly defined when George assumed the role of Windy in the Hopalong Cassidy series in 1935. The Hoppy series contract came about because Harry "Pop" Sherman, the producer, saw George in **In Old Santa Fe** and caught a glimmer of the depth of character shadings that Hayes could bring to a role. He was also, of course, familiar with George's work in the Wayne series and earlier films.

It took Harry Sherman and Hoppy star Bill Boyd four films with George (He was killed off if the first two films.) before audience response and their own instincts told them that George Hayes as Windy would bring a much needed dimension to their films—comedy relief. Then, too, Hayes could play serious dramatic scenes without losing a beat. Hayes as Windy was always believable whether telling a hilarious tall story or commiserating with Hoppy over the death of a friendly rancher. Boyd was particularly happy with George because his Windy character appealed to youngsters without alienating the large adult audience (as many of the buffoon sidekicks did) that was drawn to the Hoppy films.

As Windy, George kept his beard cropped fairly close until near the end of his twenty-two episode run from 1935 until 1939. The costume he had established as Cactus remained, but the soiled look was soon gone. The most noticeable trait that evolved during the Windy years was the character's garrulousness. Windy was, like his name, windy, and rarely stopped talking. His non-stop ramblings might take the form of grousing about the uselessness of the "young whippersnappers" who worked with Hoppy and him on the Bar 20 Ranch; then again, it might be a whopper of a story that Hoppy and the cowhands listened to with forced tolerance and a wink of an eye.

In late 1938 Sol Siegel, a Republic Pictures producer, was able to lure George away from Harry Sherman and the Hoppy series. Siegel rightly felt that Hayes would be a valuable performer not only in their B Western series, but could also lend acting weight to the planned bigger-budget efforts they had in the works with such stars as Richard Dix and John Wayne. Sherman was not happy about George's defection to Republic and retaliated by prohibiting him from using the character name of Windy at Republic. Thus the new appellation of "Gabby" was born.

The first order of business at Republic was to boost a new series of Westerns starring Roy Rogers. Roy's sidekicks seemed caught in a revolving door which moved them in and then quickly out of his series. Smiley Burnette was around to help Roy in his first two films, but then Gene Autry returned from his self-imposed studio strike and Smiley returned to Autry. Grizzled old Raymond Hatton came in to work with Roy for three films and was then hustled over to the studio's Three Mesquiteers series to replace Max Terhune. (Hatton later made a fourth picture with Roy and George Hayes.) In one

Gabby isn't too happy about washing the dishes when there are outlaws to be caught. This scene with Roy Rogers is from *Utah* (1945).

picture, ***Shine On, Harvest Moon,*** Roy was left to fend for himself except for the musical services of Lulubelle and Scotty. The episode was deemed Rogers' weakest to that time. It was at this point that George Hayes was assigned to the Rogers series.

With the release of ***Southward Ho!*** in March of 1939, the evolution of the Gabby Hayes character was complete—"Yur durned tootin'!" All of the character nuances he had been honing for years emerged on the screen in this new series. He was the perfect sidekick for Roy Rogers because—as Roy says every time you ask him about Gabby—"He was my father, my buddy, my uncle, my brother all wrapped up in one." Gabby added pith and vinegar to the wholesome "Let's go to church" mien of Roy. They were a beautiful contrast on screen and the "chemistry" was right.

Critics praised the teaming and audiences flocked to the theatres to thrill to Roy's adventures and to

laugh at the crackling humor of the cantankerous and lovable old-timer, Gabby. It is impossible, of course, to measure the impact that the teaming of Roy and Gabby had for the Rogers series, but Roy would be the first to acknowledge that his swift rise to the top of the Western field was significantly influenced by two events: his partnership on the screen with Gabby Hayes and the loss to the studio of Gene Autry when he entered the service during World War II. Gabby added a class and style to the sidekick role that no other actor had been able to achieve, and when Autry entered the service, the studio threw all of its backing to Roy—specifically, bigger budgets and a lavish publicity campaign—to insure that the Autry departure would not hurt the studio too much. It should be quickly added, of course, that Roy brought his own distinctive star quality and personality as well as his action and singing abilities to the films. They were the "givens" around which all of the supporting factors of the studio and Gabby could work to enhance the series.

Between 1939 and the end of 1942, Roy and Gabby made twenty-eight features together. Then two events occurred which caused the studio to temporarily break up its successful team: Republic signed former Columbia Pictures cowboy star Bill Elliott to an exclusive series contract and, about the same time, Gene Autry entered the service, leaving Smiley Burnette available as a sidekick. Gabby had done his job well in the Rogers series, which was second now only to Autry's. Herbert Yates, the head of the studio, felt that Gabby could do much to help build the new Bill Elliott series into a winner, and that Smiley should move to the Rogers series where in years past he had proven his ability to work well with Rogers. The deeds were done.

Calling Wild Bill Elliott was the first of the ten pictures Gabby made with Elliott. The Gabby characterization remained the same except for a very slight fine tuning to adjust for the more serious demeanor of Elliott as compared with the more light-hearted, musical mode of Roy Rogers.

As the studio had promised George Hayes when they signed him to a contract, he was given important roles in several of their major big-budget productions. During the years at Republic Gabby was prominently featured in such productions as *The Man of Conquest* (1939) with Richard Dix, *The Dark Command* (1940) starring John Wayne and Walter Pidgeon, *War of the Wildcats* (also called *In Old Oklahoma,* 1943), and *Tall in the Saddle* (1944) again with Wayne.

Legendary stuntman and action director Yakima Canutt remembers working with Gabby on one of the big-budget Wayne pictures.

Yakima Canutt: *This was a picture called*

Gabby and Wild Bill Elliott are ready for the shoot out in this scene from *The Man from Thunder River* (1943).

Yakima Canutt and author David Rothel discuss Gabby Hayes at the 1979 St. Louis Western Film Fair.

In Old Oklahoma. In the picture we had about fourteen wagons made into tank wagons to haul oil to the railroad. They had to be delivered there by a certain time. Gabby was driving one of the wagons. The scene called for the back of Gabby's wagon to be on fire. He was to stop and fan out the fire and then get back on the wagon and leave.

Well, Gabby was always trying to better his part in a picture if he could, so just before we began the scene he said, "Yak, let's do something with this. Can you get fire or smoke in my whiskers?" I said, "We can get smoke in your whiskers, but it might be a little bother to you." "Oh, no," he assured me, "it'll be great." So I got the effects man over and he fixed Gabby's whiskers so the smoke would roll out of them.

Finally, we were ready for the scene.

Gabby drove his wagon up, stopped, jumped off the wagon, and ran around back to put out the fire as he was supposed to. Then this smoke effect in his whiskers started smothering him, and he started fighting his whiskers and screaming bloody murder. I had to jump in and hold him while they put out his whiskers. He yelled, "You're trying to kill me!" I laughed, "Gabby, it was your gag; you wanted it."

After eight episodes in his own series, Bill Elliott was asked to portray the famous comic-strip cowboy, Red Ryder, in a Republic series. Elliott agreed to the switch and Gabby continued with him in the first two Ryder adventures.

Now again the studio stepped in to juggle its supporting players to get maximum benefit from their skills. Elliott as Red Ryder had the Indian boy, Little Beaver, as a juvenile sidekick, but Gabby's function in the series was not clearly defined; therefore, it was felt that better use should be made of his abilities. A few months before this, an inexperienced young cowboy named Sunset Carson was signed for an action series and was in need of a comic sidekick. The studio felt that Smiley Burnette should co-star with Sunset until the awkward young fellow got comfortable in pictures. Smiley's new assignment left Roy Rogers without a sidekick again. Roy used Guinn "Big Boy" Williams for a couple of pictures, but the chemistry was wrong between them. The decision was easy: team Roy and Gabby again.

The popular duo was reunited for *Lights of Old Santa Fe* (1944) and continued together through *Heldorado* in 1946—a total of fourteen films during their second teaming. Although Gabby had appeared many times on Roy's radio program, in 1946 they officially teamed for "The Roy Rogers Show," a weekly half-hour of music, comedy, and adventure on NBC. Dale Evans and the Sons of the Pioneers were also on hand for the radio series.

During this period of the mid 1940s Gabby Hayes reached his peak of popularity and maintained it for several years. Evidence of Gabby's popularity was established by the Motion Picture Herald poll of film exhibitors regarding their ranking of the top money-making Western stars. In 1943 Gabby ranked fourth among all cowboy stars and sidekicks. Only Roy Rogers, Bill Boyd, and Smiley Burnette ranked higher. By 1945 Gabby ranked second only to Roy Rogers. Through 1950 (when he quit films and moved into television) Gabby never ranked lower than fifth in the yearly poll.

Gabby's most memorable films with Rogers came during their second series. In *Don't Fence Me In* (1945) Gabby's role as the legendary outlaw Wildcat Kelly was pivotal to the plot. Gabby was given free rein to steal the picture from Roy and Dale with his colorful portrayal. The film was tremendously popular with audiences initially, no doubt, because of the popularity of the title song by Cole Porter. Once the crowds got into the theatres, it was mostly Gabby who captivated them for the next seventy-one minutes.

In 1946 Gabby played the crusty old owner of a palomino horse breeding ranch in the picture *My Pal Trigger.* Roy and director Frank McDonald have told me they consider the film one of the best they ever made, and it certainly is. In this big-budget episode Gabby had the opportunity to play a mostly serious role with the comedy content toned down considerably. In the picture when his prized palomino stallion, Golden Soverign, is shot and killed, Gabby movingly expresses his anger and grief in a memorable scene. Throughout this well-structured film Gabby walks a tightrope of dramatic emotion and comic relief without a falter. The film is an acting lesson for all future character actors.

Two pictures later Gabby had another exceptionally strong part in *Roll on Texas Moon* (1946)—this time with an emphasis on comedy. The highly-respected action director, William Witney, directed this film and all of the Rogers films that were to follow. Witney told a film festival audience a few years ago that he ranks *Roll on Texas Moon* as his favorite Rogers film, primarily because of Gabby's performance. Witney was quite taken by Gabby's portrayal of a cantankerous old cattleman who cannot abide sheep or sheepherders. Much to Gabby's chagrin a baby lamb from a neighboring sheep ranch becomes enamored of him and follows wherever he goes. The exasperated Gabby threatens to shoot the "walking lambchop." As he tells the lamb, "I gotta' do it; I can't afford to be seen around with anybody like you." But Gabby's a softy inside and can't bring himself to shoot the little critter. He furtively tries to hide the lamb so that his cattlemen friends won't learn of his weakness. Gabby's performance is both touching and hilarious as he tries to resolve his perplexing problem, but can only cry out in frustration, "Ya dad-blasted woolies!"

When I talked with Roy Rogers about Gabby, he told me the story he loves to tell about Gabby—the time he decided to shave off his beard.

Roy Rogers: *Gabby decided to shave his beard because he knew I was going to be on the road for about three months. He didn't have anything to do since he was working just in my series at the time. He told me the story when I got back. He said, "Roy, I knew you was going to be gone for quite a while, and I haven't seen my face without a beard on for about thirty years. I just got the urge to do it. So I went in the bathroom and got my shaver and shaved my beard off. I took one look at the mirror and never saw such an ugly so-and-so in my life."*

He was so ashamed of how he looked that he put his wife in the car and they drove to their place in Palm Desert. He didn't come out of the house for six weeks, until his beard grew out. His wife told me he didn't even go out into the backyard; he wouldn't go out of the house. He didn't want any neighbors or anybody to see him without his beard. When he cut the beard off and he saw his face sunken in a little bit, why, it shocked him. That story stands out in my mind so much about Gabby.

Dale Evans co-starred with Roy and Gabby in all fourteen films they made between 1944 and 1946.

With the completion of **Heldorado** in late 1946, Gabby decided not to renew his contract with Republic. He wanted the freedom to pick and choose his film roles in the future and to cut down on the heavy schedule Republic had set for him. In 1946, alone, he had made seven pictures with Roy Rogers plus a loan-out picture for RKO entitled **Badman's Territory** with Randolph Scott, a close personal friend.

Between 1947 and 1950 (when he left films for television) Gabby made only seven films, four of them with Randy Scott. **Trail Street** (1947), his first with Scott after leaving the Rogers series, co-starred Robert Ryan as the baddie and provided Gabby with one of his best roles as the irascible tall-tale-teller, Deputy Marshal Billy Burns. Scott played Bat Masterson, whose job it was to clean up the town of Trail Street. Many of Gabby's by now trademarked expressions were sprinkled generously throughout the script:

> *"Why you old horned toad."*
> *"This jail will be more populous than a hound dog with the fleas."*
> *"Before you know it this town will be as hot as a two-dollar pistol on the fourth of July."*
> *"Thicker'n flies around a molasses barrel."*

And then there were his tall tales:

> *(To Scott) "You think you had some pretty tough people over there in Dodge City. I guess you never heard of Drygulch Curly, have you? You see, old Brandyhead Jones, he was a United States Marshal, too. He done all the hangin' over in our neighborhood. This Drygulch Curly I'm tellin' you about—he was so tough that when old Brandyhead hung him, his trigger finger kept jerkin' for two hours after he was dead."*

> *(To Ryan) "You talk about winds and cyclones. Back where me and Brandyhead Jones was born, one time the wind blowed so hard it blowed the chicken feathers right off the chickens onto the ducks and the duck feathers onto the chickens. Funniest thing you ever saw. (laugh) To hear them ducks crowin' and the chickens a quackin'...."*

Although **Trail Street** is a typical Western with

plenty of action and a slam-bang climactic shoot out, the final scene is left for Gabby. With the town cleaned up, Bat Masterson is leaving and Gabby is named the town marshal, a job which he takes very seriously. Suddenly the stage comes thundering into town with someone inside shooting off a pistol. As the stage stops, Gabbys grabs the gun through the stage window and opens the door to discover his cousin, Brandyhead Jones (Gabby in another costume). Gabby expresses his extreme consternation ("consarned scalawag") and tells his cousin—in no uncertain terms—that if he intends to stay in town he will have to obey the law. The background music rises and the scene fades to THE END.

Gabby brought his movie career to a close with the 1950 production of **The Cariboo Trail** starring Randolph Scott. He was sixty-five years old and ready to retire. Little did he realize that a whole new career was about to open for him in television.

During 1950 the Quaker Oats Company was looking for a television format for a proposed Sunday afternoon children's show. NBC presented a plan to star old-time cowboy sidekick Gabby Hayes as the host-narrator of such a program. The format would feature the comedy of Gabby's tall tales, the educational appeal of dramatized stories of our American heritage, and Gabby's unique delivery of the sponsor's commercials. Quaker Oats liked the idea, and Gabby was off to New York for the September 30, 1950, premiere of "The Gabby Hayes Show." A special coup for the opening stanza was the guest appearances of Roy Rogers, Dale Evans, Trigger, and Bullet the dog. **Variety** commented in its favorable review that Gabby had so many guests on his opening show that he had very little to do on the program.

"The Gabby Hayes Show" was an immediate success with kid *and* adult audiences. Gabby's comical manner and ease in front of the live NBC cameras made him a natural for this new medium. For Gabby the show's success was particularly gratifying since it was the first time in his career that he was truly the star of his own series. He was no longer a sidekick helping a star to carry a movie or film series.

The slogan for Quaker Oats stated that their cereal was "shot from guns." Gabby would close each program by shooting the cereal out of a cannon aimed at the television camera. He would first warn the kids watching not to sit too close to their television sets because they might get hit during the explosion. Then he would shoot the cannon and the picture would cut to the closing credits. This bit of closing excitement was always a highlight for the kiddie audience and made for a big finish on each

Gabby Hayes—he's a television star, by cracky!

program.

With the success of the Sunday program, NBC launched a daily early-evening program where Gabby hosted a serialized old Western movie. Each evening the viewer would listen to Gabby joke around in his grandfatherly manner, see a few minutes of the Western film, and then receive the sponsor's message as only Gabby could render it.

Gabby did his NBC shows for two successful seasons and then took some time off. When Howdy Doody's pal, Buffalo Bob Smith, had a heart attack in 1954, Gabby was asked to take over the popular "Howdy Doody" program until he could return. Gabby hosted the program well into 1955.

After his "Howdy Doody" duty, Gabby felt that it was time to hang up his tattered old black hat and retire. He had worked in just about every form of show business in a career which had lasted over fifty years. When his wife Olive died in 1956 and his own health was becoming unsteady, his decision was made.

When I was researching this chapter, I remembered that Carolyn Grant, Kirby Grant's wife, had recounted an incident regarding Gabby one time while I was visiting them at their home near Orlando. I called Carolyn and asked it she would repeat the details of her meeting with Gabby years before.

Carolyn Grant: Character actors, of course, quite often look very different in their private lives compared to how they look on the screen. Around 1959 we lived on a lake just outside of Los Angeles, and it was not unusual to run into a movie star in that area.

At that time we were doing a lot of entertaining, and this particular day I was fixing my favorite shrimp curry dish for company we were expecting that evening. I went to the Lakeside Market, where everybody shopped, to select a nice wine to have with the dinner. I was having trouble deciding on just which one would go best with the shrimp curry when I looked over and saw this very dapper-looking gentleman. He had gorgeous gray hair, a very neatly trimmed goatee, and was wearing a gray flannel, obviously custom-made, suit. He was looking at the wines.

I said to him, "You certainly appear to be a connoisseur of wines. Would you help me?" He said, "Well, I'd be charmed, little lady. What is your problem?" I told him that I was having twelve people for dinner that evening. He asked what I was

serving, and I told him. I explained that I wanted to choose an appropriate wine.

He looked around and studied the different wines. Finally, he picked out a wine and took me by the arm to the lady at the check-out counter. He told her, "You give this lady as much of this particular wine to go with her dinner as she needs. If she doesn't like it, I want you to put it on my bill." With that, he left.

I said to the lady, "Boy, that was terrific! Who was that?" She said, "That was Gabby Hayes." I couldn't believe it. He certainly didn't look like the Gabby Hayes I was familiar with in the movies. I knew that he and Kirby were friends, but I had never met him before. He just helped me out like a good Samaritan.

I never saw Gabby again, but Kirby and I became good friends with his nephew, Clark Hayes, and we, of course, relayed the story to him. Clark and his wife thought it was very nice that Uncle George, as they called Gabby, would help me with my wine problem.

That was my experience with Gabby Hayes. He was completely charming, and the thing that really affected me was that he was gorgeous. He was a beautiful man; I mean, so well-groomed and well-dressed. He was dapper Dan. You wouldn't recognize him. And my friends enjoyed the wine.

Carolyn's reference to Gabby's nephew Clark Hayes was one of those happy accidents that sometimes occur when you are researching a book. Carolyn and Kirby told me that Clark had been very close to Gabby—"like a son"—and that they were sure that Clark would be happy to discuss his Uncle George with me. They gave me his California telephone number.

I called Clark Hayes the next evening and spent several hours talking with him. In his soft-spoken, unrushed manner he covered a wide range of information regarding his uncle that only a close member of the family would possess.

Clark Hayes on Gabby's education and early career: *In terms of his education Uncle George was a self-educated man. He dropped out of school in the eighth grade and hung around the theater in his hometown of Wellsville, New York, which is in western New York state. I always felt*

In private life Gabby was meticulous about his grooming and clothing—much more so than in this publicity photo done for laughs.

54

that for someone who didn't have a formal education, he was very well-educated. He was very well-read and "up" on almost any subject. In his travels he loved to talk to people about their work and was a very good listener and learned from everybody.

He went from school into vaudeville. He used to say that over the years he had probably played in every opera house in the country. He traveled for years and years. He was born in 1885, and he left home just after the turn of the century. He didn't get into Hollywood and pictures until sometime in the late 1920s, so he was traveling continually in burlesque and vaudeville for over twenty years. He was pretty much a song and dance man, but he did skits and short plays as part of his vaudeville work.

I know there are stories that he accumulated a small fortune during his years in burlesque, vaudeville, and early pictures and that he lost it during the stock market crash. That wasn't true. He was a struggling young actor who never had a great deal during those years, and Aunt Dot (Gabby's wife) worked for a while as a clerk in a five-and-dime store so that they had enough money to exist. This was during the burlesque and vaudeville years.

On Gabby's hobbies and personal interests: He was vitally interested as a spectator in all sorts of sporting activities. I think he probably followed baseball more than the other sports. He was good friends with a lot of the major league ballplayers. He was particularly close to Jackie Robinson. Uncle George was also a very avid prize fight fan. Here in California they used to have Friday night fights at the Hollywood Legion, and he was regularly in attendance. When he was younger, he loved to fish and go duck hunting.

He made quite a hobby of wines and considered himself very knowledgeable in terms of wine, especially French wines. On several trips to Europe he spent time in the wine country.

He loved to travel. He made a number of trips to Europe and cruise trips to the Far East. I guess much of that was in his later years. Some of it was after his wife passed away. He liked to spend a lot of time in the desert in the Palm Springs, Palm Desert area.

On Gabby's marriage: He and his wife were married forty-some years. She was a Ziegfeld Follies girl, a dancer. They met while they were both on the road and were married around 1914. Her name was Olive. I think her maiden name was Dorothy Olive Ireland. Her side of the family always called her Aunt Olive and the Hayes side always called her Aunt Dot. They had no children. She retired from show business after they were married.

On Gabby's friends: He made quite a number of pictures with John Wayne, of course. John and George were good friends over the years. He always had good things to say about Bill Elliott, too. Randolph Scott was really one of the finest gentlemen he ever had any dealings with. They not only worked together on screen, but they were close friends off screen.

One time I had an opportunity to meet Randolph Scott while he and Uncle George were making one of their pictures on location outside of Hollywood. I was introduced to Randy while Uncle George was doing some scenes. They were having to repeat them because some of the horses were not doing what they were supposed to do. Finally the director came over to Randy and said, "I don't think that we're going to get to you any more today. Why don't you go home; there's no sense hanging around here." Randy agreed and started to leave. When he got about a hundred yards away, he turned and came back and apologized for leaving without saying goodbye and for not telling me how nice it was to have met me. I looked upon him as a real gentleman for doing that.

As you know, Gabby worked a long time with Roy Rogers. I never knew any of the details, but I always had a feeling that somewhere along in that association there was a falling away between Roy and Gabby. There was something that didn't appear to be quite right between them, but I'm not sure what it was, and neither of them would talk about it. And yet I can recall when Gabby was in poor health, Roy came to the apartment where Uncle George lived to visit him. That would have been within the last year that he lived.

Roy and Dale have been doing publicity for Far West Savings and Loan whose home office is nearby in Orange County. When they were here one day last year, I went up and introduced myself. They were both very nice to me, and both had nice things to say about what a wonderful man Gabby was.

I believe the closest friend Gabby ever had in show business was Bill Boyd. I know there have been stories that they did not get along, but that is wrong. He quit the Hoppy series because of problems with Harry Sherman, the producer. I never knew the details, but the problems were certainly not with Bill. He and Bill Boyd and Gracie (Boyd's wife) remained very close friends. I can recall visiting my Uncle George on his birthday one year when Bill and Gracie, who were on a vacation trip in Europe, called to wish him a happy birthday. That was long after both of them had retired. It would have been in the late 1950s.

Bill had property down in Palm Desert, and Gabby bought what you'd call today a small, one-bedroom condominium in one of the little developments Bill had there. They weren't the type of people to spend a great deal of time together; they respected each other's privacy, and yet they often talked by phone. Whenever George was in the Desert, he would stop in on Bill and vice-versa. I would say he was probably closer to Bill Boyd than anybody, even Randolph Scott.

On being "Gabby" in Western films: He worked in Westerns for so long that they just became a part of him, and he became comfortable working in them. He made that character of Gabby and it made him. He was very happy with it.

I think he enjoyed the fact that everybody called him Gabby rather than George Hayes. He also loved to be recognized and loved to be asked for his autograph. He was always very gracious about that. He felt that he owed that to his fans, to be nice to them. He felt that

you should start worrying when they stopped asking.

On working with horses: He was very comfortable with horses. For a non-Westerner he became a good horseman. He was also a good driver of a team—a four-up. He developed into a horseman; the pros that were around horses all of the time respected him for what he had been able to accomplish with horses. He used to own some horses that were just pets. I learned to ride on one of his horses when I was a kid.

On Gabby's demeanor off screen: He loved to kid around among the family. In his kidding he would use his Gabby mannerisms. He'd played that character for so long that it was a part of his life. He was very likely to come out with a "Yur durned tootin'," and he would talk with his stage voice. He loved to call my wife a "city slicker" and kid her a great deal about being a city gal. He loved children even though, of course, he didn't have any of his own.

He loved to be light-hearted, but among strangers he was always more serious. He would love to get people to talk about themselves and their jobs and careers, because that was the method he always used to learn. He didn't always want to talk show business. Obviously, he talked show business, but he didn't want to bore people talking about himself and about the trade.

I would not at all describe him as an extrovert. At a party he would not be the life of the party. He was more apt to be off on the fringes of the party, seeking out groups of two or three people to whom he would talk seriously. Off stage he didn't want to be on stage. I think if someone asked him to perform—sing or dance—at a party, he would have a tendency to beg off. He wasn't a shy man at all and he wasn't introverted, but he wasn't extroverted, either.

He was a staunch conservative and was a very pro-American and staunch anti-communist. He wasn't a John Bircher, but I guess he easily could have become one. He didn't like people who had anything bad to say about this country. He had no racial prejudice. I mentioned that Jackie Robinson was a close friend. I remember that when Jackie had a home up in Westchester, my uncle was a house guest of his. Being in show business he worked a lot with people of the Jewish faith, and he had a lot of Jewish friends.

On Gabby's last years: He was pretty much retired by the late 1950s. There were a couple of attempts years after that to get him to go on a talk show as a guest. He just never felt that he wanted to do that. He had a heart condition and he didn't want to undergo any additional strain.

At the time he retired, he owned some apartments. By apartments I mean two adjoining buildings with a total of ten or twelve two-bedroom apartments in them. They had built them, he and my aunt, and they were quality apartments. Uncle George and Aunt Dot had a three-bedroom unit that they lived in.

That was the extent of his real estate holdings. He made all of his money at the wrong time. He also never got any residuals out of his movies when they ran on TV. He was comfortable, but not well-off.

Gabby lived about ten years from the time he retired. He was in poor health much of that time—at least the last five or six years. He didn't do much socializing. He read a lot and enjoyed his nephews and nieces and grand-nephews and grand-nieces. Another thing he enjoyed very much was going to good restaurants. We used to do that with him frequently. When you get to be along in years, your circle of friends shrinks, and he didn't have a lot of friends during his last two or three years.

He died of a heart attack. He had one heart attack which he got over. We brought him back to his apartment on a Saturday and on the next Monday he had another heart attack. He was taken back to the coronary care unit, and it was obvious he wasn't going to make it. I arranged with them to keep him in the coronary care unit as long as they didn't need his bed for a more serious case. All the nurses had cared for him previously and knew and loved him. It just seemed appropriate that he stay there. He died in that unit on February 9, 1969.

He was known in his films for being cantankerous, but that was all part of the pictures; that wasn't him at all. He was a pretty easygoing guy. I can't remember ever seeing him get angry and fly off the handle. I'm prejudiced, of course, but he was just a charming guy, a great guy.

One day Roy Rogers confessed to Gabby that he really did not consider himself an actor, that he talked the same on and off the stage, just like an "ol' country boy." "No, Roy, you're wrong about that," Gabby assured him. "Your cowboy talk is the real thing. All you have to do is just be natural. The most successful actors are those that act so real the audience forgets they're acting."

Gabby Hayes was real and a natural.

GEORGE "GABBY" HAYES FILMOGRAPHY

Although Gabby Hayes was featured with many Western stars, he only played continuing roles in three series. Only these series are included in the filmography.

Hopalong Cassidy series (William Boyd): (Paramount Pictures)

Hop-a-long Cassidy (8/35) George plays an old timer called Uncle Ben in this first episode.

The Eagle's Brood (10/35) George plays a character called Spike.

Bar 20 Rides Again (11/35) This is the first Hoppy film in which George plays Windy. Chill Wills and His Avalon Boys and Al St. John have small roles in this episode.

Call of the Prairie (3/36) Shanghai is the name of George's character in this episode. Chill Wills and His Avalon Boys provide some Western music in the film.

Three on the Trail (4/36) From this film through all future Hoppy pictures, George plays Windy Halliday.

Heart of the West (7/36)

Hopalong Cassidy Returns (10/36) Al St. John and singer Ray Whitley have small roles.

Hoppy and Windy ride out to adventure in this scene from one of their Hopalong Cassidy films from the late 1930s.

Trail Dust (12/36) Britt Wood and Al St. John have supporting roles.

Borderland (2/37)

Hills of Old Wyoming (4/37)

North of the Rio Grande (6/37)

Rustler's Valley (7/37)

Hopalong Rides Again (9/37)

Texas Trail (11/37)

Heart of Arizona (4/38)

Bar 20 Justice (6/38)

Pride of the West (9/38)

In Old Mexico (9/38)

The Frontiersman (12/38)

Sunset Trail (2/39)

Silver on the Sage (3/39)

The Renegade Trail (7/39)

ROY ROGERS series: (Republic Pictures)

Southward Ho (5/39)

In Old Caliente (6/39)

Wall Street Cowboy (8/39) Raymond Hatton is featured in the cast.

The Arizona Kid (9/39)

Saga of Death Valley (11/39)

Days of Jesse James (12/39)

The Dark Command (4/40) This film is not part of the regular Rogers series, but Roy is in the cast with Gabby and John Wayne.

Young Buffalo Bill (4/40)

The Carson City Kid (7/40)

The Ranger and the Lady (7/40)

Colorado (9/40)

Young Bill Hickok (10/40)

The Border Legion (12/40)

Robin Hood of the Pecos (1/41) Roscoe Ates has a bit part in this picture.

In Old Cheyenne (3/41)

Sheriff of Tombstone (5/41)

Nevada City (6/41)

Meet Roy Rogers (6/41) This ten-minute short featured Gabby, Gene Autry, Judy Canova, Bill Elliott, Bob Baker, Roscoe Ates, and Mary Lee.

Bad Man of Deadwood (9/41)

Jesse James at Bay (10/41)

Red River Valley (12/41)

Man From Cheyenne (1/42)

The Sons of the Pioneers joined the Roy Rogers series in late 1941 with the film *Red River Valley*. Pat Brady (left) was a member of the group until he entered the service during World War II. He rejoined The Pioneers after the War and later became Roy's sidekick in films and television.

South of Santa Fe (2/42)

Sunset on the Desert (4/42)

Romance on the Range (5/42)

Sons of the Pioneers (7/42)

Sunset Serenade (9/42)

WILD BILL ELLIOTT series: (Republic Pictures)

Calling Wild Bill Elliott (4/43)

Man from Thunder River (6/43)

Death Valley Manhunt (9/43)

Bordertown Gunfighters (10/43)

Wagon Tracks West (10/43)

Overland Mail Robbery (11/43)

Mojave Firebrand (3/44)

Hidden Valley Outlaws (4/44)

RED RYDER series (Bill Elliott): (Republic Pictures)

Tucson Raiders (5/44)

Marshall of Reno (7/44)

ROY ROGERS series: Republic Pictures

Gabby made two films in the Red Ryder series with Bill Elliott and Bobby Blake. The popular series was based upon the comic strip and novels illustrated by Fred Harman.

Lights of Old Santa Fe (11/44)

Utah (3/45)

Bells of Rosarita (6/45)

The Man from Oklahoma (8/45)

Sunset in El Dorado (9/45) Tom London has a featured part in the film.

Don't Fence Me In (10/45) Tom London plays the sheriff.

Along the Navajo Trail (12/45)

Song of Arizona (3/46)

Rainbow over Texas (5/46)

My Pal Trigger (8/46)

Under Nevada Skies (8/46)

Roll On Texas Moon (9/46) Tom London has a featured role.

Home in Oklahoma (11/46)

Heldorado (12/46)

★   ★   ★

Al St. John as his most famous character, Fuzzy Q. Jones.

AL "FUZZY" ST. JOHN
"Fuzzy was an angel unaware."

—Lash LaRue

Fred Scott: You ask who was the most fun to work with. Al St. John was by far the easiest of all, a great actor, comedian and athlete. One has only to watch some of his pratfalls and his work with the horses to realize how marvelous he was. It was on one of our pictures that Al got the name of Fuzzy. The part was originally supposed to be played by Fuzzy Knight. Al took the part and the name stuck ever since because it was written in the script and was never changed.

(Favorite Westerns, 5-'83, interview by Bob Pontes)

Buster Crabbe: We made thirty-six Westerns together in the Billy the Kid series over a period of six years. I think without a doubt that Fuzzy was far and away the best of all the Western comics. That includes a lot of people: Gabby Hayes, Andy Devine, Smiley Burnette, and Fuzzy Knight.

Lash LaRue: He could stumble over a match stick and spend fifteen exciting minutes looking for the match.

Al St. John was born in Santa Ana, California, on September 10, 1892, to a family of vaudeville troupers and spent much of his early childhood on-the-road with his parents. He literally knew almost nothing but show business since his schooling was a hit and miss affair as he tagged along with his family from theater to theater across the country.

Early on Al discovered that he had acrobatic skills and a proclivity for doing stunts with a unicycle and bicycle. His trick riding was so spectacular that he was soon performing his "act" with the family. Eventually he went on to headline in vaudeville on his own.

By 1914 his acrobatics and general knock-about talents had come to the attention of film producer Mack Sennett, who was looking for another fellow to join the group of zanies he was calling the Keystone Cops. Al fit the bill perfectly and was soon one of the boys in the tremendously popular comedy series of silent shorts.

During this same time he worked with such other luminaries of the silent screen as Buster Keaton, Charlie Chaplin, and his uncle, Roscoe "Fatty" Arbuckle. Although Al's parents looked askance at film making—as many vaudevillians did—Roscoe's wife, Al's Aunt Minta, encouraged him and helped to open studio doors by dropping good words about him in the proper places.

Mack Sennett used Al's talents not only for the Keystone Cops, but also for any stunting that was needed in the Sennett pictures—remember that there were no trained stuntmen in films at that time. Al, with his acrobatic rubber body was a natural. High dives, trick car driving and wrecks, falling off cliffs, and, of course, bicycle/unicycle spinning and wheeling were almost daily St. John occurrences on the Mack Sennett lot.

By 1916 Al left Sennett to join his Uncle Roscoe who had begun to produce his own films. He told Al he wanted to use him as a second banana in the films. All did not go so well in this family association, and soon Al was demoted to a lower banana on the bunch as Buster Keaton took over as the new second banana.

By the beginning of the 1920s Al had left his uncle and was making comic shorts for companies such as Fox Studio, Paramount, and Educational Studio. Eventually he was to accept smaller roles in silent

During the time Al St. John was working with his uncle "Fatty" Arbuckle, he developed this country rube character in contrast to Arbuckle's screen persona. It is quite apparent that Al's costume here is only a few modifications away from his later "Fuzzy" outfit.

features of the late twenties. Al was doing all right in the film business, but he wasn't exactly dazzling anyone with fantastic success. The freshness of his early days with Mack Sennett had dulled somewhat, and he was fast becoming just a journeyman comic in silent films.

During this time Al St. John rejoined his Uncle Roscoe for a series of shorts that were made by Vitaphone. Arbuckle had, by this time, gone through his famous rape scandal and was attempting to get his career going again. Al was sympathetic to his uncle's ambitions and wanted to help in every way he could, but, as they soon discovered, it was too late for Fatty Arbuckle to resurrect his broken career.

By the time of his uncle's death in 1933, Al had discovered a vehicle that was just perfect for carrying his talents to the public—Western films. In fact,

he was so pleased with them that, except for a few early sashays out of the genre, Al St. John was to stay in the saddle from about 1930 until 1951 when the Lash LaRue series faded into the sunset.

Al St. John found that the transition to sound pictures posed no problems for him. As a comic he was not expected to have any particular type of voice. The fact that he could play the comic fool was expected. That he could also play a straight role and even act a death scene with pathos, as he did in the early Hoppy film, *Bar 20 Rides Again* (1935), was an added plus to his early Western career.

For the first ten years or so of his Western career [if we arbitrarily date his Western start with Tom Mix in the Fox productions of *Hello Cheyenne* (1928) and *Painted Post* (1928)] Al worked constantly in Westerns with probably more Western stars than any other sidekick—not that he was necessarily a

Right: Fred Scott was the singing cowboy star of the series in which Al St. John developed his "Fuzzy" character.

Below: A young-looking Al St. John is ready for action alongside Guinn "Big Boy" Williams in one of Guinn's few starring features, *Law of the 45's* (1935).

"sidekick" during this time. His roles were often comic, but also often minor in importance. The cowboy stars with whom he appeared include Tom Mix, Bob Steele, Bob Custer, Bill Cody, Big Boy Williams (before he became a sidekick himself), William Boyd (in *Painted Desert* in 1931 before Bill became Hopalong Cassidy. The film also featured the first appearance of Clark Gable on the screen.), John Wayne, Tom Tyler, Rex Bell, Johnny Mack Brown, Tex Ritter, Jack Randall, and Buster Crabbe (in a Zane Grey Western, *Wanderers of the Wasteland* in 1935, for Paramount).

Although Al appeared several times with one cowboy star or another during the early 1930s, the first series he co-starred in was a one-year stint with movie singing cowboy, Fred Scott. The seven low-budget Scott features were released by Spectrum Pictures from April of 1937 through May of '38. Their main distinction was that in the series Al created his Fuzzy Q. Jones character which he could utilize

for the rest of his career—in fact, fans and his fellow actors called him by the "Fuzzy" moniker more then by his real name.

For the Scott series Al's beard was little more than a stubble compared with the jutting-out-from-the-chin style he would wear in later Fuzzy incarnations. He freely utilized his acrobatic attributes as in *The Roaming Cowboy* (1937) where he dismounted hurriedly from his horse and dived head first into the dirt in an attempt to avoid the shots of owlhoots. When pulled to his feet a few moments later by hero Scott, Al used his rubber-legged comic routine to show how frightened he was from the wild goings on.

Al's costume was still evolving during the Scott films. The baggy-to-the-crotch, patched-in-the-seat pants of later Fuzzy films were hitched higher here. The vest he wore did not yet have the dark triangle insert in the back. The light-colored, pushed-up-in-the-front hat was black at this point and less tattered

Fuzzy, Christine McIntyre, and Fred Scott share some close harmony in this scene from their 1938 production of *Ranger's Round-Up*. Fuzzy played the guitar to accompany Scott in several of their pictures. It was rare that he would join in the singing.

than the one we got used to during his best-known films of the 1940s.

Al had a comic roll-your-own cigarette routine that was good for laughs in a score of pictures. Sometimes he would make a total botch of the rolling; sometimes he would execute a one-handed roll with astounding dexterity—either way it was hilarious. (For the record, Al sometimes chewed tobacco and smoked at the same time in the Fred Scott pictures.)

Throughout the years Al honed the none-too-subtle shadings of the Fuzzy Q. Jones character: he was the little guy who recklessy talked tough to the big bad guys—as long as the cowboy hero was close by. When he and Fred Scott had the drop on the outlaws in **Songs and Bullets** (1938), Fuzzy warned them: "All right, boys, I reckon you can take your hands down now, but don't try anything funny or I'll jump down your throats with my spurs on and rake you from tonsil to toenail."

Fuzzy was a brave little cuss as long as he knew the hero was on hand or would arrive in time to save his hide; then, of course, he'd brag about how he "could have whipped all of them single-handed" if Fred/Billy/Lash/or whomever had not come along to interfere.

When in a fight, he used his acrobatics to fell his opponent, frequently by intertwining his legs around the outlaw's middle, pulling the villain's ten-gallon hat down over his eyes, and then pummeling him into submission. A stray barroom spitoon invariably found itself in the path of Fuzzy's footfall, resulting in much kicking, hopping, stomping, prying, and closeup facial exasperation before final release. In all, the comic escapades were cowboy variations of routines that Al had mastered years before in the silent two-reelers he made for Mack Sennett. The bits still worked and were loved by audiences all over the world because they didn't rely on words for their humor; they evoked a universal language—laughter.

After the Fred Scott series folded in mid 1938, Al St. John made a couple of films for Monogram with another singing cowboy, Jack Randall (brother of Robert Livingston with whom Al would later co-star). Then there were a few stray pictures with such other also-ran heroes as George Houston, Art Jarrett, and James Newill and Dave O'Brien in a Renfrew of the Mounties picture.

By then it was 1940 and Producer's Releasing Corporation (PRC), another shoestring production company, put Al under contract with Bob Steele for a Billy the Kid series. Al was happy to be back with Steele; he had been in a number of Bob Steele pictures in the early 1930s, and, like everyone who worked with Bob Steele, he found it a pleasant partnership. The two of them made six pictures in the series before Steele left for other pastures and was replaced by former Olympic swimmer and Tarzan/Flash Gordon/and Buck Rogers film impersonator, Buster Crabbe.

Before the cast change from Steele to Crabbe occurred, the enterprising PRC studio, realizing the popularity of its star comic sidekick, Fuzzy St. John, cast him in a second, concurrent series—The Lone Rider series—with singing cowboy, George Houston. Houston could hold his own with the best of the singing cowboys in the vocalizing department, but, otherwise, he was a somewhat sobersided saddlemate playing opposite the antic behavior of Al St. John. Houston surprised a lot of people by lasting through eleven episodes in the Lone Rider series during 1941 and '42 before turning the reins over to former Three Mesquiteers star, Robert Livingston, who undertook the Lone Rider role for a final six cinematic romps which ran through 1943. Al St. John rode beside Houston and Livingston in all of the eighteen adventures.

So from 1941 through 1943 Al was simultaneously working in two series for PRC, playing the same character in each. As if that weren't enough, when he had a couple of free days, Al would slip over to Republic Pictures and co-star with one of their heroes, Don "Red" Barry, in his popular series. In all, from 1940 through 1943, Al St. John co-starred in three series, appearing on the screen in forty-three films—probably a record for a leading performer.

Buster Crabbe continued in the Billy the Kid series with Al until 1946. After eleven episodes the series was then referred to as the Billy Carson series. It was never made clear whether the change in title was due to protests regarding the despicable nature of the real Billy, or whether it was because Buster was getting a little long in the tooth to be referred to as a "Kid." Regardless, the series proceeded in its second-rate, low-budget way until mid 1946 when Buster quit.

The Buster/Fuzzy series for PRC was never well-produced; the budgets only allowed for the cheesiest of sets, static camera setups, and scripts that often seemed to be made up as they prepared to roll the film in the camera. The main thing the series had going for it (if not the only thing) was the pleasant chemistry exuded by the two stars. It was as if they knew they were entangled in a hopeless mish-mash of Western celluloid, but would, nevertheless, attempt to entertain all of us kids who had plunked down our dimes at the box office. In short, Buster and Fuzzy didn't take the series too seriously

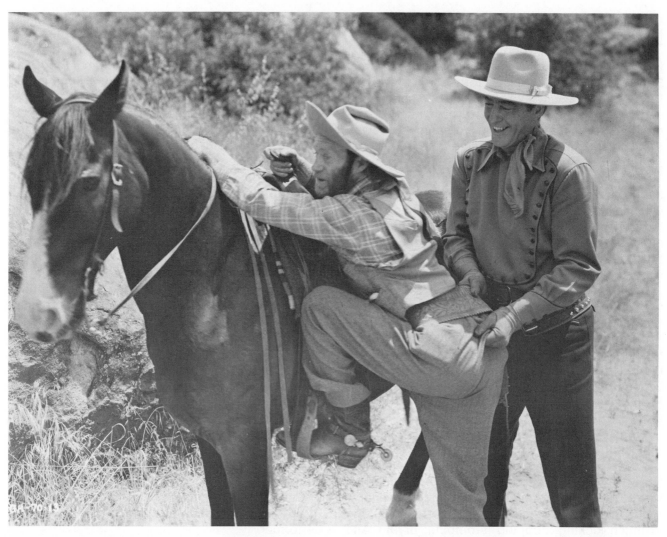

Singing cowboy, George Houston, is giving Fuzzy a boost in this scene from one of their Lone Rider films. Fuzzy was the one who gave a boost to the films.

and, therefore, just had fun with it. We in the audience could do the same.

I talked with Buster Crabbe a few months before he died on April 23, 1983. As usual, he was candid in his remarks. He said that he had loved working with Al St. John and asserted that it was about time tribute was paid to the cowboy sidekicks who helped so much to make the B Westerns popular with audiences of years past.

Buster Crabbe on Al St. John's early Hollywood experience: *He was a trick bicycle rider in the old days of vaudeville before they began to show movies at the theatre houses. He had come out to do the Orpheum circuit in California. He started in Los Angeles and was going to work up the coast.*

In those days they had no stunt women

to do stunts in the silent films. He was a real thin guy, maybe five-seven in height. So they hired Fuzzy. He'd put on a dress, get on a damned horse, and do his stunt thing.

You know, every once in a while he'd ride a bike in one of our Westerns. We'd work it in some way so he could get on it. He could really ride a bike well, you know; spin the front wheels; ride it up on the back wheels, or whatever.

The effect of the Great Depression on Al St. John: *He and his wife lived out in the valley. They had a lot of money tied up in real estate out in the valley. This goes back to Black Thursday in October of 1929. He'd been buying a lot of stock on margin—buying twice as much or three* times as much because he only had to come up with a few dollars. He'd saved a lot of money and invested it. When Black Thursday came along, he lost three-quarters of a million dollars in two or three days.

On why Al went into B Westerns: He had just been given a fifty-two week contract at $5,000 a week by Fox Film Studios, later Twentieth Century-Fox. You know he got to be a big name doing those two-reel silent comedies and some features. Sound pictures were just coming in strong at that time. All of a sudden the studio decided that there were a lot of these silent performers whose main talents would not be enhanced by the coming of sound. So the story goes that Fox called Al in and said, "Look, we'd like

to buy you off." Fuzzy said, "I have a fifty-two week contract with you people." So they hemmed and hawed and finally paid him off—every penny. Then they notified all of the other major studios not to hire the son of a bitch.

That's when he went into quickie Westerns; he couldn't get any of the big studios to hire him. He did right well, though.

On Al's off-camera personality: Fuzzy was a kind of quiet guy. Of course, if there was somebody around who would laugh, he would always put on a show for them. But he was kind of quiet. There'd usually be a little crapshooting during the lunch hour; he never went into the crap games or anything like that.

Fuzzy and Buster keep their eyes open for outlaws in this scene from *Prairie Badmen* (1946).

After shedding his image as Tarzan, Flash Gordon, and Buck Rogers, Buster Crabbe became a cowboy star. He made thirty-six pictures with Al St. John at PRC between 1941 and 1946.

On his drinking problem: *We made a lot of personals, you know. We'd go out after we'd done two or three Westerns, go up the coast, go to the Western theatres in each of the little towns way up to the Canadian border. I really had to keep an eye on him; drag him out of places. I remember one day we were playing a little Western theater in San Francisco. We were walking up the street to the theater and all of a sudden I looked around and discovered I was talking to myself. We'd passed a bar. I retraced my steps and, sure enough, there was Fuzzy holding court at the bar with a lot of people gathered around him. I had to drag him out of the place. But I kept an eye on him pretty well.*

His drinking never posed a problem when we were filming. It was when he wasn't filming that he liked the sauce. It was while he was out on tours. Touring is a rough deal. You play this date and then you have to jump three hundred miles to make a matinee at the next town up the way.

On Al's comic bits in their films: *They were mostly improvised. Fuzzy created his comedy by the bootstraps, more or less. You know, coming out of a swinging saloon door, stumbling, and falling down the stairs, and that type of thing; he was a great tumbler. I don't know how many times he fought with villain Charlie King, but they put on a hell of a battle in a lot of pictures. You know Charlie King started out originally as a comic, but then* they gave him a black hat and he played a lot of heavies. Fuzzy and he would work out a routine between them for those comic fights—funny, really funny. And when something went wrong, it was even funnier—when one of them miscued on a tumble or something like that.

On why Buster left PRC: I'll tell you what happened on a Thursday afternoon that caused me the next day, Friday morning, to go in and resign from PRC. And that's when Fuzzy took up with Lash LaRue.

I knew this outfit, PRC, like I could foresee. At about five mintues to six o'clock in the evening on this Thursday, I saw Burt Sternbeck wander over to Sam Newfield, the director—Sig Neufeld's brother [Sig was the producer]. I saw Sam

shake his head—nod his head up and down—and then he called to me, "Buster, come on over here." So I rode my horse over to him, and he told me what he wanted to do for the scene coming up.

Now the scene as originally planned was this: Fuzzy and I were supposed to be leading a posse of about ten cowboys on horseback. We were chasing the bad guys. (This was being filmed out at Iversons's Ranch in Chatsworth.) We were to ride in about two hundred yards and pull our horses to a sliding stop. My line was to be the famous one, "I think they've gone that way," indicating the hill. Then we would continue to ride after them.

So Sam told me the change he wanted me to make in the scene. As I rode back to Fuzzy and the posse, I thought to

Fuzzy seems to have stumbled into trouble once again in this scene from *Wild Horse Phantom* (1944). Buster has the situation in hand.

Song of Old Wyoming (1945) was Lash LaRue's first Western film. This title lobby card from the film lists LaRue's first name as Al, since he had not yet acquired the appellation of Lash. That's Lash standing next to the barrels on the right side of the lobby card.

myself, "Gee, I can't tell these fellows; they'll think I'm crazy." So I said to them, "When we slide to a halt, do exactly as I say." I looked at Fuzzy and Fuzzy shrugged his shoulders and so did the other cowboys riding in the posse with us.

So, "Camera, Action," and we went riding on down to this sliding halt. My new line was, "Dismount, men; we'll be faster on foot." And the reason for that new line that Sam had given me was that at six o'clock the posse horses were going to go on overtime. By leaving the horses and continuing on foot, the studio saved twenty-five dollars. Two dollars and a half overtime for ten horses; they didn't give a damn about the actors.

The following morning I went in and told Sig Neufeld that I'd had it! He didn't bat an eye. And when they started making Westerns again, Lash LaRue was working with Fuzzy.

Oh, yes, I just remembered. I got a thousand dollars a picture for the PRC Westerns; I think Fuzzy received about the same amount.

★   ★   ★

When Buster Crabbe packed his bedroll and rode out of the Billy Carson series, PRC did, indeed, have a replacement ready—a fellow dressed in black who was (for a while) called The Cheyenne Kid. Around the studio he was known as Al LaRue, and a more colorful character would be hard to locate in all the hills of Hollywood. At this point perhaps we should digress and take a look at the phenomenon of Al "Lash" LaRue for a few pages since his partnership with Fuzzy is probably the best remembered by Western fans, and Lash, himself, began in Westerns as a pseudo sidekick for singing cowboy, Eddie Dean.

Although LaRue made a few non-Western film appearances, the first real notice anyone took of him was in Eddie Dean's initial starring film, **Song of Old Wyoming** (1945). LaRue had a showy supporting role in the picture as a good/bad guy called The Cheyenne Kid. Dressed all in black and looking like a Central Casting facsimile of a cowboy Humphrey Bogart, LaRue snarled and charmed his way through the film, stopping a bullet from an outlaw just before the end credits. Eddie Dean himself should have fired the bullet since this inky-cloaked young punk had just stolen the picture from him.

Following the unexpected arrival of a few stacks of fan mail for "Cheyenne LaRue," PRC decided to cast him in another Dean opus called **The Caravan Trail** (1946). This time LaRue was called Cherokee, but the character was the same. Again Dean should have shot him, because again LaRue came through to audiences as the most interesting person in the film (which, incidentally, was probably Eddie Dean's best picture of his entire series).

LaRue's final appearance with Eddie Dean was in **Wild West** (1946), in which he played his usual "edge of the law" character, this time called Stormy. Al LaRue's fan mail popularity—with only these three sidekick roles to his credit—could not be ignored by the diminutive PRC. They had unwittingly created a Star!

I talked recently with Lash about his somewhat bizarre film career. Still active with personal appearances and occasional hosting chores on television series of old B Western films, the distinguished-looking, grey-bearded hero is always happy to talk about the good old days.

To David Rothel
1953 is a long time ago. Principles don't change, for God's sake!
your friend
Lash LaRue
1982

Lash La Rue in his prime.

Lash LaRue on getting cast as The Cheyenne Kid: *I was being interviewed by Bob Tansey, the producer of* **Song of Old Wyoming,** *in his office. Tansey said to Frances Kavanaugh, the screenwriter, "Well, he looks the part if he can act." They hadn't even talked to me; they were just looking me over.*

So I said, "I'm probably the best actor that's ever been in your office." He smiled, looked at Frances, and said, "He's either good or he's nuts." Then he added, "I had intended to use someone that could handle a whip." I said, "A bullwhip?" He said, "Yes." I said, "I've been messing with one since I was a kid." So I wound up with the part of The Cheyenne Kid.

On his whip expertise at that time: *I had never had one in my hand before. I rented an eighteen-foot and a fifteen-foot whip and practically beat myself to death trying to learn how to handle one. At the time we were filming in Cinecolor, and it took three days to get the rushes back of what we had filmed. So by three days into the shooting schedule the whip was established on camera, hanging there on my gun, but I hadn't had to use it yet.*

About that time Bob Tansey walked up to me and said, "You're doing a great job, Al. How would you like to do three pictures at three times the money you're making now?" I said, "That sounds good!" He said, "Come into my office this afternoon when you get back to the studio, and I'll have the contract set before this picture is over."

I said, "Bob, there's something I better tell you." He said, "What is it, Al?" I said, "Well, I can't use that whip." His face fell to his chest and he said, "But you said—" I said, "Wait a minute, Bob. You doubted if I could act, so I acted—I acted like I could use a whip." I pulled my shirt up and I had welts across my back and one up high on my neck where I'd really hurt myself with the whip. I told him the whole story. He thought it was the funniest thing he had ever heard.

So he hired a fellow by the name of Snowy Baker to teach me how to handle a whip. Before the picture was over, I could handle one. When the fan mail started coming in to the guy that used the whip, I figured there must be something there, so I learned how to handle the thing real good. I became the best. Every time I heard of somebody who did anything with a whip, I went to see him, no matter how far it was. I believe I was the best in the world. Not patting myself on the back, but I've had a lot of people try to copy me, and very few did. I'm very proud of the fact that Whip Wilson's series was put together because of the strength of my pictures.*

On his acting ability: *My mama went to see* **Song of Old Wyoming,** *my first Western picture, and I got killed in it. She sat there and cried like a baby. I tried to explain that I was still here, but I knew I was an actor; I'd convinced her that I was gone.*

I didn't let any of my family come out and see my pictures being made; I wouldn't let anybody visit me. So there was a—I don't know what it was—I just didn't want my family there because I was doing a job and I didn't want them; I didn't want to explain what I was doing. (laugh) Maybe I didn't know what I was doing.

The first write-up I got said, "He rides as though glued to the saddle." Bob Tansey said, "That's the only way the son-of-a-bitch could stay on!"

I picked out the wardrobe for the first picture, **Song of Old Wyoming.** *I wore a shirt that George O'Brien had used. I got it from Western Costuming. It was a black outfit and people liked it. In fact, I got fan mail addressed on the guy that wore the black outfit. I also got fan mail addressed to the guy that used the whip; they didn't even know my name!*

On his reaction today when he sees himself on the screen: *It's me—before I grew up. I was an adult adolescent for a long time. I wish I could redo the whole bunch of those films.*

On his concerns about being typed as a cowboy: *That never bothered me for a minute. When I was a little boy I used to pray to be a cowboy. Outside of my immediate family the only ones that I had respect for were the cowboys who did*

The June, 1952, Lash LaRue comic book.

good things and then rode off into the sunset. I wanted to be a cowboy. My heroes were William S. Hart, Tom Mix, Hoot Gibson, and Ken Maynard. I think there's a little cowboy in every boy.

On the Lash LaRue comic books: The comic books sold twelve million copies a year in four languages for several years. They had made a comic book out of one of my pictures that I was anxious to get—I think it was **The Vanishing Outpost.** Some kid brought it up to me at a Western film festival in Charlotte. I tried to buy it from the kid. I said, "What did you pay for it?" He said, "Twenty dollars." It was a ten-cent comic book. I said, "Well, I'll give you thirty for it." He said, "Oh, I couldn't sell it for anything!" It's amazing how these cowboy comics and movie related items—three sheets and one sheet posters, lobby cards, or anything related to me and my films— have become quite expensive.

★   ★   ★

So it was that Lash LaRue was co-starred with Fuzzy St. John in a new PRC series. In a strange, rather intriguing way, Lash and Fuzzy created a sort of surrealistic Western series. The films featured two very unlikely heroes: a black-clad cowboy who bore a striking resemblance to Bogart, who had once been a hairdresser, who had trouble staying on a horse, who at first could hardly manage a believable fist fight, and who talked out of the side of his mouth like a two-bit Chicago hood. Teamed with him was a knockabout, baggy-pantsed comedian who got his start doing tricks on a bike, who mad-capped his way through Keystone Cops shorts for Mack Sennett, who stunt-doubled for women in silent films, and who made a passel of cowboy heroes look good when, in truth, they couldn't sustain a film without him. It was a strange filmic blend over which Italian director Federico Fellini might have drooled.

As with the earlier series Al St. John had worked in, his Fuzzy character was carrying the pictures with his trade-marked comic acrobatics and laugh-getting "Fuzzy" bits—like the way he would absent-mindedly scratch the back of his head while pushing

Lash LaRue today.

his floppy hat down over his forehead, or the way he would roll his eyes and sneak a peak into the camera as if to see for sure that we were aware of his exasperation, pleasure, or chagrin at whatever was going on in the scene.

Lash and Fuzzy—the team worked well together and their films made money, especially in the South. There is no question that Lash's appeal was limited, and he was generally either loved or loathed by Western fans.

Starting with *Law of the Lash* in early 1947, Fuzzy and Lash made eight pictures for PRC in that one year. Then PRC melted into Eagle-Lion Pictures and the initial series ended. At this point a hustling producer named Ron Ormond came onto the scene. He got Lash and Fuzzy to continue as a team for his Western Adventure Productions. Twelve more films were produced under this banner between 1948 and 1952.

The early films of the Western Adventure Productions are generally thought of as dreadful by Western fans. Author Don Miller commented in his excellent book, **Hollywood Corral**, about their first effort in the series, **Dead Man's Gold** (1948): "The film consists of practically no plot, scant dialogue, but much riding around, punctuated by bursts of action. To give the riding scenes more adrenalin, composer Walter Greene had his orchestra playing at fever pitch, even though nothing was occurring on the screen at the moment. It was noisy enough to keep the patrons awake, and made the action all the more welcome when it came."

Surprisingly, the series did improve, and a later entry entitled **King of the Bullwhip** (1951) was quite satisfying—especially the climactic two-man bullwhip sequence. With the completion of **Frontier Phantom** in 1952, Fuzzy and Lash ended their film careers. (Lash did make a brief appearance in a 1969 Western porno film entitled **Hard-on the Trail**, which he says was all a big misunderstanding.)

★   ★   ★

Lash and I had met several times briefly at Western film festivals, but we had never really talked about his old sidekick, Fuzzy. I figured that he ought to have some insights on St. John that couldn't be gotten elsewhere. Since I was only able to round up an address in North Carolina for the rather peripatetic cowboy, I dropped him a note and asked if he would call me at his convenience. Within a few days I heard his familiar voice on my line. Sure, he would be happy to reminisce about old Fuzzy.

Lash LaRue on the beginning of their

working relationship: I think Fuzzy thought I had something to do with Buster leaving the series, but I had nothing to do with it at all, and Buster stepped into something else shortly afterwards anyhow. Fuzzy and I worked together almost a year before he walked up to me one time and said, "You know, I wasn't going to like you, but you're all right." From there on we became very close friends.

On making the Western series with Fuzzy: *He could do all kinds of funny things getting on and off a horse. He was very comfortable working with horses. In fact, there were some times when they thought they should double him with horse bits, and he'd say, "No, if Lash is going to do it, I'm going to do it, too." He didn't want them to double him.*

He was like a piece of spring steel; he could flip—he could stand flatfooted and flip even after he got older; he was wily. He thought of "Fuzzy" as being an entirely different person from Al St. John. When he would come across a bit of comic business, he would say, "Hey, that would be good for Fuzzy." He would talk about Fuzzy as though he were a friend— they were two different people.

They had to get his dialogue in the morning if we were working at the studio in town. Everybody recognized him, of course, and if he went out to lunch, somebody would buy him a drink and that would start it, you know. When you get to be an alcoholic, just one shot is enough to start the whole thing going again. He was an alcoholic who couldn't handle even two or three drinks at lunch time. His dialogue would bubble, and he couldn't handle it.

On Al's off-screen personality: *He loved to tell stories. We generally had a party at the end of a film. I loved to tell stories, too. Everybody would have a good time. We had to be careful not to let him drink too much because alcohol had a control over him that was not a happy one. I think he was an angel unaware. He was an older spirit, an old soul that didn't understand the game, if you can pick up on that. He was sort of a man from another* time who didn't quite fit into this period. He was a very sensitive guy, which most thinking actors and comedians are. I think men are more sensitive, probably, than they allow themselves to be thought of.

I think he was looking all of his life for love, and I don't think he ever found it. I don't think he ever understood what he was really looking for. He was looking for something to satisfy his soul, and the garbage of material excesses wouldn't do it. He was probably one of God's people who never got a chance to think about the Lord. Now that sounds a little bit far out for an old cowboy to say, but that's what I think.

On tour with Fuzzy: I had an exhibition rodeo type of thing that I played at state fairs and the expositions in Canada. I enjoyed having Fuzzy with me; the only thing was that we both were box office draws, and we didn't play much together in theaters because there wasn't **that** much money that could be made in small theaters. He could fill the house and I could fill the house, so we mostly played separately in theaters. But I was tickled to death to have him with me because I enjoyed his company and the two of us together were a recognized team for a long time.

We would take some gags from burlesque and use them on our road shows. I remember the dialogue for one of the routines went like this:

Lash: Are you really fast with a gun, Fuzzy?

Fuzzy: Oh, yes. Here is a list of all the people I can beat on the draw.

He'd go through a list of names of all the cowboy stars and my name would be on it, too.

Lash: You can't beat me on the draw.

Fuzzy: Oh, yes I can. Your name is on the list here.

Lash: We'll have to see here.

Fuzzy: How'll we do it?

Lash: Well, we'll stand back-to-back, take five paces, turn and shoot.

So I'd count and walk the five paces. When I turned around, he was right there behind me.

Lash: You're supposed to be over there ten paces away from me.

Fuzzy: Well, it was lonesome over there.

The kids just loved the routine. He was a natural; he didn't have to say funny lines in order to be funny; he could mug and get laughs.

Fuzzy was upset one time because I had a fellow working for me who had a beard. He said, "Well, I never had anybody working for me with a whip!" I've got a beard now; he'd love to see it.

On Fuzzy's personal life: He had some property out in the valley during the time we were working together in films. He could very easily have been a millionaire. We had been touring on the road. When we came back, his wife died and left everything to her son by a previous marriage. He lost a lot of money at that time. I didn't think it was right, but she had him tied up because of his previous problems with alcohol so that he didn't even get his check in his own name—her name was on his check from the studio. I asked him to get an attorney to break the will, but he said, "I've always tried to be a daddy to him, Lash." So I backed out of the situation.

His second wife married him really to get on the stage herself. She was one of these performers who plays glasses—you know, they fill each glass at a different level with water and then play a tune. She'd go out and book Fuzzy on personal appearances and then she'd come along and be in the act. I don't know very much about her. I knew that he was keeping company with her even before his first wife died. His first wife had had so many operations, one of them a colostomy. She couldn't have any physical association with Fuzzy.

He was such a sweet guy. He was just a lonesome guy that looked all of his life for love and never really found it.

★   ★   ★

Al "Fuzzy" St. John hit the road after his B Western films with Lash went out of production. His personal appearances were popular with the public, particularly in the South where his films had always packed them in. So it went, Fuzzy and his second wife, Flo Belle, playing rodeos, county fairs, and

Al "Fuzzy" St. John with his last screen partner, Lash LaRue.

What's this? The starry-eyed sidekick is getting all of the attention from the pretty heroines while hero Lash LaRue is ignored. That's popular Western character actor George Chesebro smiling in the background.

small theaters throughout the years of the fifties and early sixties. Finally, on January 31, 1963, while resting in his hotel room between shows on a personal appearance, Al "Fuzzy" St. John died suddenly of a heart attack. He was seventy years old.

AL ST. JOHN FILMOGRAPHY

The filmography includes only the series films that Al St. John made, starting with the Fred Scott films in which Al first developed his famous character, Fuzzy Q. Jones.

FRED SCOTT series: (Spectrum Pictures)

Melody of the Plains (4/37)

The Fighting Deputy (1937, no release month indicated)

Moonlight on the Range (1937, no release month indicated)

Roaming Cowboy (1937, no release month indicated)

Ranger's Round-up (2/38)

Knight of the Plains (5/38)

Songs and Bullets (5/38)

BILLY THE KID series (Bob Steele): (PRC)

Billy the Kid Outlawed (6/40)

Billy the Kid in Texas (9/40)

Billy the Kid's Gun Justice (12/40)	**Jesse James, Jr.** (3/42)
Billy the Kid's Range War (1/41)	*LONE RIDER series (George Houston):* (PRC)
Billy the Kid's Fighting Pals (4/41)	**The Lone Rider Rides On** (1/41)
Billy the Kid in Santa Fe (7/41)	**The Lone Rider Crosses the Rio** (2/41)
DON "RED" BARRY series: (Republic Pictures)	**The Lone Rider in Ghost Town** (5/41)
Texas Terrors (11/40)	**The Lone Rider in Frontier Fury** (8/41)
The Apache Kid (9/41)	**The Lone Rider Ambushed** (8/41)
A Missouri Outlaw (11/41)	**The Lone Rider Fights Back** (11/41)
Arizona Terror (1/42)	**The Lone Rider and the Bandit** (1/42)
Stagecoach Express (3/42)	**The Lone Rider in Cheyenne** (3/42)

The situation looks tense in this scene from Don "Red" Barry's film, *Texas Terrors*. Later sidekick Eddy Waller (sitting) doesn't look too healthy at the moment. Future singing cowboy star Jimmy Wakely and comic/singer Johnny Bond are standing in the background between Barry and Fuzzy.

Texas Justice (6/42)

Border Roundup (9/42)

Outlaws of Boulder Pass (11/42)

LONE RIDER series (Robert Livingston) (PRC)

Overland Stagecoach (12/42)

Wild Horse Rustlers (2/43)

Death Rides the Plains (5/43)

Wolves of the Range (6/43)

Law of the Saddle (8/43)

Raiders of Red Gap (9/43)

BILLY THE KID series (Buster Crabbe): (PRC)

Billy the Kid Wanted (10/41)

Billy the Kid's Roundup (12/41)

Billy the Kid Trapped (2/42)

Billy the Kid's Smoking Guns (5/42)

Law and Order (8/42)

Sheriff of Sage Valley (10/42)

The Mysterious Rider (11/42)

The Kid Rides Again (1/43)

Fugitive of the Plains (4/43)

Western Cyclone (5/43)

Cattle Stampede (8/43)

The Renegade (8/43)

Blazing Frontier (9/43)

BILLY CARSON series (Buster Crabbe) (PRC)

Devil Riders (11/43)

Frontier Outlaws (3/44)

Thundering Gun Slingers (3/44)

Valley of Vengeance (5/44)

The Drifter (6/44)

Fuzzy Settles Down (7/44)

Rustler's Hideout (9/44)

Wild Horse Phantom (10/44)

Oath of Vengeance (12/44)

His Brother's Ghost (2/45)

Shadows of Death (4/45)

Gangster's Den (6/45)

Stagecoach Outlaws (8/45)

Border Badmen (10/45)

Fighting Bill Carson (10/45)

Prairie Rustlers (11/45)

Lightning Raiders (1/46)

Gentlemen with Guns (3/46)

Terrors on Horseback (5/46)

Ghost of Hidden Valley (7/46)

Prairie Badmen (8/46)

Overland Riders (8/46)

Outlaws of the Plains (9/46)

LASH LaRUE series: (PRC)

Law of the Lash (2/47)

Border Feud (5/47)

Pioneer Justice (6/47)

Ghost Town Renegades (7/47)

Stage to Mesa City (9/47)

Return of the Lash (10/47)

Fighting Vigilantes (11/47)

Cheyenne Takes Over (12/47)

LASH LaRUE series: (Western Adventure Production)

Dead Man's Gold *(10/48) Former sidekick Britt Wood has a small role in the picture.*

Mark of the Lash *(10/48) Again Britt Wood has a small role.*

Frontier Revenge (12/48)

Outlaw Country (12/48)

Son of Billy the Kid (4/49)

Son of a Badman (4/49)

The Dalton's Women (2/50) Raymond Hatton has a feature role in the picture.

King of the Bullwhip (2/51)

The Thundering Trail (8/51)

Vanishing Outpost (11/51)

The Black Lash (1/52)

Frontier Phantom (2/52)

★　　　★　　　★

84

II.

Old Faithfuls:

Other Saddle Pals of the Celluloid Range

"Arkansas" Slim Andrews is seen here during the time he was Tex Ritter's film and touring sidekick.

"ARKANSAS" SLIM ANDREWS

"Great Gobs of Goose Grease!"

In 1978 when I wrote **The Singing Cowboys,** I commented that when "Arkansas" Slim Andrews took over as Tex Ritter's sidekick it was either a great comic step forward or backward, depending on your cactus comedy taste. I also quoted author Don Miller from his book **Hollywood Corral:** "There was no in-between with Andrews, one either doted on him or loathed him." Don Miller and I seemed to share the conclusion that Slim was probably more loathed than doted upon as a comic sidekick.

I think these varyings feelings about Slim Andrews were caused because his screen character was not so much Western in nature as it was hillbilly, and there was a vast difference in attitude in the minds of a lot of the audience toward Western and hillbilly. "Western" translated into cowboy, with all of the adventure of horses, ranches, cattle, wide open spaces, and outlaws that was associated with cowboys. "Hillbilly," on the other hand, translated into rube country boys, stills in the hills, half-moon outhouses, and the hills of the Southeastern United States—other things entirely from the cinema wild West we had grown to know and love. Most kids (and adults, for that matter) wanted to be cowboys; few wanted to be hillbillies. In many parts of the country the term "hillbilly" was (and still is) a term of derision.

So for all these reasons and others hard to articulate, Slim Andrews as Tex Ritter's sidekick was an enigma to many of us Western fans. He didn't quite fit the cowboy sidekick mold as we had come to know it, and yet there he was up there on the screen with Tex and several other Western stars.

Now a timeflash to Charlotte, North Carolina, and the 1983 Charlotte Western Film Fair. "Arkansas" Slim Andrews, a spry seventy-five years young, is a guest star at the Film Fair, and a more delightful, personable, and gracious Southern gentleman would be hard to locate. His outgoing, folksy manner is an immediate hit with the Western fans and, upon viewing several of his old films after meeting

the man, a new unexpected appreciation of his film work is expressed by many of the Western aficionados. The feeling seems to be, "By God, this man was (and is) really talented and was better than we thought those many Saturday matinees ago."

I had the pleasure of interviewing Slim about his career during the Charlotte Western Film Fair. Here's what the gentleman had to say.

"Arkansas" Slim Andrews: I was raised on a farm over there in the hills of northwest Arkansas. We raised strawberries. In 1924 my dad said, "Here's an acre of ground. If you'll plant strawberries on it, next year you can have what you raise off the land." Well, I did, and I made 750 dollars; that was a fortune in those days. I spent it all making a racing automobile out of a Model T Ford. That car was the darnedest thing you ever saw. I never used it for racing; I just liked to drive fast.

So I drove to Decatur, that's a little town south of Gravette where I was raised. A guy came up to me in Decatur and said, "My name is Watso the Musical Wizard." I said, "Yeah, what about it?" I was only seventeen years old and rather brash at the time.

He said, "I don't have a car and I need a partner. I play town halls every night, put on shows." I said, "Well, I can play pump organ and a piano a little bit." He asked if I'd like to get into show business and I told him, "I'd like to get into anything to get away from that farm with those rocks and strawberries."

So he suggested that we go out and ask my folks. I was under age, so he had to have their consent. They didn't want me to go because I was a pretty good farm worker, but they finally gave their okay. We took that old racer car I'd made out of the Model T and started South.

*We'd go into a town and book the town hall for maybe five dollars a night. Then we'd ballyhoo all over town, "Big show at the town hall tonight!" Watso taught me to do a Toby country boy act with a red wig and freckles. I'd come down the aisle barefoot with that wig on and overalls, singing "ice cold hot dogs, red hot pop!" He'd say, "Listen, Boy, sit down. I'm trying to entertain." I'd say, "Yeah, **trying** is right!" He'd say, "Well, can't you be quiet?" I'd say, "Nah, I was on the stage one time." He'd say, "You were?" "Yeah, feller threw my hat up there and I had to go get it." I'd usually get a big laugh on that line. We did all that kind of corny stuff.*

We'd charge a dime for the show and do pretty good. He paid me thirty-five dollars a week, which I thought was unheard of in those days. I used to work on a farm for seven dollars a week. Anyway, I was with him for about a year. We went all down through the South. We played New Orleans for nine weeks. He taught me how to play a lot of different instruments, instruments like the hand saw, one-man-band banjo and guitar and fiddle, and all that.

Finally I decided I wanted to go home for a while, so we split up. While I was home, I accumulated some instruments and decided to start out on my own. I started booking halls and doing shows by myself. Pretty soon a guy who had a big tent show out in Nebraska heard about me and hired me. I was with him for about six years. The tent show was called the Chick Boyes Players. It headquartered out of Hebron, Nebraska.

In 1929 I went back home on a visit and got married, and I'm still married to the same woman—fifty-four years now. Lucille is my wife's name. She went with me on the tent show tour and got to doing parts. She was a goodlookin' young gal then. We went with several tent shows during those years, right up to 1939 when I met Tex Ritter.

We were in a tent show down in Monticello, Arkansas; Tex was on his first tour by himself, playing theaters. He didn't have a crowd that night, and he asked the

theater manager why. The manager told him that the folks were all down at the tent show to see that country-boy Toby playing those different musical instruments.

Tex said, "Oh, I love a tent show. I wonder if I could see him? If he's that good, I'd like to hire him for my comedian." So a little later that evening some kid came to me and said that Tex Ritter wanted to talk to me, that he wanted to put me in the movies with him. I thought that was some laugh!

Anyway, I went over and talked with Tex. He said that if I came out to Hollywood that he would try to get me in pictures. That was in September. Well, my wife and I continued to travel around with the tent show. About the last week in December we had four feet of snow on the ground, so I said to my wife, "Let's go to California. Tex Ritter said he'd try to get me in the movies. She said, "You believe that?" I said, "Well, I'm going to try." We had about fifty dollars and a '38 model Ford. We loaded everything we had on that thing—trunks on top and inside and everywhere. We went.

We got out there and rented a little apartment in Los Angeles for five dollars a week. Tex had given me his phone number of where he lived out in Van Nuys; he was still single then. So I called him and he answered the phone. I said, "This is Slim Andrews. He came back with, "Who the hell is Slim Andrews?"

Well, he finally remembered me, but he told me that he had somebody as his comedian right then. He said, though, that I could come out and do an audition. He'd get the producer, Ed Finney, and the director, Al Herman, and some others to look at me. He said, "If they think you're good, they'll hire you."

So I went out to see them. I played the tire pump and the hand saw and some other instruments all by myself without accompaniment. Well, it's no good unless you have some kind of accompaniment. We didn't have tape recorders then to help out.

They sat there and thought it was terrible. I played the one-man band and they kind of grinned a little bit. Finally, they got up and left. As Ed Finney went by Tex, he made a face and said, "That guy couldn't be funny to nobody. That's terrible!"

Tex said to me, "Well, they didn't like you." I said, "What do I do now?" He said, "Go back to Arkansas." I told him that I liked it out there and that it was too cold back East.

A few days later I got a job putting on my act at a theater down at Long Beach. It got going along real good. I had a pit band playing for me, and I was stopping the show every night and taking encores.

I called Tex on the phone again. He said, "Are you still here?" "Yeah," I told him, "and I want you to bring that guy that said I couldn't be funny down here to see me and to tell me what he thinks now." Tex said, "Oh, I don't know, but I'll see what I can do." That's the way we left it.

Well, there had been a long rainy spell in Los Angeles, and we were about a foot deep in water in the dressing rooms downstairs at the theater in Long Beach. The last night I was doing the show there I took about five or six encores, stopping the show. I walked down to the dressing room and there stood Ed Finney and Tex Ritter—Tex with his boots in his hands. They had waded through the water. Finney spoke up, "I said you couldn't be funny to nobody, but that was the funniest act I ever saw in my life. Are you busy tomorrow?" I said, "No, sir." He said, "Well, you come down to my office."

They signed me up to a seven-year contract. On the first movie I made twenty-five dollars; the next one, fifty; then seventy-five. It finally got up to two hundred and fifty dollars and no more. That was it. That's the way I got into pictures.

The "Arkansas" Slim comic character I played in the movies wasn't written into the script. It was something I ad-libbed, and then they'd leave it in. The mule, Josephine, was my idea. I couldn't ride a horse, so I figured if they got an old slowed-up mule I'd be all right. I named her Josephine; her real name was Red.

I think my humor in Tex's pictures was more on the hillbilly side, which they didn't really have with the other sidekicks, of course. My character was on the verge of Gabby Hayes, Fuzzy Knight, and Al St. John—he was my favorite, Al St. John. My character was kind of a mixture of them,

but still my own. It was really an extension of the Toby character from the tent shows. I talked the same and everything. My humor was mostly verbal; not like Al St. John who was an acrobat before he got into the movies.

A lot of the comics developed expressions that they used in pictures. Gabby had his "Yur durned tootin'," for example. I had "Great gobs of goose grease!" And when I would jump on Josephine, I'd say, "Hi ho, Josephine," and whistle.

I think my favorite of all the pictures I made was **Take Me Back to Oklahoma** with Tex Ritter. I had the best part in it. I had pretty good parts in all of them with Tex, but some of them I've never seen. We had to make those films in about five days. You'd start as soon as the sun come up for outdoor scenes, and you'd shoot until sundown. Then you'd go inside and shoot studio scenes until midnight. There wasn't much time for fun; it was all work.

In one scene in the **Take Me Back to Oklahoma** picture I'm hanging onto Josephine's tail as she's pulling me. I'm hollering, "Whoa, Josephine, are you trying to make a sled out of me?" While we were shooting it, I hit one of my feet on something and darned near broke my ankle. They practically had to cut my boot off to get it off my foot. There was a scene right after that where I went into a blacksmith shop and got a job. I sang a song in there. Here I was trying to look funny and happy singing this song, and the pain from my foot was just killing me. It wasn't very funny at the time. I had to do the rest of the movie limping on that sprained ankle.

After I left Tex, I did about four movies with Tom Keene and two with Don Barry. Don "Red" Barry wouldn't do a scene with me unless he was sittin' down or I was sittin' down. That was because I was tall and he wasn't.

I never will forget the first day I met Don Barry. I was standing outside Republic Studios with the producer of Red's pictures. Red came riding up on a bicycle. The producer said, "Don, I want you to meet your new sidekick, Slim Andrews." Barry looked at me and he gave a take and said, "What clown hired that giant?

"Arkansas" Slim Andrews and his mule Josephine as they appeared in the Tex Ritter films.

Slim is seen here with a sitting Don "Red" Barry in a scene from one of their Republic Pictures' Westerns. Because Barry was sensitive about his short height, he would avoid doing scenes where he had to stand with Slim. After two films together, Barry got little Emmett Lynn for a sidekick.

I'm not going to do any scenes with him." He never would speak to me after that, only when he had to. Don Barry was temperamental, I guess you would call it. Tom Keene was the same way; he never said a word to me. Once in a while Tex would get a little hot under the collar, but very seldom. He was easy going and never talked about anybody else; he never had any enemies that I know of. Everybody like him.

I was never particularly close with the other comic sidekicks. I would hardly ever see any of them because I would either be shooting a film or would be out on the road. Unless you worked with one in a picture, you didn't get to see him. I got to know Smiley Burnette when I worked in

a Gene Autry picture, **Cowboy Serenade**, in 1942. I had a real good scene with Smiley in that picture. He was dressed up as a woman and I was supposed to make love to him. I wasn't supposed to know that he was a man dressed up as a woman. Boy, the scene turned out real funny. When the scene was finished, Smiley said, "Hey, Bud, you won't be in any more of these." I thought he was kidding. I said, "Probably not." He said, "I know you won't." I asked him why. He said, "Because you're too funny, I'm the comedian on this show." And I wasn't in any more of the Gene Autry pictures. He had an in with Gene, you know.

I was with Tex from 1940 until 1950, either in films or touring with him. I hated those tours. I started out touring with Tex for fifty dollars a week. I was keeping up a home in Hollywood, and I had a boy about a year old at the time. Then, too, I had to pay my own bills on the road. My gosh, I was living on hamburgers and hotdogs and staying in crummy hotels trying to save enough to send some money home to keep Lucille going. It was rough!

I finally said, "I'm not going any more for no fifty dollars a week." So Tex raised me to a hundred, doubling it. Well, that was pretty good. I could send home fifty a week and live like a human being. I finally got up to two hundred and fifty a week on tour, and I started saving some money.

When we got a little money saved, we started buying old houses which I would fix up. I'm one of those jackleg carpenters; I can fix anything. We'd work those old houses over and sell them. We bought and sold twenty-three houses out there in California. We made a little money, and we've still got it!

When I left Tex, I went to Channel 5 television in Los Angeles. I was there until 1953 with a children's program. Then I got a job in Fresno on television. I was on the air for an hour every day, five days a week, for ten years. Then I went back home on a visit and found out about this station up in Pittsburg wanting somebody, and I got the job up there. That's Pittsburg, Kansas, KOAM. I'm still there.

★   ★   ★

"Arkansas" Slim Andrews poses here with author David Rothel at the 1983 Charlotte Western Film Fair.

Slim Andrews used this poster to advertise his own personal appearance tours during the 1940s and TV guest stints during the '50s.

Slim is a dunce in this film in more ways than usual. The scene is from Tex's picture, *Rainbow Over the Range.*

"ARKANSAS" SLIM ANDREWS FILMOGRAPHY

TEX RITTER series: (Monogram Pictures)

Rhythm of the Rio Grande (3/40) Slim has only a bit part in this film. He does his one-man band routine. Frank Mitchell has the main comic sidekick role.

Pals of the Silver Sage (4/40) Slim is given the name Cactus for his sidekick role.

Cowboy from Sundown (5/40) Roscoe Ates (later with Eddie Dean) has the main sidekick duties, playing the role of Gloomy. Slim has the character role of Judge Pritchard.

The Golden Trail (7/40) Here's a reverse: Eddie Dean has a small role in this picture as a character called Injun. Dean, of course, later starred in his own singing cowboy Westerns with Roscoe Ates as his sidekick. Slim for the first time plays a character called Slim, as he would through the rest of the Ritter series.

Rainbow Over the Range (7/40) The leading lady is Dorothy Fay. She would soon become Tex's wife in real life.

Arizona Frontier (8/40) Former football player Jim Thorpe has a role in this film.

Take Me Back to Oklahoma (11/40) This is Slim's favorite film from all that he made.

Rollin' Home to Texas (12/40) Eddie Dean has an important role in this film.

Ridin' the Cherokee Trail (2/41)

The Pioneers (5/41)

TOM KEENE series: (Monogram Pictures)

Wanderers of the West (7/41)

Dynamite Canyon (8/41)

The Driftin' Kid (10/41) Slim shared comic duties with Frank Yaconelli who later provided humorous relief in the Cisco Kid series of movies.

Ridin' the Sunset Trail (10/41) Frank Yaconelli again shares comic honors with Slim in this picture. Slim left the series after this picture.

DON "RED" BARRY series: (Republic Pictures)

The Cyclone Kid (5/42)

The Sombrero Kid (7/42) Slim is listed next to last in the cast and just plays a comic townsperson. Rand Brooks (of the later Hopalong Cassidy series) plays an important role in this film.

★   ★   ★

Which way did they go? Roscoe Ates displays a typically perplexed expression in this scene from an Eddie Dean film.

ROSCOE "SOAPY" ATES

Roscoe Ates was a comic sidekick in only one Western series, the Eddie Dean films of the 1940s, but his pop-eyed, Silly-Putty face had been a familiar sight to filmgoers from 1930 on. He didn't have to do much to be funny—just screw his face around into a perplexed expression and let his overly prominent eyes do the rest. The look on his face could be counted on for audience chuckles and sometimes, depending on the film situation, belly laughs.

Roscoe's face and eyes could do the job for his silent comic bits, but his bag of verbal laugh-getters included a stuttering routine that would generally convulse any holdouts who didn't break up at just his facial contortions. (This, of course, was back in the years when sensitivities were not so disturbed by the use of stuttering for comic effect.)

Born in Grange, Mississippi, on January 20, 1895, Roscoe Ates was afflicted with a real stuttering problem which he finally cured by himself by the time he had reached his late teens. Even though he was always a cutup, Roscoe did take one thing seriously—his violin playing. During his early years he had hoped to become a concert violinist. That was not to be, however, and by the time he had reached maturity, he was playing vaudeville houses around the country as a stuttering song and dance comic who would also rip off a lively ditty on his fiddle.

By 1930 Hollywood had discovered his talents and he began to appear in a wide variety of films: **Billy the Kid** (1930), **The Champ** (1931), **Alice in Wonderland** (1933), **Gone With the Wind** (1939), and **Captain Caution** (1940), just to name a few. Most frequently he would show up in small parts as a townsperson or a ranch hand. He would quite often get a chance to use his stuttering routine for a few laughs. The fact that he could produce laughs so quickly and easily (with just a slight facial contortion and/or a quick stutter) gave him the reputation among other actors for being a scene stealer. Not everyone wanted to share the screen with him in a scene. They knew they were likely to go unnoticed by the audience once the camera found Roscoe.

In early 1946 singing cowboy star Eddie Dean was looking for a new comic sidekick to replace Emmett Lynn who was leaving his series. Eddie chose Roscoe Ates, who would be called Soapy Jones in all of their pictures. I asked Eddie Dean how he happened to select Roscoe and to reminisce about working with him in the fifteen films they made together.

Eddie Dean: I was asked to come to the studio to talk with Roscoe about working in my pictures. The producer wanted to see if we would be compatible. Roscoe had on his Army uniform when I first met him. He had been a Major in the Army in Special Services. He was an entertainer, you know; that was the Special Services field. He was just getting out of the service and he wanted a job. I liked Roscoe right away.

Roscoe had been famous in vaudeville and in films before my series. In fact, he made himself famous with his stuttering. He had a different way of stuttering. He'd start to say something; then he'd stutter and couldn't say it; then after his stammering and stuttering, he'd say another word which had the same meaning. And that's what made it funny.

In a comic routine you might ask him where he had been. He'd say, "I went across the str-str-str-str-; I went across the road." By changing the stuttering word he always made it much funnier. Roscoe's stuttering was different, consequently, from Fuzzy Knight's. Fuzzy didn't usually use the substitute technique for his laughs.

Singing cowboy star Eddie Dean and author David Rothel reminisce about Roscoe Ates during the 1983 Memphis Film Festival.

I'll tell you something interesting about that stuttering thing Roscoe did. We used it in about two or three of my pictures, and then the Parent-Teachers Association put up a squawk about it and we had to stop it. He felt bad about it because it was one thing that had helped his career from the very beginning. He said that if they only knew he stuttered as a child and that through therapy—mainly on his own—he was able to quit stuttering, they might not be so critical. He proved that stuttering could be cured—at least in some cases—if one wanted to really work at it. He was a very bad stutterer as a child, he told me. Because he had been a natural stutterer, he felt it was natural for him to use it in his act.

Roscoe liked to tell jokes and he had a great sense of humor, but the writers on my pictures never seemed to write too much comedy material for him. It bothered me. I'd say, "Hey, you have nothing to do here; we've got to work something out." So we'd get together before a scene and figure out funny things for him to do. When we had something worked out that we liked, we'd then ask the director if it was okay to do it. A lot of times we'd end up completely away from the script. So, many of Roscoe's comic bits were improvised on the set right at the moment before shooting.

Roscoe could ride a horse all right. He respected horses, which everybody should. He had his old horse that they picked out for him (I can't think of the horse's name right off hand). Oh, how he loved that horse; they got along just great together. He used the same horse all of the time in our pictures. Like I said, Roscoe respected horses, but he wasn't afraid of them.

98

On the set Roscoe was always busy. He mixed a lot with the other actors and crew, and if they had a crap game going, he'd try to get into it. Sometimes the guys would go off into a little corner, have a toddy, and shoot a little. He'd always enjoy getting into something like that. But when he had a scene with somebody, he always did his best, and he was always very comfortable to work with.

It may seem funny to you, but I always thought I would have been better as a comic sidekick. I don't know why, but I always felt that I could do comedy. In fact, we had a comedy scene in one of my pictures where Roscoe had a dream and in the dream we changed clothes and played each other. In the dream sequence I ended up in the horse trough.

The producer didn't go for the sequence even though they shot it. The dream was in the film when it was released, but they didn't complete the whole sequence to where I ran out, like Roscoe would do, and fell into the horse trough, which I really did. The producer said it wouldn't be right for the hero to do. I said, "This is ridiculous; why wouldn't it be?" He said, "Well, people out there have a lot of respect for you and we don't want to lose that." I was really dumbfounded when I saw the picture and it was cut out.

Roscoe was a very happy guy. He enjoyed life and enjoyed having a good time. He had a wife who was one of the sweetest little gals that you'd ever want to meet. Barbara was her name; she had been an actress. Roscoe loved her very much. We and our wives would occasionally socialize. We were friends, good friends. He and Barbara had a daughter named Dorothy, but I never really got acquainted with her. Roscoe's wife died of leukemia during the time we were making our series.

During and after the series Roscoe and I talked a lot about going out on personal appearances together, but we never did. He had name value at the box office, of course, and it wasn't necessary for us to go together to draw an audience. Also, in those days it was kind of difficult to get enough money in the smaller towns for two well-known people. We did a few
local shows together, but that's all; most of them were benefits.

You know, I always respected and admired the sidekicks. They had to take second billing all of the time, yet without them the cowboy hero would really have been in bad straits.

After the series with Eddie Dean concluded, Roscoe continued to make appearances in films. He was usually featured down in the cast in a small role, but he was a familiar, friendly face that audiences remembered fondly. You never forgot Roscoe Ates once you had seen him on the screen.

His later films included *Thunder in the Pines* (1948) with George "Superman" Reeves, *Hills of Oklahoma* (1950) with singing cowboy Rex Allen, *Honeychile* (1951) with Western comedienne Judy Canova, *The Stranger Wore a Gun* (1953) with Randolph Scott (and featuring fellow former sidekicks Guy Wilkerson and Britt Wood), and *Those Redheads from Seattle* (1953) with Rhonda Fleming and Gene Barry. Roscoe's last screen appearance was a bit part in Jerry Lewis' 1961 production of *The Errand Boy.*

On March 1, 1962, Roscoe Ates died of lung cancer in Hollywood; he was eighty-seven. On July 6, 1982, his only daughter, Dorothy Ates, a former singer and dancer, died in Van Nuys, California. Her obituary in *Variety* mentioned that she had worked with her father in vaudeville as a youth, and that she had been under contract to MGM for three years. There were no other survivors in the family.

★　　　★　　　★

ROSCOE ATES FILMOGRAPHY

EDDIE DEAN series: (Producer's Releasing Corporation)

Colorado Serenade (7/46)

Driftin' River (10/46)

Tumbleweed Trail (10/46)

Stars Over Texas (11/46)

Wild West (12/46) This feature was in Cinecolor and had Al LaRue in an important role.

Wild Country (1/47)

Range Beyond the Blue (3/47)

Watch out, Roscoe, Eddie Dean's packin' a full house.

West to Glory (4/47)

Black Hills (10/47)

Shadow Valley (11/47)

Check Your Guns (1/48)

Tornado Range (2/48)

The Westward Trail (3/48)

Hawk of Powder River (4/48)

Tioga Kid (6/48)

Prairie Outlaws (1948) This feature is a re-edited, re-released, black and white version of **Wild West**, which was originally released in 1946.

★　　　★　　　★

Roscoe Ates accompanies Eddie Dean as he sings about the wide open spaces out West. Occasionally, Roscoe would sing a comedy tune in their series.

Two-gun Pat Buttram as he appeared with Gene Autry in his films and television series.

102

PAT BUTTRAM

The Sage of Winston County, Alabama

With a caption that proclaimed, "Romeo of the Huskin' Bees - Billy of the Hills," a 1949 printed program for the national personal appearance tour of "The Gene Autry Show" introduced sidekick Pat Buttram in this manner:

When the Melody Ranch programs get off to a merry start on the air in each weekly broadcast, Gene Autry's first and major concern is to see that a tall, husky, awkward fellow, who comes ambling out on the stage with a round-eyed stare and a bumpkin grin doesn't trip over the microphone and fall flat on his face. This character is Pat Buttram, and radio audiences all over the country are aware that when he of the cracked corn larynx plaintively whines, "Mister Ar-tery," the comedy is about to begin.

A typical example of the Autry/Buttram brand of comedy can be found in this excerpt from the September 17, 1949, broadcast of the radio "Melody Ranch."

P. Buttram: Say, Mr. Artery, you are looking at Patrick J. Buttram, genius.
G. Autry: Do I have to?
P. Buttram: Now, I'm serious. I'm going to open me a roadside store.
G. Autry: Sounds very enterprising, Pat. When is the big event going to take place?
P. Buttram: Just as soon as possible. And I'm goin' to do it up in a big way, too. For instance, you know in the city when they open a new store they have search lights which go a thousand feet into the sky.
G. Autry: Yeah, but don't tell me you're going to have search lights that go a thousand feet in the sky.
P. Buttram: No, I can't afford a search light, but I'm going to get the same effect. I'm gonna' have a firefly back into a hot stove. (laugh)
G. Autry: Sounds very, very brilliant.
P. Buttram: Well, that's me.
G. Autry: Say, by the way, do you think you've got enough stock to operate a store like that?
P. Buttram: Well, I must say that that's a problem now. For instance, like this morning I went down to my chicken roost and I found one egg. I was so discouraged I almost give up right then and there.
G. Autry: But, Pat, you shouldn't be discouraged. Instead, you should look to the future. Why just think, one egg could hatch one chicken. And that chicken could lay more eggs, and they'd hatch more chickens. Pretty soon you'd have two thousand chickens laying four thousand eggs a day. Then think how much money you'd have—and all from just one egg.
P. Buttram: I don't think it'll work.
G. Autry: Why?
P. Buttram: I ate the egg for breakfast this morning. (laugh)

Such was the comic banter that went on for years on Gene Autry's "Melody Ranch" radio program. If you liked Gene, Pat, or bucolic humor, the weekly half-hour broadcast was a must.

Gene Autry, in his autobiography, ***Back in the***

Pat was hailed as the "Romeo of the Huskin' Bees - Billy of the Hills" when he toured with Gene Autry in 1949.

Saddle Again, reminisces about Pat Buttram and their years together.

His first break came in a fashion that sounds like the plot for a situation comedy. In 1934 Pat went to Chicago to see the World's Fair, and reporters from WLS were interviewing people to get reactions. Pat was picked out of a crowd, and he gave them a flip answer to each question. With each answer he drew a bigger laugh. Soon he had the audience howling for him.

The manager of WLS offered him a job on the "Barn Dance," virtually on the spot.... That was where we first met, at the old theater on Eighth and Wabash.... Pat teamed with me on radio for fifteen years and through most of my movies at Columbia and the "Gene Autry Show" on television.

Pat Buttram's first film with Gene Autry was **The Strawberry Roan** (1948), in which he was cast in a relatively minor role and was listed far down in the cast. In his next picture, **Riders in the Sky** (1949), Pat became Gene's sidekick and remained so for fifteen more films, running through 1952. He was Gene's sidekick throughout the "Gene Autry Show" television series, which was produced from 1950 until 1954.

Pat's humor in the films was not far removed from the buffoon-type comedy of Smiley Burnette, who, of course, preceded and succeeded Pat in the Autry movie series. Buttram was comfortable with the physical comedy a la Burnette, but it can be seen that he had a sharper edge to his verbal banter than most of the cowboy sidekicks in films and television. He knew how to read a line to get the maximum comic effect—perhaps more than just about any other cowboy sidekick, Gabby Hayes being the possible exception.

"My voice never quite made it through puberty. It has been described as sounding like a handful of gravel thrown in a Mix-Master."

104

Pat Buttram, as Mr. Haney on "Green Acres."

Pat had proven years before on the "National Barn Dance" and then Autry's "Melody Ranch" program that he didn't need a camera to sell his humor. He could deftly deliver the cactus comedy written for him regardless of the medium.

In the Autry film *Valley of Fire* (1951) Pat is at first a gold prospector. When his panning produces a nugget, he joyously exclaims to his burro, "Gold! A pure nugget as big as your eyeball. It's a bonanza! I've hit paydirt. Maybe the mother-in-law lode." Later, when a well-dressed stranger claims to have found a gold mine, Pat remarks, "If that dude ever turned a spade, it was in a deck of cards." No one would confuse the above lines with the writing of Noel Coward, but in Buttram's snappy style of delivery they *do* produce laughs.

Pat proved in later years that he was even better when delivering lines he had written for himself or while exchanging ad libs with fellow toasters and roasters at tribute banquets all over the country. In the years following Pat's tenure with Autry, he acquired a reputation as a country humorist and wit which greatly transcended the barnyard humor of

the "National Barn Dance," "Melody Ranch," and Gene Autry films. Buttram is the reigning court jester of the rubber chicken and peas celebrations in show business.

Since the mid-1970s I have had the opportunity to observe Pat in action at many informal personal appearances, on television talk shows, and in the print media. On these occasions Pat has reminisced about his career in show business and his friendship with Gene Autry and other personalities he has come to know during his long career.

When chronicling the various comments of Pat Buttram over several years, one cannot help realizing that he has become, in his own way, our modern-day Will Rogers. A similar homespun humor and sharp wit mark his style of delivery. Watching and listening to Pat in his quest for the elusive laugh is a lesson in the art of stand-up comedy that many of our young comedians today should (and many do) study. Pat Buttram is a funny, funny man who speaks best for himself. Here are some samples:

On the subject of Gene Autry: I first met Gene in Chicago at WLS at the "National Barn Dance" radio program. He was appearing on the show and I was on the show, and little Georgie Gobel—a little kid—was on the show, too. Gene was singing on the "Barn Dance" before he came out to Hollywood. I used to play tricks on him. I would get one string of his guitar out of tune and I wouldn't tell him which one it was; I'd mix him up. (chuckle)

Smiley Burnette would rarely work radio; it wasn't his medium, so I did radio with Gene. When Gene was in the service, Smiley went with Charlie Starrett. When Gene came out of the Army in '46, he didn't have a sidekick in pictures, so he just put me in the pictures.

*Mule Train: [Pat's third picture with Autry] shows you the character of Gene Autry, to let a guy come in and just take the whole part—it's **my** picture; it's the sidekick's picture for a change. Gene just encouraged it and helped out all he could to see that it held up as a picture rather than trying to hog it all for himself. A lot of guys in Westerns, if the sidekick happened to get a little ahead of the star on his horse—now this is no joke—the star would stop the scene and say, "You get back; I want to be six feet ahead." This was often the rule of a lot of them had, but Autry wasn't that way at all.*

Gene Autry and Pat Buttram in scene from *Valley of Fire* (1951).

We're very close; just like brothers today. He's interested in the ballclub right now, of course. He's crazy about that baseball team and he travels with them all of the time.

Gene was one of the real great guys of the West, and he was the president of the Cowboy Hall of Fame in Oklahoma City. Gene's heart is still with the Westerns, and we talk all of the time. Of course, what Autry liked most was the tours, the personal appearances. He says, "Let's go on one more tour, just one more time."

On comedy routines: When I first started with Autry, I knew Buster Keaton very well. I went out and talked with him, and he showed me how to do some falls. He said, "If it's possible to do a stunt in comedy yourself, do it—in a water trough, a cactus, or wherever you're to fall." He said, "It's not the fall that gets the laugh; it's your reaction as you hit the ground or whatever, and then getting up. If they have to cut to a double and then cut back to you for your reaction, it's not as effective as if it's one big take." Keaton also said, "There's going to be kids watching your picture, so when you fall get up real quick because if kids think you're hurt, they won't laugh. When they see you're okay, then they'll laugh like hell." He helped me a lot.

I always tell kids in college when I make lectures, if you want to be in show business and do comedy, just never pass up an opportunity to perform. You can go to school to learn to be a dramatic actor,

Would you buy a bottle of elixir from this sidekick? Gail Davis (TV's Annie Oakley) is center. Gail was a favorite Autry heroine.

but comedy you can only learn by doing it, learning the timing, fluffing. You can get out on a stage and do a joke and it flops; a wall of silence, a big wave of silence comes right up and knocks you right through the back wall of the theatre. You have to learn to pick up a joke and get out of situations—like this right now. (laugh)

On stunt doubles for the sidekicks: The doubles made more money than we did, the sidekicks. I wish I'd had a double all the time. I was twice close to death because of accidents in pictures. Once in about 1951 we were making a picture up in the desert and a cannon blew up and blew me all to pieces and almost cut off my foot. I was about a year in the

hospital. In the film I was supposed to be a rainmaker. I pulled a little string which was supposed to set the cannon off to shoot up into the clouds to make rain. The cannon just went into a million pieces, and I got it all through me. Those scenes can be rough, especially with explosives. Autry was in the scene with me, but he wasn't hurt.

Then I had another accident in which I almost lost one arm in a picture, so my experience with movies has been a little bit drastic, and I've gone further West than I really wanted to go a couple of times. But I guess it has been worth it. Autry used to say before every scene we'd have where it would be pretty rough, "Just remember that you will mend and you will heal, but this film is going to be

(½ page photo goes here)

Gene and Pat shoot it out with the bad guys in this action scene from one of their last films together.

108

it look good." So we did the best we could.

On the subject of horses: I didn't get along too well with horses. At the beginning, not too well; at the end, terrible. I always say that horses are hard in the middle and dangerous at both ends.

On his film, Mule Train, and the leading lady: Autry says **Mule Train** is the best Western he's made [Gene has said this about several of his films], and it is in the library in New York City as the best B Western ever made. Columbia University has it as an example of the best B Western. I met Sheila Ryan on this picture, and we started going together during the picture, and, afterwards, we got married. As you know she passed away in 1975. She did a lot of pictures— Westerns towards the end, and she was at 20th Century-Fox for years. We have a daughter who looks just like Sheila, but she's not in pictures. Everyone wanted her to, but she didn't. She went into banking.

On his favorite roles since the Autry series: I haven't been doing a regular series lately. The big series, of course, was "Green Acres." I did Mr. Haney. That was a lot of fun to work on. It was a very happy cast, good writing, and everything you need for a successful series.

I did three pictures with Elvis. I did the best picture I think Elvis ever made, **Roustabout.** I played his in that.

They just aren't making Western pictures. I don't know. For a while it got to where Hollywood was making sex pictures and Italy was making the Westerns. The big thing for me is personal appearances, because I like a live audience, laughs. If you do a TV series, they put a laugh track in there. You don't have any contact with people, and a lot of the young comics on TV are very funny and they get a lot of laughs on the show. When they get out in front of a live audience, they find out the people don't necessarily laugh in the place like in a laugh track on TV.

On using his own name when he was

Pat as Mr. Haney on the "Green Acres" television series. The series premiered on CBS in September of 1965 and ran until September of 1971.

Gene's sidekick: Well, I can play Pat Buttram better than anybody else. Ol' Gene had trouble remembering names, and they'd have a different name for me in every picture. On the TV shows we were doing two or three a week. Finally, Gene just said, "Call him Pat Buttram." Roy and Dale had the same thing. They had a sidekick, Pat Brady, in their TV show, and they called him Pat Brady.

On getting started as a toastmaster: Well, they had a Western dinner at the Masquer's Club, a big show business club. They had to pick the guy to emcee it, and they settled on me. **Variety** and the other show busines papers [gave me] great reviews. I remember I introduced Roy Rogers and Dale Evans as the Lunt and Fontanne of the fetilizer set.

On the plight of the cowboy sidekick: I'm the last sidekick left, just about. Gabby's gone and Andy Devine and Chill Wills, Pat Brady—and it's getting lonely.

In the summer of 1983, I saw Pat at the Memphis Film Festival; I hadn't seen him in person since the '78 St. Louis Western Film Fair. He was looking healthier and much happier, due in no small part, I'm sure, to the attractive lady on his arm. Autry had commented earlier that Buttram had "soul of a blithe spirit" when it came to women. Now in his sixties, the cowboy sidekick seemed much enamored of his female sidekick. Pat Buttram is one sidekick who is not yet ready to ride off into the sunset.

★   ★   ★

PAT BUTTRAM FILMOGRAPHY

Pat served only as a sidekick for Gene Autry. (He did make some radio appearances with Roy Rogers, but never any films.) He was Autry's pal for seventeen movies and most of ninety-one half-hour television shows.

GENE AUTRY series: (Columbia Pictures)

The Strawberry Roan (8/48) Pat is listed fifth in the cast and is not really a sidekick in this film. Rufe Davis and Eddy Waller also appear in the film.

Riders in the Sky (11/49) Tom London plays an important role in the film.

Mule Train (2/50) Future wife Sheila Ryan is the heroine in this feature which also includes Syd Saylor in a small role.

Beyond the Purple Hills (7/50)

That's Clayton Moore (television's Lone Ranger) holding the gun on Pat in this lobby card scene from *Barbed Wire.*

110

The Sage of Winston County and author David Rothel at the 1983 Memphis Film Festival.

Indian Territory (9/50)

The Blazing Sun (11/50) Tom London is again featured in the cast.

Gene Autry and the Mounties (1/51)

Texans Never Cry (3/51)

Silver Canyon (6/51)

Hills of Utah (9/51) Tom London again shows up in the secondary cast.

Valley of Fire (11/51) Syd Saylor has a brief scene as a drunk.

The Old West (1/52) Tom London and Syd Saylor are once again employed by Autry.

Night Stage to Galveston (3/52)

Apache Country (5/52) Tom London is here again in a small role.

Barbed Wire (7/52)

Wagon Team (9/52) Gordon Jones and Syd Saylor are featured in the cast.

Blue Canadian Rockies (11/52) Tom London makes a few more bucks in a featured role.

★   ★   ★

ANDY CLYDE

ANDY "CALIFORNIA" CLYDE

Tommy Farrell: Being a juvenile sidekick gave me a great opportunity to study from some of the masters of comedy. By that I mean people like Andy Clyde, Fuzzy Knight, and Al St. John. Those three guys, given absolutely nothing to do—nothing written in the script whatsoever—could eat up thousands of feet of film if left alone to their own inventive minds.

Rand Brooks: We had an affinity for one another. I learned a lot about comedy from Andy. He fell more into the type of comic that could do straight dramatic material. He was a fine actor, and he could hold his own in the action scenes.

Andy Clyde was born on March 25, 1892, in Blairgowrie, Scotland. He was almost literally born in a show business trunk, since his parents were prominent Scottish performers. They brought young Andy and his brother David to America in 1912 when the family was asked to tour the United States in a vaudeville circuit.

By 1919 Andy was seen and signed by Mack Sennett for appearances in his popular comedy film shorts, including the Keystone Kop series. Andy's abundant mustache caused him to be dubbed "the little comic with the big mustache." When Andy's own series of shorts turned out to be only moderately successful, he turned to supporting roles where he found the work steady, the pay good, and the audience approval grew and remained loyal through his long career.

He had no difficulty transferring from silent shorts and features to sound shorts and features as the evolution of film making wound through the 1920s and into the 1930s. Andy worked for just about all the film companies during those years and established himself as a capable, serious actor as well as a comic. He also worked with a myriad of famous performers: W.C. Fields in *Million Dollar Legs* (Paramount, 1932), Barbara Stanwyck and Preston Foster in *Annie Oakley* (RKO, 1935), Jimmy Stewart in *It's a Wonderful World* (M-G-M, 1939), and Raymond Massey in *Abe Lincoln in Illinois* (RKO, 1940). Little did he realize that with the coming of 1940 his show business career was about to make a long-term change to the wide open spaces. He was about to be ambushed by Hopalong Cassidy.

At Paramount Pictures Harry "Pop" Sherman had been producing a Hopalong Cassidy series of Western pictures since 1935. The series was well-produced and starred William Boyd as Hopalong with James Ellison and George Hayes in major support. In 1937 Russell Hayden replaced Ellison as the youthful sidekick, and by 1939 George Hayes left the series to sign with Republic Pictures—leaving the comic sidekick slot vacant. For the next two years several would-be successors to Hayes were tried and discarded—among them Harvey Clark, Frank Darien, and Britt Wood.

When the 1940-41 Hoppy series was in pre-production, a suitable comic sidekick had not yet been selected. Screenwriter Norton S. Parker, who had admired Andy's film work for years, suggested to Pop Sherman that he might fit into the series very comfortably. Parker had, in fact, written the first script for the 1940-41 series, *Three Men from Texas,* and knew that the role of California Carlson, a cantankerous old desert rat, would fit Andy's acting style like the proverbial glove. Parker's suggestion was heeded, Andy was cast, and *Three Men from Texas* was a big success—considered by some to be one of the very best episodes in the long series. It was an auspicious start for what would eventually be an eight-year run for Andy as California Carlson.

As with most of the comic sidekicks whose roots went back to knockabout vaudeville and comedy silent shorts, Andy Clyde's forte was taking incidental moments and turning them into memorable comedy vignettes. I think two of his funniest bits

Andy "California" Clyde is seen here with Bill Boyd and Russ Hayden in a shoot-out from his first Hopalong Cassidy film, *Three Men from Texas.*

that exemplify this are in his Hoppy film, ***Riders of the Deadline*** (1943).

At one point in the film the script calls for Andy to dismount his horse at a town hitching post along with Hoppy and Jimmy Rogers—nothing funny in that as written in the screenplay. But wait, Andy Clyde is at work. Andy dismounts; ties the rein to the rail; and then, inadvertently, puts his leg over the drooping rein as the horse takes a step back, causing the rein to become taut. As a slightly exasperated look comes over Andy's face, he lifts the rein and puts his head under it in an attempt to extricate himself, but now he finds that his leg and his head are tangled in the rein. In his frustration he almost falls head-over-heels into the dust. Finally, in total exasperation, he figures out how to disengage himself and catch up to Hoppy and Jimmy.

Later in the film Andy is so frustrated by the events that have occurred that he decides to hang himself. (I won't bother with the details which lead to this rather extreme decision.) Andy plans his demise very carefully—strong tree limb, knotted noose around his neck, box to stand on prior to the deed. When Jimmy shows so little concern for his drastic action and even humorously offers advice to insure success, Andy angrily changes his mind. In a fit of high dudgeon Andy proclaims that he won't give anybody the satisfaction of his suicide. Forgetting that he still has the noose around his neck, he steps off the box, does a tumble backwards as the noose tightens, and squawks a "Help!" to Jimmy, who extricates him from his latest misadventure.

These hilarious bits of inventive comedy business—lasting no more than a couple of minutes on screen—are a good example of why Andy Clyde was so valued in the Hoppy pictures.

114

This portrait of Rand Brooks is from the time when he played Lucky Jenkins in the Hopalong Cassidy series.

Rand Brooks played Lucky Jenkins, the juvenile part of the threesome, in the last twelve episodes of the Hopalong Cassidy series, which were made from 1946 until 1948. (Russell Hayden, of course, had originally played the part from 1937 until 1941.) Rand is a popular guest at Western film festivals these days, and it was at several of the festivals that I had the opportunity to talk with him about working in the Hoppy series and, specifically, about Andy Clyde.

*Rand Brooks: I was under contract to Metro for three years just before the war. I did some Hardy family films and **Babes in Arms** with Rooney and Garland. Then M-G-M loaned me out to Selznik for **Gone With the Wind;** I was Scarlett's first husband, Charles Hamilton. They also loaned me out to Warner's for **The Old Maid** with Bette Davis. I worked with little Jane Withers; I did a lead with her at Fox in a film called **Girl from Avenue A.** Then I*

went into the service for almost four years, and Hoppy hired me when I got out.

There was a lot more production in the earlier Hoppys—the ones with Russell Hayden, for instance. When I got the role as Lucky, Russ's old role, I ran into Russ. He said, "I wouldn't do that role again for $5,000 a week." I thought it was sour grapes, but I found out Bill was tough to work for. He wanted things his way.

Andy Clyde and I would read the script the way it was, and then the way we'd like to do it, and then the way Bill would want it. And that's the way we did it—Bill's way! Through Andy I was able to get along pretty well with Bill.

Andy was my favorite sidekick in films. He was, I guess, the finest gentleman I ever knew in my life. One of the interesting things about Andy Clyde was that he started playing old men when he was about twenty-eight years old. People couldn't believe he still looked the same all those years because he just made up a little less as he grew older.

He did thirty-six Hoppys. He did them when Pop Sherman produced them, and he did them when Bill Boyd produced them. Andy and I rode in parades and did all kinds of personal appearances together. We used to share a bathroom in Lone Pine where they shot a lot of the pictures.

Andy was almost like a father to me. He had lost a son at ten years of age to spinal meningitis. He knew that I had had spinal meningitis, too. I would have been about his son's age. He never said anything about it, but he always seemed to treat me like the son he lost. He advised me and, as a matter of fact, helped me when I had financial troubles.

He was just a very kind, fine gentleman. He was a high Mason. He would devote three or four nights a week to Masonry. I asked him one time why he had never asked me to join and he said, "You're supposed to ask me." I said, "Andy, I don't think I could ever live up to it the way you have—the time you've given." I was married and had a couple of children—a struggling actor. He said, "Well, you don't have to give up that much time. I'm just doing it because I love it." I never joined, but sometimes I regret it because I believe Andy would have liked that. Everybody loved Andy!

He would create and improvise much of the comedy in the Hoppy films. He would think of things and try them out. Bill would let him do pretty much what he wanted to. Bill didn't seem to be concerned that there would be too much comedy or that it would be overdone. You can always cut the film, you know.

Andy was a great horseman, but he was always doubled, as he should have been. Even a good horseman can have his horse step into a prairie dog hole awfully quick. His double was Clem Fuller.

After the Hoppy films, he did some of the Whip Wilson pictures. He got me a job on one of them. Then I went with the TV "Rin Tin Tin" series, and I got him in

about ten of those.

I told you Andy was a Mason. We did a show one time for the Eastern Star Old Ladies' home. I used a bullwhip pretty well, so we worked up a gag where Andy rigged his pants with some weights on them. He would pull a string which would break the suspenders loose and the pants would drop. He had red flannel underwear on underneath, which would always get a laugh. Anyway, we went out to the Eastern Star home and did our little routine. They had one of their flags on this little stage; I got the whip mixed up with the flag and it was the most embarrassing thing in the world. But Andy and I pulled it off, and they loved it. I'd wrap the whip around him, the buttons would pop off, and his pants would fall down.

Hoppy sheds light on some evil doings for Rand Brooks and Andy Clyde in this scene from *The Marauders* (1947). In re-release the film was entitled *King of the Range*.

Rand Brooks poses for the author's camera at the 1982 Charlotte Western Film Fair.

We had it all rigged for the gag. It was fun! They all loved him.

Andy's wife is still alive, still very bright. She lives in the old family home.

When the Hoppy film series folded in 1948, Andy was asked to help enliven a new series that was starring an unknown named Whip Wilson. The series was quite a comedown from the well-produced Hoppy films, but Andy signed on and eventually made twelve pictures with Wilson during 1949 and '50. He played a character called Winks, but he was still California Carlson, only this time in a stovepipe Stetson.

Whip Wilson died of a heart attack in 1964 at the age of forty-five. Monica Meyers, Whip's widow, comments in her book entitled **Crashing Thru—My Life with Whip Wilson** on the friendship they had with Andy during the time that Whip and Andy worked together.

Monica Meyers: Andy Clyde was the most adorable person I had met in Hollywood. To know Andy, out of character, was the surprise of a lifetime. He was a very proper English-Scots gentleman and spoke very proper English. He was a member of the Lakeside Country Club, Hollywood's finest. You never just "dropped by" his home; you needed an invitation. We were his guests on numerous occasions for dinner and cocktails. Andy's wife, Elsie, was an ex-Max Sennett show girl. . . .

Andy Clyde had a special room in his home that no one was allowed in. This room contained mirrors and props so that he could constantly rehearse his character. When he entered the room, he became the familiar figure that we so much enjoyed on the screen.

Whip Wilson and Andy "Winks" Clyde ride to adventure in their Monogram Western series.

118

Tommy Farrell, the son of the famous actress Glenda Farrell, was a guest at the 1983 Charlotte Western Film Fair.

In a few of the Wilson films Tommy Farrell played a role not unlike the Lucky character in the Hoppy series. Tommy talked with me about working with Andy on the Whip Wilson series.

Tommy Farrell: Andy was an extremely inventive comic. There was a sequence in a picture called **Outlaws of Texas** *where Whip and Andy had to fill some time— they were waiting for some event to happen. So Whip says to Andy, "Help me fix this fence." All he has to do is say that, get out of the way, and let Andy go to work. Well, Andy walks over to the pile of fence board and promptly selects a board that is about six feet too short to fit in the fence. For about the next three minutes on screen he's trying to fit this board. There's no way it's going to work and everybody in the audience knows it. In the meantime he was absolutely hysterical to watch. This was sheer comedy invention on the part of Andy.*

When he'd think of something funny, he'd giggle to himself. If you sat with Andy while waiting for a scene to come up, you could tell when he was thinking of something because he would start to do that high-pitched giggle of his. I'd say, "Have you come up with a goody, Andy?" He'd say, "I think I got something." Then he'd giggle some more. You could be sure then that something funny was going to happen.

Off camera Andy was not a zany person. He was very quiet and a studied professional. He was a very dignified man, an avid reader, and a very intelligent man.

At the same time Andy was doing the Whip Wilson film series, he was still playing California Carlson on the Hopalong Cassidy radio series. As the announcer usually said, "The same California you've laughed at a million times." The series ran from 1950 until 1952 on Mutual and then CBS.

Andy was surprised and disappointed when Bill Boyd did not use him as his sidekick in the Hoppy 1951-52 television series. According to Andy, Boyd had promised him the role and then reneged in favor of Edgar Buchanan. Reportedly, Boyd never told Andy about his change of mind; Andy read about it in *Variety.*

Andy moved into television full time starting in 1957 when he began a seven-year stint as an old codger named Cully on the "Lassie" series. At the end of the 1963-64 season it was decided to drop the human cast (Timmy and his mother and father) by having them move to Australia. Then the scriptwriters on the series had Cully suffer a heart attack in the first episode of 1964-65, forcing him to give the dog to a forest ranger. The new "Lassie" series was off and running; Andy was briefly out of work.

Andy's last television series role was in "No Time for Sergeants" during the 1964-65 season. He played the grandfather of Millie Anderson, the love interest on the short-lived series.

Andy Clyde died on May 18, 1967. He had spent most of his seventy-five years running the gamut of what show business had to offer: stage, screen, radio, and television. He had done it all and, in the process, had made a lot of people happier.

★   ★   ★

ANDY CLYDE FILMOGRAPHY

HOPALONG CASSIDY series (William Boyd): (Paramount Pictures)

Three Men from Texas (11/40) Russell Hayden co-stars in the first six pictures in which Andy appears.

Doomed Caravan (1/41)

In Old Colorado (3/41)

Border Vigilantes (4/41)

Pirates on Horseback (5/41) Former Hoppy sidekick Britt Wood has a small part in this picture.

Wide Open Town (8/41)

Riders of the Timberline (9/41) Brad King replaces Russ Hayden starting with this film and continues for the next four episodes. Brad plays Johnny Nelson, the role Jimmy Ellison originated in the series.

Twilight on the Trail (9/41) Sidekick Tom London and Jimmy Wakely's Trio have small roles in this picture.

Stick to Your Guns (9/41) The Jimmy Wakely Trio and Tom London are around again in this film.

Outlaws of the Desert (11/41)

Secrets of the Wasteland (11/41)

Copyright 1943, United Artists Corporation. "Property of National Screen Service Corp. Licensed for display only in connection with the exhibition of this picture at your theatre. Must be returned immediately thereafter."

Harry Sherman presents "FALSE COLORS" featuring WILLIAM BOYD with Andy Clyde · Jimmy Rogers · Douglass Dumbrille · Claudia Drake Tom Seidel · Bob Mitchum · Released thru United Artists

Permission is hereby granted to newspapers, magazines and other periodicals to reproduce this photograph. Printed in U.S.A.

43/395

Tom Seidel looks awfully worried in this scene from *False Colors* (1943). He has little need to fear, however, with friends like Hoppy, Jimmy Rogers, and California on hand.

Hoppy has just come to an understanding with Robert Mitchum (Rip Austin). Mitchum usually ended up looking like this in his Hoppy film appearances. This scene is from *False Colors* (1943).

HOPALONG CASSIDY SERIES (William Boyd):
(United Artists)

Undercover Man (10/42) Jay Kirby completes the threesome by playing Breezy Travers in this episode.

Hoppy Serves a Writ (3/43) Bob Mitchum plays a heavy in this Hoppy film. Jay Kirby is called Johnny Travers.

Border Patrol (4/43)

The Leather Burners (5/43)

Colt Comrades (6/43) This is Jay Kirby's last Hoppy film.

Bar 20 (10/43)

False Colors (11/43) Jimmy Rogers (Will's son)

joins the cast as the youngest of the threesome. Jimmy has the tough job of playing Jimmy Rogers for six episodes.

Riders of the Deadline (12/43) Bob Mitchum makes his third appearance as a Hoppy heavy. He plays a character called Drago.

Lost Canyon (12/43) Jay Kirby is back for this film. It is very likely the picture had a delayed release for some reason.

Texas Masquerade (2/44) Jimmy Rogers is again with Hoppy and California.

Lumberjack (4/44)

Mystery Man (5/44)

Forty Thieves (6/44) Jimmy Rogers completes his

stint in the Hoppy pictures with this episode.

Fool's Gold (1/46) Rand Brooks joins the cast of the Hoppy series for the last twelve episodes. He plays Lucky Jenkins.

Devil's Playground (11/46)

Unexpected Guest (3/47)

Dangerous Venture (5/47)

The Marauders (7/47)

Hoppy's Holiday (7/47)

Silent Conflict (3/48)

The Dead Don't Dream (4/48)

Sinister Journey (6/48)

Borrowed Trouble (7/48)

False Paradise (9/48)

Strange Gamble (10/48)

WHIP WILSON series: (Monogram Pictures)

Crashing Thru (1/49)

Shadows of the West (1/49)

Haunted Trails (8/49)

Riders of the Dusk (11/49)

Range Land (12/49)

California never did have much luck with the ladies. Ethel Wales doesn't seem to understand that California is just trying to come to her rescue in this scene from *Lumberjack* **(1944).**

122

There were several horses that were used for Hoppy's horse Topper. The horse pictured here was Bill Boyd's favorite. This horse can be distinguished from the others by the gray shading on its neck and a brown spot on its ear. The scene is from *Unexpected Guest* (1947).

Fence Riders (1/50)

Gunslingers (4/50)

Arizona Territory (7/50)

Silver Raiders (8/50)

Cherokee Uprising (10/50)

Outlaws of Texas (12/50) Tommy Farrell appears in this episode.

Abilene Trail (2/51) Tommy Farrell is again on board to give Whip and Andy a hand in capturing the outlaws.

★   ★   ★

Wait a minute, Whip! Andy's one of the good guys. This fooling around is from *Arizona Territory* (1950).

ANDY "JINGLES" DEVINE

To the 1950s TV buckaroos the happy yell, "Hey, Wild Bill, wait for me!" became a catch-phrase to announce the opening of a popular early television series, "Wild Bill Hickok," starring Guy Madison and Andy Devine. It also served to introduce to these first-generation kids of television an actor who had already been around for several decades to delight the dads, moms, and even grandparents of these kids of the '50s—Andy Devine. When I talked with Andy's co-workers, I found out how much they admired and liked the man, too.

Dale Evans: *Oh, I loved Andy Devine; a lot of other people loved him, too. I would say that he was one of the most popular characters in pictures.*

Tommy Farrell: *Andy was a good friend of my mother, Glenda Farrell. Andy Devine was a very close neighbor. He was a wonderful clown but a very serious man off screen. He was not a zany; he was a very serious guy. He had that marvelous voice, and whatever they gave him to say, when it came out, you had to laugh. If you look at some of those old things he did, a lot of the lines were not funny lines—I mean if given to somebody else. But when Andy said them, they were funny.*

Jock Mahoney: *Andy was one of the most beautiful people in the whole world and his wife Doggie (Dorothy), too.*

Oliver Drake: *I worked with Andy at Universal. He was very well-educated. He was born in Arizona, was a cowboy. John Ford was making a picture down there of some kind and he needed somebody to drive a stage. They brought Andy Devine in and he worked for Ford and Ford liked him. Ford gave him some lines, so Andy*

Devine became an actor and came to Hollywood. Now, this was long before **Stagecoach,** *which he did for Ford years later.*

Jim Bannon: *Andy I just loved—a wonderful guy. I had great respect for Andy. I thought he conducted himself real well as a performer and as a big star. I loved Andy because his kids never got into any trouble. He ran a tight ship and was a good father.*

Rand Brooks: *I did some "Wild Bill Hickok" programs with Andy. What a man! He had a memory that just used to kill me. I knew him from being a kid watching him on the screen, but I'd walk on the set and he'd see me and say, "Hi, Randy, how you been." And it wasn't just me; it was everybody—a fabulous memory. He was a lovable man who was also married to a nice lady and had some fine sons.*

Roy Rogers: *You know, he always had a problem fighting weight. At one time he weighed over 300 pounds. On one of my pictures we had a green man [a person responsible for the "outdoor" studio sets] who was a big guy, and we had a gaffer who was also big. We were out on a ranch that had one of these scales where they weighed the wagons of hay when they came in. Somebody got the idea of getting these three guys on the scale and weighing them. Do you know what the three of them weighed? Over a thousand pounds—about a thousand and forty-some pounds! We had a lot of fun kidding them about that.*

Andy "Jingles" Devine doesn't look in any mood to be fooled with in this publicity still from one of his pictures with Roy Rogers.

126

Kirby Grant: Andy was a lovely person. I used to do those pictures with that dog for Lindsley Parsons at Monogram in the late '40s and early '50s. We'd go up to Big Bear and Cedar Lake up above Big Bear to do them. At that time Andy had a place called The Wagon Wheel, a bar and restaurant in Big Bear City. We used to hang out there. Like everyone else who knew him, I loved the man.

With his scratchy, high-pitched voice (the result of a childhood accident with a piece of curtain rod—"Don't put dangerous things in your mouth," Mom warned us, "or you'll sound like Andy Devine.") and his rotund, bullfrog-like physique, Andy was blessed with a comedy voice and appearance which immediately brought a smile to the faces of his audience. What separated him from other comic sidekicks with similar traits was the warmth and depth of character which he exuded in his many screen roles.

Andy could play comedy for chuckles or belly laughs; he could also bring tears to the eyes with a slight modulation of his voice and a change in his physical demeanor. His Cookie Bullfincher role in the Roy Rogers film series and Jingles in "Wild Bill Hickok" were mostly played for laughs with only occasional serious moments. The latter day TV generation who only knew Andy as Jingles Jones could not even guess at the depth of tragic characterization he brought to his first sound Western role in **Law and Order** (1932). In this classic film depiction of the early West with all its harsh reality, Andy played a simple-minded young man who is hanged for an accidental killing. The role was small, but one cannot shake from the mind the memory of Andy's moving depiction of this dull-witted, overgrown youth who accepts the fact that he must hang for what he has done, but is not able to fully comprehend this thing called "law and order" that is just arriving in the West.

Andy Devine was born in Flagstaff, Arizona, on October 7, 1905. Andy's father was a hotel owner; his grandfather was Admiral James Harmon Ward, one of the founders of Annapolis.

When Andy was only sixteen, his father died, leaving the family in a precarious financial state. It was only through his athletic ability—mainly football—that Andy was able to enter Arizona Teachers College. Later he attended Santa Clara University where he made quite a name for himself as a football player. His football prowess led to a brief stint as a pro player, but acting was what the husky youth really wanted to tackle.

It took Andy two years of odd jobs and knocking on studio doors before he landed his first Hollywood film role as an extra in the silent film two-reelers, **The Collegians** (1927). Soon he was playing featured roles in such long-forgotten pictures as **Red Lips** (1928), **Lonesome** (1928), and **Hot Stuff** (1929). He feared that the coming of sound pictures might put him out of the business because of his peculiar voice, but a comedy role in Universal's **The Spirit of Notre Dame** (1930) demonstrated that the raspy voice could actually be an identifying asset for a character actor—you certainly couldn't forget him once you had heard him. His performance in **The Spirit of Notre Dame**—that of a dumb student being coached so his grades would permit him to play on the varsity for a championship game—was very popular with audiences, and the studio was flooded with letters asking that he be given bigger parts.

Andy was put under contract by Universal in 1930 and continued with the studio for seventeen years. Although he was occasionally loaned to other film companies, Andy made most of his movies during these years at his home studio.

Former actor and now film executive Ewing "Lucky" Brown recalled for me some of the events of Andy's Universal years.

Lucky Brown: Richard Arlen was a big star at that time, and Andy and Dick became very good buddies. They wound up doing a whole lot of flying pictures at Universal because they were both pilots. When they both were sitting around with nothing to do, they would start putting together ideas for an airplane picture. They would do this, of course, because they had their own planes. They'd go to the studio and say, "We got an idea and this is what we'd like to do. We'll furnish the planes and fly them." That's how they'd get a film assignment. When they were a little bit broke and things were quiet, they'd put together one of their airplane specials. That was way back in the '30s, of course.

Andy owned a flying school called Provo Devine and during World War II his school was training pilots for the government. As a matter of fact, I bought a plane that Andy owned. It was one of the training planes that was made for the government called an Interstate. I think the engine was about sixty-five horsepower, and I know the wingspan on the thing was a third larger than a Cub; it was like a big

Andy was a utility actor during his seventeen years under contract to Universal. He played everything from zany comedies to aviation pictures to Westerns. This scene with Leo "Pancho" Carrillo is from *Texas Road Agent* (1941) which starred Dick Foran.

glider. *That plane was so slow that on a windy day you could watch the cars down below drive off and leave you.*

Andy and I used to hang around together because I had bought a plane from him and I liked to fly. A whole bunch of us would get together—Jackie Cooper, Andy, Dick Arlen, myself, and some others—for what we called "coffee flights." Just for the sheer fun of flying we'd take off and fly to San Diego or up to Bakersfield and have a cup of coffee. Maybe the guys would go out hunting for a couple of hours and then hop into the planes and fly back.

With the financial security of the Universal contract in his pocket, Andy took some bold steps in his personal life. While he was appearing with Will Rogers in *Dr. Bull* in 1933, Rogers introduced him to a young actress named Dorothy Irene House, whom Andy married later that year. Two sons, Denny and Tod, resulted from the long and happy union. Both children appeared with their father years later in *Canyon Passage* (1946).

A landmark Western for Hollywood and for Andy during these years was John Ford's *Stagecoach* (1939) in which he played Buck, the stagecoach driver. The classic film allowed him to demonstrate brilliantly his ability to portray the gamut of human emotions.

In addition to his successful film career, Andy also became very popular on radio. For years he was a semi-regular on Jack Benny's popular radio series. Andy's appearances on the program always produced hilarious results. Oliver Drake reminisced with me about those old radio shows.

*Oliver Drake: Andy's Buck Benny routines with Jack were some of the funniest bits ever to air on the radio. Andy was really a funny guy, and he didn't have to try to be funny. And it wasn't just because of his voice—the gravel voice he used with Jack Benny when they did the Buck Benny scenes. In radio, TV, and movies he was funny just because he was Andy Devine. He was so natural about his funniness; it wasn't like a Benny making a take or something. Andy was so natural with his funniness because he **was** funny. He was like an overgrown kid, and you could see that he enjoyed what he was doing.*

*When Andy came onto the scene there was almost a feeling of fun or silliness, and yet he could play as serious as you wanted him to. In **Stagecoach**, for example, he was very comic and also serious. That's because he was an actor first.*

Kirby Grant spent several years under contract to Universal during the time that Andy was there. Later Kirby would become famous as TV's Sky King. While at Universal Kirby got to know Andy quite well.

Kirby Grant: Andy was a jovial and outgoing person on screen and in real life. I have a funny story about him. Frankie Van, who used to be a world champion boxer, had a health club at Universal. Everybody at Universal used to go there to work out occasionally at the gym. Andy would go, but he wouldn't work out. He'd

Andy's got the six-up winding through Monument Valley as George Bancroft keeps a lookout for Apaches or maybe even the Ringo Kid. The scene, of course, is from John Ford's *Stagecoach* (1939).

strip down to the nude and lie down on one of those army cots. He'd cover himself with a sheet and go to sleep. He'd be like a beached whale snoring away there. We'd all leave, and Frankie would tell him before he left, "Andy, be sure and lock up." So one day Andy was left by himself, snoring peacefully on the cot. When he finally woke up, he turned around on the cot to get up, stretch, and all that kind of thing. Well, as he started to do this, all of his very private parts—to put it delicately—fell between the edge of the angle iron of the cot and the springs. He tried to get up and the springs came up to meet the edge of the angle iron and there he was; he was hooked! Of course, there was not a soul around. He screamed and carried on until, finally, the old watchman came around, heard him bellowing, and turned him loose. Andy never went back there to sleep. The whole experience must have been a little disconcerting for poor Andy.

When Andy left Universal in 1947, he moved over to Republic Pictures for his first continuing character sidekick role, Cookie Bullfincher in the Roy Rogers series. His first Rogers picture was *Bells of San Angelo*, which is considered by many B Western fans as the best episode in the long-running Rogers series and one of the best B Westerns ever made—at least of the musical Westerns. The film featured the direction of action ace, William Witney; it contained more slam-bang, violent action than anyone had ever seen in a Rogers film—or most other B Westerns, for that matter; and it was filmed in Republic's Trucolor process.

Border investigator, Roy Rogers, and Sheriff Cookie Bullfincher keep their eyes peeled for silver smugglers in this scene from *Bells of San Angelo* (1947).

Although Dale Evans co-starred in many of the Roy Rogers films, she only appeared in one of the nine films in which Andy was Roy's sidekick. That was Andy's first, *Bells of San Angelo* (1947).

Andy played his Cookie role for laughs, but always kept the character realistic enough to be believable in serious moments and during action scenes. It was always a delight to see Andy with Roy in a climactic shoot out. Andy had a comic yet forceful way of throwing his pistol arm and wrist in the direction of his shot so that he appeared to be helping the bullet eject from the gun with more force.

Andy made nine films with Roy Rogers during 1947 and 1948. They were all in color, all action-packed, all beautifully produced on large budgets (for B Westerns), and probably represent—as a package—the best string of films Rogers ever made.

Jock Mahoney told me of a funny incident that occurred about the time Andy was completing the Rogers series.

Jock Mahoney: *Andy and I had never met*

at the time a whole bunch of us cowboys went up to San Francisco on a train for a personal appearance. It was a money raiser of some sort. Russ Hayden, Bill Boyd, Roy Rogers, Gene Autry, Andy, myself, and a lot of others were on the train. Just before we arrived in San Francisco, I ran out of money because I'd been buying lots of rounds of drinks and food for the gang.

About that time I ran into Doggie [Andy's wife Dorothy] on the train. She said, "What's the problem, Jocko?" I said, "I'm tapped; I need some bucks." So she loaned me a twenty-dollar bill.

As soon as we got to San Francisco, I got some money and I took it right up to Doggie's room to pay her back. Now I had never met Andy formally; we both knew about each other, but I had never met him personally. Andy opened the door of their room. I said hello to him and just walked across the room to Doggie—she stood up as I approached. I gave her the twenty dollars and said to her, "You were absolutely marvelous, wonderful; you were great; I loved every moment of it."

Andy just stood there with his mouth hanging open. I gave her a kiss, turned around, and walked out. (laugh) Andy was beautiful; they don't come like him anymore.

After the Rogers series, Andy appeared in fewer films, freelancing in whatever roles came along. He appeared in **The Traveling Saleswoman** (1950) with Joan Davis; **Never a Dull Moment** (1950) with Fred MacMurray and Irene Dunne, and three fairly big-budget Westerns: **The Slaughter Trail** (1951), **New Mexico** (1951), and **Montana Belle** (1952). He played the small role of the talkative soldier in John Huston's production of **The Red Badge of Courage** (1951), the only memorable picture of the bunch.

In 1951 Andy was approached with a proposal to co-star with Guy Madison in a half-hour Western television series entitled "Wild Bill Hickok." The producer, William Broidy, acknowledged to Andy that the pay was no good, only $250 per show, but he was willing to offer a ten percent piece of the show if Andy signed a contract. Andy agreed and the show made him a wealthy man. Over the next few years 113 episodes were produced, thirty-nine of them in color. They ran in syndication starting in 1952 and on ABC during the 1957-58 season. As of this writing, the old series has been revived on the CBN

THE LATEST THRILLING
WILD BILL
HICKOK
ADVENTURE

"THE
**MATCH-
MAKING
MARSHAL**"

starring

GUY
MADISON
as WILD BILL HICKOK

and

ANDY
DEVINE
as JINGLES

Produced by WESLEY BARRY
Directed by FRANK McDONALD
Screenplay by MAURICE TOMBRAGEL and BILL RAYNOR

A NEWHALL PRODUCTION

Guy Madison and Andy shoot it out with the bad guys in this scene from a "Wild Bill Hickok" episode. Many programs from the television series were edited into feature film versions and distributed to theatres, primarily in the European markets.

cable network as a Saturday afternoon program for a new generation of youngsters.

During the years that the television series was in production, a "Wild Bill Hickok" radio series with Madison and Andy was running on the Mutual network. From late 1951 through 1954, "Wild Bill Hickok" was a three-a-week half-hour program sponsored by Kellogg, which also sponsored the television series. In 1955 and '56 the radio series was unsponsored and ran on Sundays.

Oliver Drake wrote a lot of the scripts for the "Wild Bill Hickok" television series. He talked with me about those years.

Oliver Drake: Bill Broidy was not a real smart producer, but he knew people and he was lucky. Just through accident he made the "Wild Bill Hickok" pilot with Guy Madison and Andy Devine; took it to New York, and got Kellogg to sponsor it. In his time he had the best TV contract in the business with Kellogg; he made a fortune. Guy Madison and Andy got well paid for it, of course. I think without Andy they wouldn't have had the series. I don't think that Madison—as much as I like him and as much as I know he's a good actor—would have been enough to sell the series on his own. Guy and Andy were good for each other, a good team, just like Leo Carillo was with Duncan Renaldo in "The Cisco Kid" series.

The contract that Bill Broidy got with Kellogg was great because of the amount of money he got and the duration of the contract. He got probably three times as much money out of a single program as was put into the program to produce it. This was unusual because it usually takes about three runs of a television show before the producer even breaks even. Broidy more than broke even; he made a hell of profit off the first run. Everybody just drooled over the contract. He could have sold it, probably, for five million dollars, but Broidy liked to gamble—he'd go to Las Vegas and lose twenty or thirty thousand dollars on a weekend. He'd then go to the bank and borrow on his contract with Kellogg.

Guy Madison was a nice guy, but not too friendly. You never got too well acquainted with him; he was sort of cool. Andy and I would try out certain gags for the series before I'd turn in the script, so

Andy got a chance to have some of his comedy in the "Hickok" series built right into the scripts. I enjoyed working on things like that with Andy. He could improvise his comedy, but he usually didn't. He'd stick close to the script.

Lucky Brown, Jock Mahoney, and Jim Bannon remembered the horse that Andy rode in most of his films and the television series.

Lucky Brown: Andy had a horse that belonged to the Fat Jones Stable. I can't think of its name. [The horse was called Joker in the TV series.] Andy was a big man, so there were only a couple of horses that he could ride. There was one horse that was his lead horse. Andy used to say that this horse would just look at him and sigh every time he walked towards the horse. Andy said that when they had to do a chase, he'd always lean down and pat the horse and say, "Well, old fellow, hang in there. We'll both make it."

Jock Mahoney: Andy's horse hated him. Every time Andy would go to get on him, the horse would put his ears back and act as if he would bite him. If the horse got the opportunity, he would! Well, Andy was a big, heavy man. I wouldn't want him getting on my back either.

Jim Bannon: For a man as big as he was, Andy did pretty good on those horses. There was a big, old bay that he used to ride all the time, a horse called Banner. He rode that horse in most of his pictures and the "Hickok" series. It was kind of a choice of Banner or get a Clydesdale! You know, Andy was something to hold up.

Rand Brooks acted in many of the "Wild Bill Hickok" television adventures.

Rand Brooks: Andy was very cat-like for his weight and size. He moved well and handled himself well. He'd been a good athlete in his day, so this came naturally to him. Guy Madison was very, very quiet, but they got along well, were good friends.

Andy was the extroverted, jovial-type person he exuded on the screen, but he

THE LATEST THRILLING
**WILD BILL
HICKOK**
ADVENTURE

"THE
**MATCH-
MAKING
MARSHAL**"

starring

**GUY
MADISON**

as WILD BILL HICKOK

and

**ANDY
DEVINE**

as JINGLES

Produced by WESLEY BARRY
Directed by FRANK McDONALD
Screenplay by MAURICE TOMBRAGEL and BILL RAYNOR

A NEWHALL PRODUCTION

Andy's horse doesn't look too happy about the passenger astride his back. Those ears aren't turned back just to hear the sparkling dialogue between Andy and Guy Madison.

did it without always being "on." He was a very open person, never a complainer, always a positive thinker.

Jock Mahoney loves to play practical jokes on people, especially his fellow actors when they are in a public situation and can't immediately retaliate.

Jock Mahoney: As I was driving down Santa Monica Boulevard one day years ago, I saw a huge tent set up on the side of the street. Andy and Guy Madison were signing autographs in a personal appearance for their "Wild Bill Hickok" series. I saw them as I passed the tent on my way to Santa Monica.

When I came back about two hours later, the crowd had dwindled out because everybody was going home for dinner. Andy and Guy were just at the end of about a five-hour session of signing autographs as fast as they could sign them. When you get to that point in signing, everybody looks alike and you don't even look at the people.

Andy was sitting at one table and Guy Madison was just a few feet away at another. The fans would get a picture of Andy and Guy from a publicity man and then hand it to Andy for an autograph. After Andy signed it, the fan would take it over to Guy and he would sign it.

So I got out of my car and got in a line that gradually got me to Andy. The minute I got in front of Andy I started gushing. I said how thrilled I was. He said, "Oh,

134

thank you, thank you." At the same time he was writing his autograph for me. I said, "Boy, You sure thrilled me to pieces; you really thrilled me"—I just went on and on. I picked up my picture, the next person moved in, and I moved over to Guy Madison.

"And you, too, Mr. Madison," I said in my most unctuous manner. "I sure am a big fan of yours!" Guy looked up through his foggy brain, and it began to sink in what he had been hearing over at Andy's table. Suddenly he realized it was old Jocko funning them. They never did swear in public, of course, but this time Guy couldn't resist. He said, "Oh, shit! It's Jocko. Will you get the hell out of here?" Both he and Andy wanted to come out of there like bulls in a china shop and lay

into me. Oh, I did have fun with them that day!

While the "Wild Bill Hickok" series was still going strong, Andy was asked to take over the kiddie show called "Smilin' Ed's Gang" when Smilin' Ed McConnell died in 1954. The program was retitled "Andy's Gang" and ran on NBC-TV starting in 1955 with the same characters and format that McConnell had made popular—Froggie the gremlin, Midnight the cat, and a serial-type filmed adventure. The show was poorly produced in every way, but it was fairly popular with very young children.

During the 1960s Andy began to slow down the pace of his career. He still made an occasional feature picture—(most notably John Ford's **Two Rode Together** (1961) and **The Man Who Shot Liberty Valance** (1962). During the 1964-65 television season he appeared in a few episodes of the

Andy seems a little worried about exploring this spooky, old ranch house with Wild Bill Hickok (Guy Madison).

"Flipper" TV series as a character named Hap Gorman. It's very likely that he did the "Flipper" programs so that he could enjoy some Florida fishing. The Ivan Tors series was produced in the Miami area.

All during his career Andy took a great interest in community activities wherever he lived. He served as the mayor of Van Nuys, California, for seventeen years. When the family moved to Newport Beach in 1957, he quickly became a pillar of that community. He served on many important committees, but he was particularly proud of being a member of the Board of Directors for the Boy Scouts of Orange County. Never afraid to take a political stand, he was a staunch Ronald Reagan supporter and campaigned actively for the candidate in the 1976 California presidential primary.

In 1976 the Orange County Press Club tossed a testimonial dinner for Andy at the Disneyland Hotel in recognition of his years of worthwhile endeavors. The affair was held on his seventieth birthday. John Wayne hosted and the speakers included Ronald Reagan, Buddy Ebsen, Roy Rogers, and Claire Trevor.

Andy's health was not good during the 1970s. He suffered for several years from cancer, diabetes, and leukemia. In late 1976 his health severely worsened. In critical condition he was admitted to a Santa Rosa, California, hospital under treatment for kidney failure and pneumonia.

On February 18, 1976, Andy Devine died. His wife and two sons and hundreds of hours of his audio and filmed entertainment survived him.

★   ★   ★

ANDY DEVINE FILMOGRAPHY

ROY ROGERS series: (Republic Pictures)

Bells of San Angelo (4/47)

Springtime in the Sierras (7/47)

On the Old Spanish Trail (10/47)

The Gay Ranchero (1/48)

Under California Stars (5/48)

Eyes of Texas (7/48)

Night Time in Nevada (9/48)

Grand Canyon Trail (11/48)

The Far Frontier (12/48)

WILD BILL HICKOK series: (Newhall/Allied Artists)

Episodes from the "Wild Bill Hickok" television series were edited into feature film versions and released to theatres.

Behind Southern Lines (11/52)

Ghost of Crossbones Canyon (11/52)

Trail of the Arrow (11/52)

The Yellow-Haired Kid (11/52)

Border City Rustlers (11/53)

Secret of Outlaw Flats (11/53)

Six-Gun Decision (11/53)

Two-Gun Marshal (11/53)

Marshals in Disguise (12/54)

Outlaw's Son (12/54)

Trouble on the Trail (12/54)

The Two-Gun Teacher (12/54)

Timber Country Trouble (5/55)

The Match-Making Marshal (5/55)

The Titled Tenderfoot (5/55)

Phantom Trails (5/55)

★   ★   ★

137

Yes, you're right! It's not a ukulele; it's a guitar that Cliff "Ukulele Ike" Edwards is strumming in this scene from the 1941 Charles Starrett film, *Prairie Strangers*. Cliff Edwards' songs and gentle humor added much to the Charles Starrett and Tim Holt films of the early 1940s.

CLIFF "UKULELE IKE" EDWARDS

I suppose that most people remember Cliff Edwards as the voice of Jiminy Cricket in Walt Disney's 1940 animated cartoon feature *Pinocchio.* His poignant rendering of "When You Wish Upon a Star" was a hit in the movie, and the song became the signature theme for the Disney television series and, in truth, the entire Disney empire. Because the Disney identification so overwhelmed Edwards' other work, it is often forgotten that he had a topflight career before Disney and, for a two-year period in the early 1940s, was a comedy sidekick for Western stars Charles Starrett and Tim Holt.

Cliff Edwards was born in Hannibal, Missouri, in 1895. By the time he was a teen-ager, he was singing in bars around the St. Louis area for whatever coins the tipsy patrons would toss to him. Luck struck Edwards when he teamed up with a fellow named Bobby Carlton who had written the song "Ja Da." The song became one of the hits of the twenties and sparked the careers of both men. Soon Cliff was a hit on vaudeville circuits.

Edwards got his nickname of "Ukulele Ike" during the time he was playing an extended engagement at a Chicago nightspot. One of the waiters had trouble remembering Cliff's name, so he called him "Ike." Since Cliff played a ukulele to accompany himself, he was dubbed Ukulele Ike. The name stuck and soon Cliff officially billed himself that way.

During the 1920s and '30s, Ukulele Ike became a big star by virtue of his best-selling records. His recordings of such tunes as "June Night," "Sleepy Time Gal," "Fascinating Rhythm," "Toot, Toot, Tootsie," and "I Cried for You" (and the later "When You Wish Upon a Star") sold a reported seventy-four million copies. Soon Hollywood beckoned, and Cliff had the distinction of introducing the song "Singing in the Rain" in the MGM musical hit, *Hollywood Revue of 1929.* Throughout the 1930s Cliff worked constantly in films doing featured roles. He was also popular on many radio shows—probably best remembered for the Rudy Vallee program.

By the time of his Jiminy Cricket role in *Pinocchio,* Cliff's career had started to fade. He found he was no longer in demand at the studios. In early 1941 Warner Brothers put him in a ten-minute filler called *Cliff Edwards and His Buckaroos,* which suggested his potential as a musical Western comic sidekick. It was from this short subject that Cliff segued into the Charles Starrett Western series at Columbia Pictures, an association that would last for eight pictures during 1941 and early 1942.

I talked with Charles Starrett about his remembrances of Cliff Edwards as a cowboy sidekick.

Charles Starrett: Cliff was just a wonderful person. It was a sad thing about his career. Everything had been going along great for Ukulele Ike—of course, his career went back to the theatre in New York; he was a big name at the Gardens and with Ziegfeld. In 1929 he had come out to MGM and had been a big star in his own right there. Then he had marital trouble and he and his wife split. His wife married her lawyer, and they really fleeced poor Cliff. He finally had to declare bankruptcy. He was behind the eightball for a long time.

He was available in 1941, so he came over to Columbia and I had him in my pictures. I just loved Cliff; he was such an asset in a picture. It finally came time for his option, and I had a producer (that I won't mention by name) who said to Cliff, "Oh, you're just a comedian. We get you guys for a dime a dozen." Cliff said, "Go get 'em!" And he walked out on us. It was a hell of a loss because he went right over to RKO and started working with Tim Holt at double the salary that Columbia was paying him.

David — I rode 33 white horses in my 17 yrs with Columbia Pictures. This gelding was the best — he was a "scene stealer" too! Your friend — Charles "Durango" Starrett

Cliff Edwards worked as Charles Starrett's comic sidekick in eight films during 1941 and 1942.

Cliff's comedy was more appealing to adults, I think. He was not a slapstick artist, you know. Just using his own gentle, joshing sort of manner he was marvelous; we were going along good. As a matter of fact, the writer that we had began to really understand and appreciate Cliff's style of comedy. And, too, Cliff could take a piece of material and tailor it for himself—he knew what was good for him and what wasn't. Sometimes there might be a little argument about changing this or that in the script. I'd say, "Let Cliff alone; he knows what he's doing, and there may be an improvement in the scene. We'll try it Cliff's way." I found that Cliff's way was generally right. So we worked very well together. I wish we could have kept him. Things were going along great for us; I saw good times ahead working with Cliff. I hated to lose him.

As Charles Starrett indicated, Cliff left Columbia Pictures and went over to Tim Holt's popular series for RKO. He replaced Lee "Lasses" White who was leaving the Holt pictures. In the first Tim Holt film, **Bandit Ranger,** Cliff played a character named Whopper. For the rest of the pictures he was called simply "Ike."

Cliff's sidekick tenure with Tim Holt was of short duration, however, because World War II was beginning and Tim was enlisting in the army as an aviation cadet. The six features Cliff made with Tim were filmed in a grueling fifty-four days prior to his call to duty. Upon hearing of his son's fifty-four day ordeal, Tim's father, famous screen star Jack Holt, joked, "I know why you're going in the Army; you're a coward to stay at RKO." The studio's real reason for rushing the production of the features was that it wanted to be able to release Tim's films gradually while he was away in service. In this way they could keep their star in front of his public while the war was going on.

After the Tim Holt series, Cliff Edwards was through as a cowboy sidekick. During the succeeding years he worked sporadically in radio and then television. From May through September of 1949, he had a fifteen-minute television series called "The Cliff Edwards Show." It filled the remaining fifteen minutes in the 7:30-8:00 p.m. half-hour which included the CBS Evening News—long before

Walter Cronkite or Dan Rather had earned their anchor spots. On his show Cliff sang, told homespun stories, and often modeled funny hats from a huge collection he had.

Cliff made occasional guest appearances after his brief series, but he was now considered "over the hill" for major responsibilities. In the late 1960s Disney Records released an album called "Ukulele Ike Happens Again," which did not sell very well.

During the final years of his life, failing health (he had difficulty walking) and very limited funds kept him somewhat of a recluse. He did not ever remarry. He was living in a partly furnished apartment above Hollywood Boulevard when he died in 1971.

★　　　★　　　★

CLIFF EDWARDS FILMOGRAPHY

CHARLES STARRETT series: *(Columbia Pictures)*

Thunder Over the Prairie (7/41)

Prairie Stranger (9/41)

Riders of the Badlands (12/41)

West of Tombstone (1/42)

Lawless Plainsmen (3/42)

Riders of the Northland (5/42)

Bad Men of the Hills (8/42)

Overland to Deadwood (9/42)

TIM HOLT series: *(RKO)*

Bandit Ranger (9/42)

Pirates of the Prairie (11/42)

Fighting Frontier (1/43)

Sagebrush Law (4/43)

Avenging Rider (5/43)

Red River Robin Hood (7/43)

★　　　★　　　★

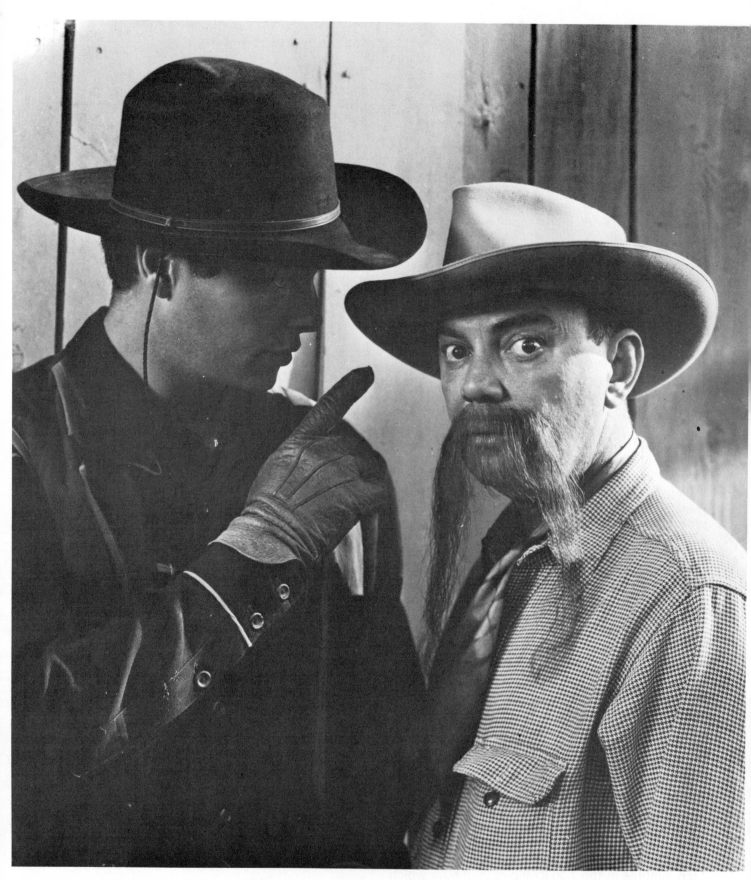

I don't think Tim Holt is fooled by Ike's disguise in this scene from one of their RKO features.

The old pie-in-the-face comedy routine was not typical of Cliff Edwards' type of humor. An indication of this is that he is not the one wearing the pie. The scene is from *Overland to Deadwood* starring Charles Starrett.

This early publicity photo of Raymond Hatton was taken during the late 1920s when he was co-starring with Wallace Beery in a series of comedy features for Paramount Pictures.

144

RAYMOND HATTON

Don "Red" Barry: Raymond Hatton was a doll; he was one of the wonderful, sweet men of the business and a great professional actor.

Oliver Drake: He was a wonderful person. Raymond Hatton was a real gentleman, a nice guy, and a nice family man. His first big pictures were the silent comedies he made with Wallace Beery. They made a series in the 1920s that was a big money maker. Beery was hard to get along with, so they finally separated and Hatton went his way and Beery went his.

Raymond was a far more serious sidekick than most. He did some comedy, but he wasn't a screwball comic like Al St. John or Fuzzy Knight or others like those. Raymond's roles were mainly serious in his pictures, and he was serious about his work. He was not one of those smart-off comedians that are "on" all of the time. He'd been in vaudeville and on the stage. But Ray never felt that the B Westerns were a comedown in any way. Regardless of what kind of a part he played, he played it to the hilt.

Raymond Hatton was born on July 7, 1892, in a little four-corner town called Red Oak in the state of Iowa. By the time he reached his teens he was performing in vaudeville stock companies in cities big and small throughout the country. His versatility as both a serious and comic actor made him a valuable commodity to producers and popular with his fellow actors and audiences.

By the time he reached voting age, he had cast his ballot for films over vaudeville and was working for the Biograph Company in New York. Soon Mack Sennett heard about him and cast the fledgling film

actor in many of his comedy shorts. C.B. DeMille caught sight of Hatton in a film appearance and decided to use him in several films. By the early 1920s Raymond Hatton had a Paramount Pictures contract in his pocket and was a successful and highly regarded movie actor in Hollywood.

From 1926 to 1928 he was cast with Wallace Beery in a series of very popular comedy films. It was during the time of this series that he reached star status with the movie-going public. During the 1930s his roles began to veer more and more into the Western vein. Ray began to hone a rough-hewned, buckskin-clad frontiersman character which he would modify to be comic or serious through the set of his posture, the gait of his walk, the inflection in his voice, or any of the other acting devices he had bagged through his years of performing. Like the black sheep, he had at least three bags full.

Raymond Hatton is one of the best examples of a serious character actor who wandered into Western series sidekick roles purely by happenstance and stayed for twelve busy years. From 1938 through 1950 Hatton made seventy-three series Westerns. (By drawing the boundaries of those twelve years for my main concentration of his career, I realize that a multitude of other sidekick and Western character parts are overlooked, but Ray Hatton's roles outside the confines of this period of time comprise irregular appearances in a variety of films. In trying to deal with a career which spanned more than fifty years and some three hundred films, a writer is forced to be selective or he is apt to become lost in a cloud of cinema trail dust.)

Raymond Hatton's first Western series came about because of a feud Gene Autry was having with Republic Pictures. In 1938 Autry and Republic reached an impasse in their ongoing squabble over a new contract. Autry, of course, wanted more money and Republic didn't want to give it to him. Finally Autry called his director, Joe Kane, and told him not to expect the cowboy crooner on the set for

This extremely rare photo shows a very youthful Raymond Hatton and Wallace Beery in a publicity shot from one of their silent feature comedies of the late 1920s.

their next scheduled picture; Autry was taking a walk. In fact, he went on an extended personal appearance tour throughout the South while Republic stewed over what to do about their recalcitrant singing cowboy.

What Republic finally decided to do was launch a new singing cowboy series with a young fellow they had under contract. His name was Leonard Slye, but, of course, they changed it to Roy Rogers. For box office insurance Republic cast Autry's popular sidekick, Smiley Burnette, in Roy's first couple of pictures. When Gene finally reached agreement with Republic on his contract, Smiley returned to the Autry pictures and Rogers was left sitting astride Trigger with no sidekick—but not for long.

It was at this point that Raymond Hatton was signed by Republic to serve as Roy's sidekick. Decked out in tattered buckskin regalia and generally riding a mule named Dinah ("Hi Ho, Dinah!"), Hatton seemed to be having as much fun as the movie audiences who watched him. During

his four-picture run with Roy Rogers, Ray set the tone for his Western comedy that would carry him throughout his sidekick career.

Raymond Hatton's comedy was seldom of an overt nature. He never played the stooge or buffoon in his sidekick roles. The humor came out of his characterization and comic attitude. The only noticeable change which occurred very gradually with the passing years was a reduction in the amount of comedy within each film and a tendency to lean more and more in the direction of straight character parts with only a touch of humor.

After three films with Roy Rogers, Hatton was assigned to the Three Mesquiteers series, replacing the departing Max Terhune. (A fourth film with Rogers, **Wall Street Cowboy,** was released after Ray's first Three Mesquiteers film was already in release.) Max Terhune had played a character called Lullaby Joslin in the Mesquiteers pictures; Hatton played Rusty Joslin, presumably Lullaby's brother, but I have never been able to verify that the relationship was actually stated.

At this point in the Three Mesquiteers series (1939) John Wayne and Ray Corrigan comprised the other two-thirds of the starring cast. After two films with Ray Hatton, Wayne and Corrigan left for other film pastures and Hatton was teamed with Robert Livingston (returning after an eight-picture hiatus from the series) and Duncan Renaldo (creating a new character called Rico). Hatton provided what comedy there was in the revamped series, but he made no attempt to continue the hayseed, country cousin humor of Max Terhune. Ray played his Rusty Joslin role as a light-hearted, rattlesnake-tough, energetic old frontiersman—a colorful combination of character traits which film audiences, young and old, found fascinating. He made nine episodes in the series during 1939 and '40. Then Republic played musical chairs again with its Three Mesquiteers casting: Renaldo and Ray Hatton were out; Bob Steele and Rufe Davis were in.

In early 1941 Monogram Pictures was developing a new trio Western series. They had two Western film veterans signed—Buck Jones and Tim McCoy—and all they needed was a comic relief actor to complete the threesome for the Rough Riders series. Ray Hatton was their choice, he was agreeable, and he eventually played the assigned role of Sandy Hopkins for the nine episodes that were filmed in the series. Sandy Hopkins was basically a recostumed Rusty Joslin with just a bit less humor.

The plots of the Rough Riders films were all pretty much the same, but the sameness in this case worked to the benefit of the series. The three special

Although wounded, Roy seems to have won the day and the leading lady, Mary Hart. Ray Hatton (right), playing a character by the name of Horseshoe, seems mighty pleased with the proceedings in this scene from *Frontier Pony Express* (1939).

"All for one and one for all." Raymond Hatton made seven Three Mesquiteers films with Robert Livingston and Duncan Renaldo.

Who would be foolish enough to challenge these three fellows known as the Rough Riders? Buck Jones, Tim McCoy, and Raymond Hatton are stalking their prey in this publicity photo from the Monogram series.

U.S. Marshals would be put on a case at the start of an episode. McCoy and Hatton would generally work undercover to infiltrate the outlaw gang, while Buck would be the up-front good guy working with the local sheriff and/or long-suffering townspeople/ranchers/whomever. Buck could be counted on to have several inconclusive fights and shoot outs as Tim and Sandy were surreptitiously getting the goods on the bad guys. Buck's trademark in the films was a stick of gum he would put into his mouth and slowly chew when his temper was aroused. Finally, all the plot threads would be pulled together for a slam-bang climax.

With peace restored, the Rough Riders would gather on the trail for an "adios scene" before they headed out for their separate destinations: Buck to Arizona, Tim to Wyoming, and Sandy to Texas. Off they rode to the soundtrack strains of the Rough Riders' song. You always knew, however, that they

would be back together again when they were needed.

After eight Rough Riders episodes, Tim McCoy applied for and received a commission to serve in World War II as a lieutenant colonel. Buck and Ray made one more episode with Rex Bell as the third member of the cast. Before the picture was released, Buck Jones died tragically in the Coconut Grove night club fire in Boston. The Rough Riders would ride no more.

With Tim McCoy in the service and the death of Buck Jones, Rough Riders producer Scotty Dunlap decided perhaps it was time to drop the trio Western format and revert to the more traditional concept of a cowboy star, his horse, and his sidekick. Rather than go to the promotional expense of starting with an unknown actor, Dunlap gave veteran Western actor Johnny Mack Brown a call and asked him if he was interested in starring in a Monogram series

Nevada Jack McKenzie and Sandy Hopkins (Johnny Mack Brown and Raymond Hatton) seem ready for action in this publicity photo from their Monogram Pictures series.

with Ray Hatton as his sidekick. Brown, who was temporarily at liberty, jumped at the offer.

The concept for the series called for Johnny Mack to play Nevada Jack McKenzie, a special U.S. Marshal much in the mold of the Buck Jones character in the Rough Riders. Ray Hatton was to continue his by now well-established character of Sandy Hopkins. For the first couple of years the series was in production, Sandy continued to do much of his work undercover. He would arrive in the beleaguered town in the guise of an undertaker, snake oil salesman, newspaper publisher, or whatever type of character the scriptwriters concocted. Usually only the audience was aware of the Brown-Hatton association until late in the proceedings. Again it must be noted that Ray Hatton continued to ease the comedy out of his sidekick role in favor of a colorful, well-developed oldtimer characterization. He also continued to strengthen his image as an intelligent and shrewd operator who was also mighty handy with his dukes and a six-gun. In fact, Ray Hatton was turning Sandy Hopkins into an equal partner rather than a "Nevada, what do you think we ought to do now?" sidekick.

For three years Brown and Hatton rode the Monogram series trail with few diversions from their established path. The films were moderately well-produced considering the limited budgets that Monogram allocated, but they never compared favorably with the flashy production quality and action-full scripts that could be found in any Republic Pictures product. Many of the Brown-Hatton scripts plodded along with an overabundance of stale dialogue and a paucity of action. By mid-1946, when they dropped the Nevada and Sandy roles, the series had pretty much lost its focus and had started a long downhill slide into mediocrity or worse.

In **Gentleman from Texas** (1946), their first episode with revised character names, Brown is called Johnny Maclan. Hatton is the crusading newspaper publisher who happens to have a pretty daughter. For most of the film Hatton's character name is not mentioned. Then, as if someone suddenly discovered this oversight, he is repeatedly referred to as Idaho—an unlikely name for the somewhat distinguished newspaper publisher.

The script's snail pace is interrupted four times for meaningless musical interludes by a Western swing band and a sultry saloon singer with the name of Miss Kitty. The tempo of the film is made additionally uneven by the use of slow fades to black at the end of most scenes. Brown looks and acts bored through much of the film. Ray Hatton strives mightily to add some vigor to the proceedings, but

he is thwarted by the stodgy script. Don Miller in his book, **Hollywood Corral,** probably best sums up the status of the Johnny Mack Brown series from 1946 until its demise:

> *The Browns then assumed the dimensions of a basket of strawberries, with the viewer doing the sorting. Some were good, some were bad, and all looked pretty much alike.*

By 1948 Ray was getting extremely restless in the Johnny Mack Brown films and longed to move on to more diverse acting work. Throughout his series career he had been able to squeeze in an occasional free-lance film, and now his agent assured him that with television becoming a new outlet for work and the continued opportunities in feature films, there would be plenty of acting jobs available. The agent even predicted that he would probably make more money as a free-lance actor.

Since Ray's career did not become noticeably better or worse during the following years, the wisdom of his decision to free-lance is inconclusive. There is no question, however, that the Johnny Mack Brown series was going nowhere, even though it would survive until 1952. As his agent promised, Ray did appear in many television shows over the next few years and played small to medium-sized roles in a string of features, mostly of the second-rate variety. His last film role, though, was as the old hitchhiker in the highly acclaimed **In Cold Blood** (1967).

Ray Hatton's only obvious misstep during these years was accepting a co-starring assignment in a 1950 Lippert Pictures series with Jimmy Ellison, Russ Hayden, and Fuzzy Knight. The six-episode Western series was a dreary venture which fortunately was quickly forgotten. (More information on the series can be found in the Fuzzy Knight chapter of this book.)

On October 21, 1971, Raymond Hatton died at the age of eighty-four in his Palmdale, California, home. His wife, the former actress Francis Hatton, had died just the week before. Ray Hatton was proud of his long career in show business, and he had reason to be. He had provided entertainment for several generations of audiences, and they had responded to his efforts with a warmth of appreciation and deep respect all performers strive for. Perhaps even more satisfying was the high regard his acting peers held for him. You can't have it much better than that, oldtimer.

★   ★   ★

Raymond Hatton and Johnny Mack Brown seem very concerned about something in this scene from *Gun Talk* (1947). Perhaps their concern should be about the weak script.

RAYMOND HATTON FILMOGRAPHY

***ROY ROGERS* series:** *(Republic Pictures)*

Come On, Rangers (11/38)

Rough Riders Round-Up (3/39)

Frontier Pony Express (4/39)

Wall Street Cowboy (8/39)

***THREE MESQUITEERS* series (Wayne and Corrigan):** *(Republic Pictures)*

Wyoming Outlaw (6/39)

New Frontier (8/39) Allan Lane sidekick Eddy Waller has an important role in this film.

***THREE MESQUITEERS* series (Livingston and Renaldo):** *(Republic Pictures)*

The Kansas Terrors (10/39)

Cowboys from Texas (11/39)

Heroes of the Saddle (1/40)

Pioneers of the West (3/40)

Covered Wagon Days (4/40) Tom London is featured in the cast.

Rocky Mountain Rangers (5/40)

Oklahoma Renegades (8/40) Sidekick Lee "Lasses" White and later singing cowboy star Eddie Dean have roles in this episode.

ROUGH RIDER series (Jones and McCoy): (Monogram Pictures)

Arizona Bound (7/41)

Gunman from Bodie (9/41)

Forbidden Trails (12/41)

Below the Border (1/42)

Ghost Town Law (3/42)

Down Texas Way (5/42)

Riders of the West (8/42)

West of the Law (10/42) This is Tim McCoy's last film in the series.

Dawn on the Great Divide (12/42) Rex Bell substitutes for Tim McCoy in this film, but plays a different role.

JOHNNY MACK BROWN series: (Monogram Pictures)

The Ghost Rider (4/43)

Stranger from Pecos (7/43)

Six Gun Gospel (9/43)

Outlaws of Stampede Pass (10/43)

Texas Kid (11/43)

Raiders of the Border (1/44)

Partners of the Trail (3/44)

Law Men (4/44)

Range Law (6/44)

West of the Rio Grande (8/44)

Land of the Outlaws (9/44)

Law of the Valley (11/44)

Ghost Guns (11/44)

The Navajo Trail (1/45)

Gun Smoke (2/45)

Stranger from Santa Fe (4/45)

Flame of the West (6/45)

The Lost Trail (10/45)

Frontier Feud (11/45)

Border Bandits (1/46)

Drifting Along (1/46) (How's that for an exciting title!)

Haunted Mine (3/46)

Under Arizona Skies (4/46)

Gentleman from Texas (6/46)

Trigger Fingers (9/46)

Shadows on the Range (10/46)

Silver Range (11/46)

Raiders of the South (1/47)

Valley of Fear (2/47)

Trailing Danger (3/47)

Law of the Lawless (4/47)

Law Comes to Gunsight (5/47)

Code of the Saddle (6/47)

Flashing Guns (7/47)

Prairie Express (10/47)

Gun Talk (12/47)

Overland Trails (1/48)

Crossed Trails (4/48)

Frontier Agent (5/48)

Triggerman (4/48)

Back Trail (7/48) Snub Pollard has a small role in this film.

Fighting Ranger (8/48)

Sheriff of Medicine Bow (10/48) Max Terhune joins the cast for the final three films in which Raymond appears.

Gunning for Justice (11/48)

Hidden Danger (12/48)

JIMMY ELLISON-RUSS HAYDEN series: (Lippert Pictures)

Hostile Country (3/50) Fuzzy Knight is co-starred in all six episodes in this series.

Marshal of Heldorado (4/50)

Colorado Ranger (5/50)

West of the Brazos (6/50)

Crooked River (6/50)

Fast on the Draw (6/50)

★　　　★　　　★

Maybe the letter explains where Raymond got that silly-looking hat. The scene is from *Flashing Guns* (1947).

Fuzzy Knight turns on the sly, shy charm in this publicity still from 1939. This was during the time he was under contract to Universal Pictures.

FUZZY KNIGHT

Nell O'Day: *Fuzzy Knight was one of the most wonderful people anybody could have worked with. He was just as charming off screen as he was in all of the films you've seen him play. All of those pieces of pantomime he worked out for himself. He had a marvelous sense of timing, as you can see in his films. And he could talk to a horse and somehow you had a feeling that the horse really understood him. Old Brownie was the horse Fuzzy rode in most of the films he made with Johnny Mack Brown and me. He was a wonderful person to get along with; I never saw him cross at anyone; I never saw anyone cross at him, either. I don't know how they could have been.*

The first thing one might wonder about Fuzzy Knight is how this clean-shaven comic acquired the tag "Fuzzy." Producer-director-screenwriter Oliver Drake quickly cleared up that matter for me: "He had this very raspy, fuzzy voice, and that's where he got his name. I never heard him called anything else."

I never did either, but I did find out that his real name was J. Forrest Knight. I've tried diligently, but without success, to find out the name that goes with the initial.

Anyway, J. Forrest Knight was born in 1901 in Fairmont, West Virginia. By his early teens he was in show business, working as an end man in a tent minstrel show (not unlike fellow sidekick Lee "Lasses" White did during his early years). An education was highly prized in the Knight family, so show business had to give way, slightly, for a college education. I say "slightly" because Fuzzy played piano and other instruments in a dance band while studying at the University of West Virginia.

By the time he graduated from college, Fuzzy knew that show business ranked higher in his priorities than the practice of law, so he headed for the bright lights. It wasn't long before he was making his mark as a song and dance man in vaudeville, nightclubs, and, ultimately, Broadway. In 1927 he was featured in Earl Carroll's *Vanities;* in 1928 he played in the hit show, *Here's How;* Ned Wayburn's *Gambols* followed in 1929. By 1930 he was a "name" entertainer touring with the Keith vaudeville circuit. And then, as they say, Hollywood called.

Mae West initiated him to Hollywood in her 1933 classic, *She Done Him Wrong.* A series of films followed, including C.B. DeMille's *This Day and Age* (1933); *George White's Scandals* (1934), which featured another future cowboy sidekick, Cliff Edwards; and *The Trail of the Lonesome Pine* (1936) with Fred MacMurray and Henry Fonda.

It was shortly after *Trail of the Lonesome Pine* that Fuzzy became a contract player at Universal Pictures; he stayed there for nearly ten years. At Universal Fuzzy was a utility player, acting in a variety of pictures, but gradually narrowing in as a comic sidekick in Universal's B Western unit. That's where Oliver Drake first met Fuzzy—when Drake was put under contract to Universal as production manager and associate producer for the Johnny Mack Brown series.

Oliver Drake: *Fuzzy was at Universal when I went there. He had been playing sidekick to Bob Baker and some of the other cowboy characters. So I inherited him for the first Johnny Mack Brown pictures I made, and then for the series with Johnny Mack and Tex Ritter. Later, he was also in the Rod Cameron pictures. He was a pleasure to work with, a very funny guy. He'd usually ad lib better dialogue then our writers would write for him.*

The comedy was built into the scripts, but Fuzzy would change it. And if he changed it, he improved it. I had trouble with writers trying to write for him and

Fuzzy Knight, heroine Nell O'Day, and cowboy star Johnny Mack Brown in one of their Universal pictures from the 1940s.

trouble with some directors trying to direct him to be funny.

I remember one time when we were doing a picture and I went to see the dailies (the rushes in the projection room) with some of the studio bigwigs. In the rushes Fuzzy was the most unfunny person you ever saw. He was terrible. Afterwards, one of the front office guys sat down with me and asked what the problem was with Fuzzy. I said that I didn't know, but I agreed that he certainly was not very funny.

So I went out on the set. I had a director working for me then who was a thwarted actor. I walked in just in time to see him—Harry Frazer was his name— out in front of the camera rehearsing a scene, and he was going through all of

the contortions that he thought Fuzzy should do. I heard him say, "Now Fuzzy, I want you to do it this way." There he was in the middle of the sound stage trying to tell Fuzzy Knight how to be funny, and it was sad because Harry Frazer was a lousy actor and wasn't **anything** from a comedy standpoint.

I went over to Harry and asked him to come aside with me so that I could talk to him privately. I never would bawl out anyone on a set in front of others. I'd take them out where nobody else heard what I had to say, especially if it was a director I was talking to.

Out behind the set I said to Harry, "Leave Fuzzy Knight alone. You're a bad actor; you can't act for sour apples and you're not funny and you're trying to tell

Fuzzy Knight how to be funny; it's ridiculous. Leave him alone." Well, he left Fuzzy Knight alone from then on and Fuzzy became funny again.

When I started working with Fuzzy, he had a stuttering bit that he would do for comedy—not that he stuttered normally, but he developed this stuttering character a little on the order of Roscoe Ates. Well, the Hays Office said it didn't want any stuttering because the little kids would copy it—which was probably true—so they took the stutter away from him. [Fuzzy still sneaked the stutter into a lot of films over the years.]

But Fuzzy would work on comic bits of business himself, and then he'd come to me on the set and ask if he could do this or that comedy bit. He'd run the dialogue for me, but he'd change it or make it fun-

nier. He never hurt the scene; he always improved it. The lines were funnier than when they were written.

Everybody liked Fuzzy Knight. I was quite friendly with both him and his wife. I'd go out to his house, and we'd go out to dinner once in a while. Otherwise, I didn't know too much about his personal life. Of course, his first claim to fame was when he sang "Twilight on the Trail" in the picture **Trail of the Lonesome Pine**; that's what made Fuzzy a star, and they sold a zillion records on the song.

He was really a good singer. He did mostly comedy songs in the Westerns, and I wrote most of them. He played the squeeze box, you know, and he'd sing these crazy songs I'd write.

I'll tell you a funny story about a song I didn't write. We once bought a song,

Oliver Drake and author David Rothel at the 1983 Charlotte Western Film Fair.

According to the notice, the carrying of firearms within Red Mountain Township is now strictly prohibited. Rod Cameron is getting ready to nail up the notice as Fuzzy Knight and Ray Whitley look on. The scene is from *Riders of Santa Fe* (1944).

paid twenty-five thousand dollars for the rights to "Deep in the Heart of Texas." So I wrote an original story based upon the song which would become the picture. We were all ready to make the picture when the front office came in and took the song away from me. They said they were going to make a big picture and wanted the song.

Well, they made their picture, a big, dramatic Western. They went out and spent about forty thousand dollars—which was a lot of money in those days—for a musical score. They previewed the picture and when the music to "Deep in the Heart of Texas" came on the soundtrack, the audience clapped their hands where you're supposed to in the song. It ruined the serious mood of their dramatic picture.

Pretty soon my boss came to me and said, "We're going to give you back "Deep in the Heart of Texas." I said that I'd take it, but I wanted the score, too. He told me I could have it since it was no good to them.

I opened the picture with Fuzzy Knight on a stagecoach playing a squeeze box and singing "Deep in the Heart of Texas." I took out all of the places in the score where the audience might applaud at the wrong time. Our little picture made more money than that big picture they made, which now had a changed title, of course.

I never really noticed or felt that the action stars like Johnny Mack Brown or

Rod Cameron minded the comedy that was put into their pictures by sidekicks like Fuzzy Knight. If they did, they kept it to themselves. Actually, the Western actors were a great bunch of people to work with.

Fuzzy spent most of his screen time from 1940 through 1943 with Johnny Mack Brown. During the last year, they were joined by singing cowboy star Tex Ritter. When Johnny Mack and Tex pulled up stakes and left Universal, Fuzzy moved over to the Rod Cameron Western series, which was also produced by Universal and had singer Ray Whitley for additional support.

The Rod Cameron series lasted through 1945, when Cameron got lucky and started to move into bigger budgeted films which were not always in the Western vein. The war had just ended and one of the boys to come marching home was Kirby Grant, who had been under contract to Universal prior to the war and was looking for work—but **not** as a cowboy.

Kirby Grant (TV's Sky King) poses for the author's camera at the 1981 Charlotte Western Film Fair.

Kirby Grant: *I never wanted to be a cowboy star. I did everything under the sun to get out of that. The head of the studio finally said that he'd put me on suspension unless I did the Westerns. I had just come out of the service and I couldn't afford to go on suspension. I was upset because I had been doing musicals and comedies, and they had told me that I was scheduled for bigger things. Then along came these lousy, stinking oaters, and I wasn't too happy about it. Fuzzy was scheduled to be my sidekick in the Western series, so he talked it over with me. He said, "It's not so bad; we'll have a good time." He was very helpful to me at that time.*

Fuzzy was a very affable and funny person. He enjoyed telling stories about his time on the stage when he was doing vaudeville and things like that. He played honky-tonk piano, as you probably know. He had played in a whorehouse, as a matter of fact, back in the early days before he worked in pictures. He told me a story once about when he was in vaudeville on the same bill with a lady dwarf. He was obsessed with the idea of going to bed with this lady dwarf to see what it would be like. Well, he finally did. He just had a hankering to find out if it was any different. His description of that incident was hilarious. And that's all I'm going to tell you about that!

*Fuzzy was a genuinely funny person. Some of the sidekicks were not **really** funny. They affected humor with their appearance and in little gimmicks they used, but Fuzzy had a great sense of what was funny and was a genuinely humorous person. His comedy was not generally of the falling-into-the-horse-trough type. It was mostly confined to double takes and the occasional stuttering and the little personality traits of a humorous character.*

A lot of what Fuzzy did for comedy was improvised right on the set. The lines, the bare bones were there, but Fuzzy fleshed them out with his own brand of humor and gimmicks, double takes, and things of that sort. This was almost always the case. The Western writers just didn't know how to write sidekick comedy. I don't know whether they were just not good enough to do it or if they were under such time pressure trying to get a script out that they didn't take the time.

Unlike Gabby Hayes, who was something of a chameleon as far as his personal life and his screen roles were concerned, Fuzzy was just himself on and off screen. I don't think he could have acted any differently than he did.

I think the Westerns were an opportunity for him to chew up the scenery, which he could not always do in other pictures. I never actually had the feeling that he was trying to upstage me, but you couldn't compete with him in humor, so you had to play it straight; that was the only thing you could do. You allowed him to play off you for his reactions and humor. It would have been a mistake to try it the other way. Some of the cowboy stars tried to do that, play off their sidekicks, and it just couldn't be done.

We did one Western where we disguised ourselves as two women. The heavies fell into our trap, of course, and we were able to capture them because they thought we were a couple of women. Fuzzy camped around in his drag attire and had some fun. That turned out to be a very funny situation in the picture. Of course, it wound up where we started knocking the outlaws around and lost our sunbonnets and all that sort of thing. We got a kick out of that picture because the script was a little different. Most of them were real dogs with the same old cliches, the same old running inserts, same old

This scene from *Marshal of Heldorado,* the second of six quickie Westerns turned out by Lippert Pictures, includes the five leads who appeared in all of the films. Left to right, they are Betty (later Julie) Adams, Jimmy Ellison, Raymond Hatton, Fuzzy Knight, and Russ Hayden.

crap—you know.

Fuzzy enjoyed his booze, but I never saw him under the weather because of it. If he was, he certainly hid it. I can't ever recall seeing him come on the set with a snootful. I know he finally quit drinking. His health was so bad he just simply couldn't drink any more; his liver was shot.

I think Fuzzy was very pleased, very happy with his lot in life as a comic. I don't know too much about his personal life, but he appeared to be a happy-go-lucky, take-it-as-it-comes type of person.

When the Kirby Grant Western series ended in late 1946, Fuzzy's services at Universal were not continued. He didn't show up in another Western series until 1950 when he co-starred in a threadbare series with Jimmy Ellison, Russ Hayden, and Raymond Hatton for Lippert Pictures. If we sometimes call the standard B Westerns "oaters," then these little epics would deserve the designation of chaff. The six pictures which made up the series were (or should have been) a dismal embarrassment for all concerned. The **entire** series was shot in just a month's time using the same cast—right down to the dog heavies—in all the pictures. From a production standpoint, it looked as if the entire six pictures could have been made for a hundred dollars with change left over.

Ellison and Hayden were the only continuing characters in each of the films, going by the names Shamrock and Lucky. The rest of the cast, including Fuzzy and Ray Hatton, played a variety of characters—good guys and bad guys—in the series. Inexplicably, even though within the plots Hatton and/or Fuzzy might be in opposition to Lucky and Shamrock, the four of them rode side by side on horseback behind the opening credits, suggesting wrongly a foursome for law and order.

Getting co-starring billing in this series was no assurance of equal screen time for Ray Hatton and Fuzzy. For example, in the last of the series, **Fast on the Draw,** Hatton, who plays the serious character role of the heroine's father and a town leader, does not appear on screen for the first twenty-three minutes. Fuzzy comes on camera for the first time a couple of minutes after Hatton. The entire film only runs fifty-five minutes!

In **Fast on the Draw** Fuzzy plays a deacon in the town and is only vaguely humorous. This was, no doubt, because it was hard for Fuzzy not to be a little bit funny even when he wasn't supposed to be. And he **wasn't** supposed to be funny, because at the

end of the picture he turns out to be The Cat—the head outlaw who had killed Shamrock's parents twenty-five years before. This may have been the only time in Fuzzy's career when he ended up on the wrong side of the law. Needless to say, this was not the Fuzzy Knight of old, and all concerned with this series could find some comfort in the knowledge that few people were ever in the theaters where these pictures played.

In 1950 Fuzzy got a one-shot comic sidekick role in a quality production, Republic Pictures' **Hills of Oklahoma** starring newcomer singing cowboy, Rex Allen. Another old-time singing cowboy sidekick, Roscoe Ates, was also featured in the funny business of the picture. Fuzzy played a sidekick named Jigg and seemed a natural to continue in the series, but it was not to be.

In 1951 Fuzzy found employment in Monogram Pictures' Whip Wilson series, another sorry excuse for using up unexposed film. The series had started in early 1949 with Andy Clyde (late of the Hoppy series) providing the comic moments. By 1951 Clyde had found better things to do and left. That opened the door for Fuzzy to step in.

Tommy Farrell, the son of actress Glenda Farrell, played the juvenile lead in several Whip Wilson films during the early 1950s.

Monogram Pictures' cowboy star, Whip Wilson, is ready for action.

Tommy Farrell is a busy scriptwriter on such popular television series as "The Love Boat," "Fantasy Island," and "Hart to Hart." He is seen here with author David Rothel at the 1983 Charlotte Western Film Fair.

When I asked Fuzzy's former producer-director, Oliver Drake, about the Whip Wilson series, he sighed, shook his head, and said, "Well, nobody wanted to work in the Whip Wilsons because they figured it was a dog series. I'm surprised that so many talk about Whip Wilson today because on the job nobody cared to work with him. They didn't expect him to go any place, and he didn't."

Whip Wilson was Monogram's answer to Lash LaRue. Contrary to studio publicity, Whip was not born in Texas and was never a rodeo star. For a short while, though, he was manager of a small farm in St. Albins, Missouri, and made a little extra money at the time by selling butter and eggs—not the sort of information to be found in his studio bio. Whip, whose real name was Roland Charles Meyers, followed a circuitous route to Hollywood, stopping along the way to work at such varied jobs as opera singer, border patrolman, motel manager, and

nightclub singer before becoming a silver screen cowboy. Actor Terry Frost, who played a heavy in many of the Wilson films, once referred to Whip as "the clumsiest cowboy I ever saw."

Tommy Farrell, who played the "nice young man" role in several of the Whip Wilson pictures, watched closely how Fuzzy handled what comedy there was in the films. Tommy told me, "Fuzzy Knight had that marvelous stutter which always occurred at just the right time. It wasn't thrown in gratuitiously; it was always just where he wanted it to be to get the maximum comedy effect. It's true that in the Whip Wilsons there was never a great deal of time devoted to the comedy; however, most of the comedy was not written and Fuzzy liked to set up a situation for himself, something that would lead him into a comedy bit."

Jim Bannon, who had played Red Ryder in a short-lived series for Eagle-Lion Pictures in the late 1940s, was brought into the Whip Wilson series with Fuzzy to help provide some spark for the less than dynamic whip-wielding star. I talked with the colorful and candid Jim Bannon about the Wilson series and Fuzzy Knight.

Jim Bannon: I did five pictures with Whip Wilson and Fuzzy Knight. At that point in time it was kind of like feeding oats to a dead horse. They were trying to hype that series, and they couldn't have done it with the two Barrymore brothers. I never did know Whip very well, but as I understand it, he had been a singer with the St. Louis Muny Opera.

To me, what you basically needed in a B Western was an athlete who could read a few lines, not an actor who could barely ride a horse. It was a damned sight easier to teach an athlete a few lines than it was to teach an actor to ride a horse the way we had to ride them. I always felt that people like Johnny Mack Brown and the guys who were fundamentally good athletes were the best cowboy stars. I didn't think Whip Wilson was a particularly good athlete, and he had an awful time riding a horse. God, that old horse he rode! The poor son-of-a-bitch couldn't run fast enough to scatter his own dung.

Anyway, they brought Fuzzy and me in to try to hype this series, and it was really a lost cause. By then Scotty Dunlap [the producer] had figured out that he'd made a bad deal because Whip wasn't particularly handy with that whip either— the way Lash LaRue was. Lash was never one

WHIP **WILSON** in *Stagecoach Driver*   A MONOGRAM RELEASE   **FUZZY KNIGHT** JIM BANNON · GLORIA WINTERS

Jim Bannon and Fuzzy Knight seem to be having a good time as they bring the stage into town for this scene from *Stagecoach Driver* (1951).

of my favorite people, personality-wise, but he could handle that by-God whip. There was no question that he knew what he was doing with that whip. He can still handle it pretty well today if you can catch him when he can see the victim. You know, Sunset Carson used to try to do something with the whip. Sunset was about as handy as a bear cub in boxing gloves. Well, he wrapped that whip around Peggy Stewart [popular Western film heroine] one day and I thought it was going to cut her in half. "Don't worry about it, Peggy. I've been handling this whip a long time," he'd tell her. Then "whap!" All of a sudden she's wrapped up.

Fuzzy was a very cooperative person to work with. He was a much bigger star than I ever was, and I kind of felt a little bit like it was a comedown thing for him to go into that kind of a series. As I say, it was a dying series. Scotty Dunlap was trying to make Whip into another Buck Jones; he was trying to make **everybody** into another Buck Jones. Fuzzy was pleasant to work with; I never did get to know him too well. By the time we got together for those films, he'd straightened himself out, because he was a big booze fighter at one time.

Lew Collins, who had directed me in the Red Ryder films, was directing the Whip Wilsons. I had to speak to him because he was ignoring Whip and treating me like the star of the series. I said to him, "Lew, damn it, it's not **my** series; it's Whip Wilson's series. Stop telling me what to do and then saying, oh, yeah, and Whip, you do the same thing."

When Lew and I did the Ryders together, we got along like a dream. So all of a sudden I show up in this new series, which he'd just taken over, and he's still directing me as if I'm the star. It was an embarrassing thing. Finally, after one picture, we got it to where he stopped doing it, but it was almost as though it were my series. I thought, "Hey, that ol' boy's got a whip in his hand; he may wrap that around my neck!"

There wasn't really that much comedy in the Whip Wilson pictures. Fuzzy was not a slapstick guy; Fuzzy was kind of a situation guy. Emmett Lynn, who I'd worked with in the Red Ryder films, was just out and out slapstick. As I say, it was almost an embarrassing thing for me to see Fuzzy Knight in the pictures because it was such a bad series; it was on its last legs.

In 1951, between the Wilson pictures, Fuzzy free-lanced in any pictures in which he could find a few days work. The films ranged from a spoof called **Skipalong Rosenbloom** (1951) with Slapsie Maxie Rosenbloom to a film called **Gold Raiders** (1951) with George O'Brien and (of all people) the Three Stooges. In MGM's 1951 version of **Show Boat** starring Howard Keel, Kathryn Grayson, and Ava Gardner, Fuzzy played the piano as Kathryn Grayson struggled through "Can't Help Lovin' that Man." His one line in the picture was "Keep tryin', sister; you'll make it."

In early 1952 Fuzzy wrapped his final Whip Wilson picture, **The Gunman.** It was no better or worse than the others in the series. Then things brightened for Fuzzy Knight as he saddled up once more and rode alongside William Elliott in his series for Monogram, later to be called Allied Artists. By this time it was late in the day for the B Westerns. Most of the series had succumbed to the havoc wreaked on the film industry by the thriving newcomer, television.

The Elliott series was not like most of the Western series of old where you generally had the star and sidekick play the same characters in each film. In this final Elliott Western series each story and its characters were totally unrelated. Fuzzy was not in all of the pictures, and the importance of his role varied from picture to picture. Also, since Elliott was trying to give the series a more adult appeal and the production look of an A series, he did not want the broad humor of the typical B Western sidekick. Fuzzy was, therefore, called on to be more of a humorous character actor than a comic sidekick. He was well-suited for the approach Elliott wanted to take with the series. Broader comics like Smiley Burnette, Dub Taylor or Al St. John would likely have had trouble fitting into this situation.

Because he was just an irregular regular in the Bill Elliott films, Fuzzy had no tight commitment to the series and was free to take a better offer if one came along—and one did. He was offered the role of Buster Crabbe's comic orderly in the television series "Captain Gallant of the Foreign Legion."

Gary Grossman in his excellent book called **Saturday Morning TV** comments on the "Legion" series' similarity to the old B Westerns:

As Captain Gallant he [Crabbe]

portrayed a swashbuckling Foreign Legion officer. But the series had all the earmarks of a Western. Instead of wearing a ten-gallon hat and chasing down cattle rustlers, Crabbe searched for camel thieves. He worked for an unnamed "mother country," and policed feuding Arabs instead of warring Indians.

Like all good Western heroes he needed a comic sidekick. Cowboy veteran Fuzzy Knight fit the bill after having ridden with Johnny Mack Brown, Russell Hayden, and Tex Ritter. For human interest the show relied on a ten-year-old scene-stealer played by Crabbe's son, Cullen. The first production season, legitimate French Foreign Legion officers played supporting roles.

In early 1954 the crew filmed at an outpost on the edge of the Sahara Desert, six hundred miles southeast of Casablanca. Other backgrounds during the premiere year included ancient French forts, Moroccan streets, Marrakech, Paris, and Athens. . . .

Crabbe explains that the show was shot abroad not so much for realism, but to cut expenses. "It took us four days to shoot a half-hour episode overseas. That was a day more than a Hollywood crew working on the show if we had filmed in the Mojave Desert. It took longer, but it was cheaper abroad by six or seven thousand dollars per show," he says.

The total budget for each installment was approximately $21,500.

I talked with Buster Crabbe shortly before his death in 1983 about the "Captain Gallant of the Foreign Legion" series and working with Fuzzy Knight.

Buster Crabbe: *Oh, he was a peach! I never had to worry when Fuzzy was on the set; I never had to worry about somebody keeping an eye on my son if I had to go out in the desert to do a shot away from where the regular location was. Fuzzy was just like a second father to my son Cuffy; he was great with him. My whole family loved Fuzzy Knight.*

When we were looking for a fellow to play the sidekick role in the "Foreign Legion" series, I said to Harry Saltzman, the producer, "When you get out to

California, look up Al "Fuzzy" St. John." Al had, as you know, been my sidekick in the Westerns I made in the 1940s at PRC. I thought he would be good as an old legionnaire with a beard and everything.

So when Saltzman got out to Hollywood, he called Fuzzy St. John in. Poor old Fuzzy went in loaded. That threw him out of the series. When I called Harry to check on things, I said, "Well, Harry, did you find somebody?" He said, "Yeah, Fuzzy Knight." Well, you know, Fuzzy Knight had had a drinking problem, too, but I sure admired his work in pictures and was glad to have him for my TV series.

At the time Saltzman told me he'd hired Fuzzy Knight, Fuzzy hadn't had a drink in a year and a half. What had happened was that Fuzzy had gone to a woman out in the Valley who dried out people with alcohol problems. When he was dried out, he said goodbye to the lady and she said, "I'll be seeing you, Fuzzy." Now something just snapped in Fuzzy and he told her, "You'll never see me again." He stopped drinking entirely. He didn't even take a glass of wine when we were on location doing the "Foreign Legion" series. No sir, he was teetotaler.

The series was all filmed overseas. We made thirty-nine half-hours the first season; then in 1956 we went back and made twenty-six more—making a total of sixty-five shows, and Fuzzy was in all of them.

Fuzzy played it fairly straight, subtle, in his role as my orderly; it couldn't really be played too broadly. He was as much a character actor as he was a comedian, so he was just great for the kind of character we wanted. He was quite different from Al St. John in my Western series. Fuzzy Knight wasn't running around the place all the time; he was a quieter guy. Al St. John was more adept at the zany kind of comedy, but there was more feeling, maybe more heart, more warmth in the Fuzzy Knight kind of comedy.

Some years back, but way after the "Foreign Legion" series, I got a call one day from an outfit in New York, an agency for a candy outfit that wanted to get a hold of Fuzzy Knight for a commercial. I told them I would get Fuzzy on the phone and have him call them. I called Fuzzy's number and found that it had been disconnected for a long time. I thought that that would be no problem; I'd just call the Screen Actor's Guild and they'd give me Fuzzy's new address and phone number.

So I called SAG, identified myself, and explained that a candy company wanted Fuzzy Knight to come to New York to make a candy commercial. The person I was talking with at SAG said that Fuzzy wasn't working any more, wasn't active in the business.

What I didn't know was that he was at the old actor's home. It was for health reasons, but I didn't know exactly what his problem was. I didn't see anything in the papers, but a short time later a friend of mine in New York called and told me that Fuzzy had passed away.

★   ★   ★

FUZZY KNIGHT FILMOGRAPHY

The Fuzzy Knight filmography is a little more difficult to compile than most because he tended to jump around as a sidekick from one cowboy star to another, frequently returning to do a few more pictures with a particular star after the lapse of a few months or even years.

KERMIT MAYNARD series: *(Ambassador Pictures)*

Song of the Trail (3/36) Sidekicks George Hayes and Horace Murphy have featured roles in the film.

Wildcat Trooper (7/36)

TEX RITTER Series: *(Grand National Pictures)*

Song of the Gringo (11/36) This is Tex's first series Western.

Fuzzy and the other musicians provide background music for some spooning by Johnny Mack Brown and Nell O'Day in this scene from *Ragtime Cowboy Joe*. (1940).

168

Fuzzy is ready for the shoot out in this scene from *Rawhide Rangers* (1941).

BOB BAKER series: *(Universal Pictures)*

   Courage of the West (12/37)

   The Singing Outlaw (1/38)

   Border Wolves (2/38)

   The Last Stand (4/38)

JACK RANDALL series: *(Monogram Pictures)*

   Where the West Begins (2/38) Ray Whitley is in the cast.

JOHNNY MACK BROWN-BOB BAKER series: *(Universal Pictures)*

   Desperate Trails (9/39)

   Oklahoma Frontier (10/39)

   Chip of the Flying U (11/39)

   Riders of Pasco Basin (4/40)

   West of Carson City (5/40)

   Badman from Red Butte (5/40)

JOHNNY MACK BROWN series: *(Universal Pictures)*

   Son of Roaring Dan (7/40)

   Ragtime Cowboy Joe (9/40)

Law and Order (11/40)

Pony Post (12/40)

Boss of Bullion City (1/41)

Bury Me Not on the Lone Prairie (3/41)

Law of the Range (6/41)

Rawhide Rangers (7/41)

Man from Montana (9/41)

Masked Rider (10/41)

Arizona Cyclone (11/41)

Fighting Bill Fargo (12/41)

Stagecoach Buckaroo (2/42)

The Silver Bullet (8/42)

Boss of Hangtown Mesa (8/42)

JOHNNY MACK BROWN-TEX RITTER series:
(Universal Pictures)

Deep in the Heart of Texas (9/42)

Little Joe, the Wrangler (11/42)

The Old Chisholm Trail (12/42)

Tenting Tonight on the Old Camp Ground (2/43)

Cheyenne Roundup (4/43)

Heroine Jennifer Holt seems a little dubious about Fuzzy's attempt to fly in this scene from the 1942 Universal series.

This shoot out may be briefer than Fuzzy expects. The scene is from the 1942 Universal Picture entitled *The Old Chisholm Trail.*

Raiders of the San Joaquin (6/43)

Lone Star Trail (7/43)

TEX RITTER series: (Universal Pictures)

Arizona Trail (9/43)

RUSSELL HAYDEN series: (Universal Pictures)

Frontier Law (11/43)

TEX RITTER-RUSSELL HAYDEN series: (Universal Pictures)

Marshal of Gunsmoke (1/44)

Oklahoma Raiders (3/44) Dennis Moore replaced Russell Hayden in this episode.

ROD CAMERON series: (Universal Pictures)

Boss of Boomtown (5/44) Musician and sometime sidekick Ray Whitley is featured in all of the entries of the Rod Cameron series.

Trigger Trail (7/44)

Riders of the Santa Fe (11/44)

The Old Texas Trail (12/44)

EDDIE DEW series: (Universal Pictures)

Trail to Gunsight (8/44) Ray Whitley is featured in the cast of the picture.

ROD CAMERON-EDDIE DEW series: (Universal Pictures)

Beyond the Pecos (4/45) Ray Whitley continues in the series.

Kirby Grant, the reluctant Cowboy hero. Kirby never wanted to do Westerns; he had been promised comedies and musicals at Universal, but he was more often seen with a shooting iron in his hand and a Stetson on his head.

Renegades of the Rio Grande (6/45) Ray Whitley

KIRBY GRANT series: *(Universal Pictures)*

Bad Men of the Border (9/45)

Code of the Lawless (10/45)

Trail to Vengeance (11/45)

Gun Town (1/46)

Rustler's Roundup (8/46)

Lawless Breed (8/46)

Gunman's Code (8/30/46)

JIMMY ELLISON-RUSS HAYDEN series: *(Lippert Pictures)*

Hostile Country (3/50) Raymond Hatton co-stars with Fuzzy in all of the episodes of this series.

Marshal of Heldorado (4/50)

Colorado Ranger (5/50)

West of the Brazos (6/50)

Crooked River (6/50)

Fast on the Draw (6/50)

REX ALLEN series: *(Republic Pictures)*

Hills of Oklahoma (6/50) Former Eddie Dean sidekick Roscoe Ates is also featured in the cast.

WHIP WILSON series: *(Monogram Pictures)*

Wanted Dead or Alive (4/51) Jim Bannon is featured with Fuzzy in all of the Wilson pictures except *Stage to Blue River, Night Riders,* and *The Gunman.*

Canyon Raiders (4/51)

Nevada Badmen (5/51)

Stagecoach Driver (6/51)

Lawless Cowboys (11/51)

Stage to Blue River (12/51)

Night Riders (2/52)

The Gunman (4/52)

WILLIAM ELLIOTT series: *(Monogram Pictures)*

Kansas Territory (5/52)

Fargo (9/52)

Topeka (8/53)

Vigilante Terror (11/53)

★   ★   ★

Emmett Lynn, in appearance alone, was one of the funniest of the cowboy sidekicks.

EMMETT LYNN

Chill Wills: I think Emmett was one of the finest comedians there ever was in Westerns. (Florida Western Film Round-Up, 1976)

*Lash LaRue: I worked with Emmett in **Song of Old Wyoming**. He was a fine fellow. His career was held down because he had epilepsy. They were afraid that he might throw a fit and not be able to finish a picture. Emmett always had something funny to say. He was like Pat Buttram, who was always funnier in person than he ever was allowed to be in pictures. I don't think the writers ever really caught Emmett's or Pat's comic qualities or possibilities.*

*Eddie Dean: Emmett was the type of guy that would chew up the scenery around you if he didn't like you. But if he **did** like you, he would be very helpful. He liked me, and he was a great guy to work with.*

Emmett Lynn—with his banty rooster cackle of a voice and laugh; his taffy-jointed body, which seemed to move in all directions at once; his whip-like tongue, flashing in and out and around his mouth when he was excited; and his squinty right eye contrasted by the left which peered eagle-like when he was alerted to danger—was to many Western fans the personification of the comic "oldtimer" sidekick.

Emmett Lynn's acting range was almost unlimited. No spittoon-over-the-head, falling-into-the-horse-trough sight gag was beneath his dignity, and yet he could give Gabby Hayes competition in wringing out every audience tear duct while playing a death scene—as he did in Roy Rogers' **Grand Canyon Trail** (1948). He could play equally well a riotous old drunk or a cuddly codger tenderly lulling a baby to sleep.

If Emmett had a fault as an actor, it was that he didn't always recognize the line which divided acting from overacting. Sometimes his enthusiasm would carry him over the line, much to the frustration of his fellow actors, but, no doubt, to the hilarious delight of youngsters—especially when he was careening headlong towards a laugh.

As good as he generally was on screen, his sometimes cantankerous behavior off screen, plus serious drinking and health problems, caused his career to run an unsteady course. He never remained long with any one series as a cowboy sidekick. Eventually, he was limited to brief bits in a multitude of films. A regular filmgoer might see Emmett often in a number of pictures, but not for long in any one film. As brief as his appearances became, he always made an impression. **Jubilee Trail** (1954) is a good example of his later bit parts. Emmett is only on the screen for approximately ten seconds doing a sourdough bit during Vera Ralston's barroom song and getting embroiled comically in a subsequent brawl in the bar. He serves no other purpose in the film, but it is a delightful bit even if you had never seen Emmett Lynn before.

Emmett Lynn was born on February 14, 1897, in Muscatine, Iowa. He started his career in films with the Biograph Company production of **The Imp** in 1913, but theatre acting, vaudeville, burlesque, and radio comprised the major part of his early show business career. Singing cowboy Eddie Dean remembered working with Emmett in the early 1930s.

Eddie Dean: I had a radio show on CBS out of Chicago called "Modern Cinderella." I was starring in it, playing the part of a cowboy. Emmett was the comic relief on the show. The program was about a girl trying to get a break in show business and her cowboy from Texas. I, of course, was doing the cowboy. It was one of those soap operas, you know.

We were sponsored by General Mills for CBS, Coast to Coast. We had to do the show in the morning for the East and in the afternoon for the West, because in those days they weren't set up to tape programs. We had to do the same show twice a day.

When I came out here to Hollywood, I did bit parts in Westerns, and for some reason a lot of people remembered me from the radio program. As a result, I was asked to go down to a theatre on Hollywood Boulevard where they were running a Western picture I had a part in. While I was making an appearance there,

who should walk in but Emmett Lynn with a beard way down to his belly. I didn't recognize him until he started to talk.

Emmett Lynn's first cowboy sidekick role was as a character called Whopper in the early 1940s Tim Holt series for RKO. The Whopper character had originally been played by Chill Wills in the 1930s George O'Brien series at RKO. Emmett did four pictures with Tim before he was replaced in the role by Lee "Lasses" White. Singer Ray Whitley was top-featured above Emmett in the Tim Holt films, playing his pal and occasionally throwing out a wry line or two, but the bulk of the comedy fell to Emmett.

Oliver Drake wrote the script for the last Holt picture in which Emmett worked, **Robbers of the Range** (1941). Oliver, who produced, directed, and/or wrote dozens of Western films, reminisced with me about Emmett Lynn.

Emmett seems to be telling a whopper of a story about Ray Whitley (left) as a bemused Tim Holt listens. The scene is from *The Fargo Kid* (1940), the second film in which Emmett appeared with Tim Holt.

GANGSTER'S DEN

PRC Pictures presents
Buster CRABBE
KING OF THE WILD WEST
and His Horse Falcon

with
AL (FUZZY) ST. JOHN

Gangster's Den (1945) had three of the funniest men in Western pictures in its cast: Emmett Lynn, Charlie King (center), and Al "Fuzzy" St. John (right). King was generally cast as a mean outlaw with no funny stuff; occasionally, however, he was cast as a comic outlaw and the results were always hilarious, as in the scene above.

Oliver Drake: *Emmett Lynn was a very interesting character and a good actor, but, unfortunately, like some of the others, he got so that he did a little too much elbow bending and wouldn't show up on time, so they let him go.*

When I was at Universal, his agent came in one day to talk to me about his client. Emmett hadn't been doing anything and was living in a trailer out near the studio. His agent pleaded, "Will you please give Emmett Lynn a bit in the picture you're working on? He needs the money."

So I said that I would. I wrote about a page or so in the script for him which would pay him about two hundred dollars.

The agent read it and said, "Can't you make it a little bigger? You know, Emmett has been out for quite a while."

So I added to it until I got about four pages of scipt for Emmett. In the meanwhile I'd made a deal for a day's work for him. I think the agreement was for him to get about $350 for the day. Just when I had everything all set, the agent came back and said that Emmett had read the script and wanted a thousand dollars to do it because the part was now bigger. I said, "You tell Emmett Lynn what he can do! I'm going back to the original script and there's no Emmett Lynn in it." I never used him again.

He was an all-around good entertainer

and actor in vaudeville and films, but like so many of his contemporaries, he wasn't big enough to get by with his drinking. Some that I worked with were big enough to do it, but he wasn't and so they let him go.

Emmett Lynn's longest stint in a Western series was six episodes he did with Don "Red" Barry for Republic Pictures during 1942 and '43. Don Barry, one of the more accomplished actors among the Western stars, no doubt appreciated the fact that Emmett was even shorter than he was—height being a particularly sensitive issue to the diminutive Barry. The series was well-produced, with scripts in some instances a cut above the usual B Western fodder. Their fifth picture together, **Days of Old Cheyenne** (1943), provides a good example of their working relationship, with scenes ranging from slapstick to touching drama—a feat not usually attempted in sixty-minute Westerns.

During the first ten minutes of the film, Emmett (Tombstone Boggs), in typically inept sidekick fashion, causes Barry to become embroiled in two fist fights. One fight is the result of Tombstone bungling the theft of a roasting chicken from three desperadoes at their trailside camp; the other occurs when Tombstone smashes a tough dude's pocket watch while attempting a magic trick in a Cheyenne saloon. In both instances Barry intercedes to save his beleaguered buddy.

After these fast-paced opening sequences of comedy and fisticuffs, the storyline settles into the more serious concerns of Barry to thwart the plans of outlaws who are attempting to gain political control of the Cheyenne Territory—an epic scope also not usually attempted with skimpy B Western budgets. In this instance it is pulled off quite successfully.

Late in the film Emmett and Barry have a plot reason to stage an apparently serious argument in front of the corrupt town leader. An angry, drunken Tombstone arrives to tell the now Governor Barry that the acquisition of political power has changed him and that he is no longer the true-blue cowboy pal he used to know. Barry strikes Tombstone, who then completes his impassioned speech and stalks out. The scene is played straight with no hint to the bad guy or the audience that it is merely a ploy to allow Tombstone to possibly infiltrate the outlaw gang. Emmett demonstrates in this serious scene his ability to play dramatic scenes extremely well. It is unfortunate that his career only afforded him the opportunity to do occasional serious scenes and never let him display the dramatic potential he had

within him.

After the Don Barry series, Emmett spent the next couple of years playing small roles in a variety of films. He appeared in two episodes of the Trail Blazers series (the last film gasps for veterans Ken Maynard and Hoot Gibson). For the record those films were **The Law Rides Again** (1943) and **Blazing Guns** (1943), both for Monogram Pictures. In the Texas Rangers series (starring James Newill, Dave O'Brien, and Guy Wilkerson) he appeared in **Return of the Rangers** (1943). Other roles included bits in **Cowboy Canteen** (1944) with an all-star Western cast including Charles Starrett and Tex Ritter; **Gangster's Den** (1945) in the Buster Crabbe/Fuzzy St. John series for PRC; and **Both Barrels Blazing** (1945) with Charles Starrett at Columbia Pictures.

In 1945 Emmett got the sidekick role of Uncle Ezra in Eddie Dean's new series of musical Westerns for PRC. As had happened before, Emmett was difficult to get along with right from the start. Eddie explained the situation to me.

> **Eddie Dean:** *When I got my series in pictures, I asked for him. The producer said that was fine, but Emmett didn't get along with Bob Tansey, the producer and director. Because of this, Emmett walked off my first picture,* **Song of Old Wyoming.** *I stopped him at the door as he was going and I said, "Emmett, I've been out here a long time and I've worked hard to get something going. Now I've got it and you're walking out; you're really walking out on me." He turned and said, "Eddie, I'll do it for you until you find somebody else." So we did three pictures and then Roscoe Ates came in as my sidekick. Emmett wanted to go his other way, so we hired Roscoe.*

From 1946 through 1948 Emmett again freelanced in a variety of films, the most noteworthy being his five Republic Red Ryder films with William Elliott and Allan Lane—two with Elliott and three with Lane. The size of his contributions to the Republic Ryder films varied considerably, but, as usual, when he was on screen, you couldn't take your eyes off him. One of his better roles in the series was as Coonskin in Allan Lane's **Stagecoach to Denver** (1946).

Emmett's last series was the Eagle-Lion Red Ryder series starring Jim Bannon. There were only four pictures in the low-budget series, the first being **Ride, Ryder, Ride** (1949) in which Emmett played Buckskin Blodgett, his typical squirrelly old codger.

"Well, Eddie, you see it was this way," cackles Uncle Ezra (Emmett Lynn) in this scene from *Song of Old Wyoming* starring Eddie Dean.

The main distinction of the series was that it was shot in Cinecolor, the poor man's Technicolor.

I talked with Jim Bannon about working with Emmett on the Red Ryder series.

Jim Bannon: *Emmett was a pleasure to work with. He was cooperative to the point of dedication in my Red Ryder films. I guess Emmett probably fought the booze a little and lost, but practically all of the sidekicks drank some. I don't guess Gabby drank much; I never did know him real well, but I don't think Gabby put it down. But Emmett did, and you'd run onto him at eleven o'clock at night down on Ventura Boulevard. You'd have to decide whether to just let him lay there and sleep, or to pick him up and take him home.*

Emmett's comedy in my Red Ryder series was almost a Western conversion of the burlesque/farce type of comedy— overboard. If he did a pratfall, it was a BIG pratfall. He always worked with no teeth, and that tongue of his—God All Mighty, it was like a whip! In some cases it was funny, and in some cases it was kind of a repulsive thing. Emmett didn't really have all that much great taste, but when he did, by God, it was primarily to entertain kids and, boy, they laughed.

I always tried to make a point of appearing with my own pictures because it helped at the box office. At this time— the late 1940s and early '50s—you would have had trouble filling the theatre with Christ and the twelve apostles doing a bicycle act standing on their heads; the theatre business was getting so bad. So it did help if you went with your own pictures, and I always tried to book myself with the films. I can remember those kids getting hysterical about old Emmett and the things he'd do. I'm speaking about Emmett's comedy on the screen. I never took Emmett with me on personal appearances. I was pretty careful about that because of the booze problem.

I have no idea whether Emmett was married or not because I didn't see him socially. [Eddie Dean told me that he thought Emmett had been married, but that he wasn't sure. Nobody that I talked with knew anything about Emmett's personal life.] I was never a big joiner in Hollywood; I was not part of the big Hollywood crew. I used to kind of mind my own business and go my own way.

After the Red Ryder series, Emmett's roles were, with rare exceptions, bit parts in films ranging from top budget epics like Clark Gable's *Lone Star* (1952) to medium budget programmers such as Bill Elliott's *The Homesteaders* (1953) to the low budget *Northern Patrol* (1953) with Kirby Grant and the dog Chinook. One of Emmett's last films was *Living it Up* (1954) with Dean Martin and Jerry Lewis.

Emmett Lynn died of a heart attack on October 20, 1958. As Eddie Dean recalled it for me, "Emmett died in a motel. I think it was about three days before anybody knew it. It was very sad."

★   ★   ★

Emmett has done it again! The Duchess (Martha Wentworth) is none too happy to have her unmentionables dumped on the sidewalk for all to see. Little Beaver (Bobby Blake) and Red (Allan Lane) try to suppress their laughs in this comic scene from a Republic Red Ryder episode.

Here we see Emmett's whip-like tongue start to go into action as he squints with his right eye and peers eagle-like for danger with his left. Get ready to laugh!

EMMETT LYNN FILMOGRAPHY

TIM HOLT series: (RKO)

Wagon Train (10/40) Singer Ray Whitley co-starred with Tim Holt in all four of the films in which Emmett Lynn appeared.

The Fargo Kid (12/40)

Along the Rio Grande (2/41)

Robbers of the Range (4/41)

DON BARRY series: (Republic Pictures)

Outlaws of Pine Ridge (10/42)

Sundown Kid (12/42)

Dead Man's Gulch (2/43)

Carson City Cyclone (3/43)

Days of Old Cheyenne (5/43)

Outlaws of Santa Fe (4/44) Emmett has a small role in this film. Wally Vernon had taken over as Barry's sidekick.

EDDIE DEAN series: (Producers Releasing Corporation)

Song of Old Wyoming (11/45) Former Tex Ritter sidekick, Horace Murphy, has a small role in the film.

Romance of the West (3/46)

Caravan Trail (4/46)

RED RYDER series (Bill Elliott): *(Republic Pictures)*

Wagon Wheels Westward (12/45)

Conquest of Cheyenne (8/46)

RED RYDER series (Allan Lane): *(Republic Pictures)*

Stagecoach to Denver (12/46)

Oregon Trail Scouts (5/47)

Rustlers of Devil's Canyon (7/47)

RED RYDER series (Jim Bannon): *(Eagle-Lion Films)*

Ride, Ryder, Ride (2/49)

Roll, Thunder, Roll (8/49)

The Fighting Redhead (10/49)

Cowboy and the Prizefighter (12/49)

★   ★   ★

Emmett finally gets a smile out of the Duchess (Marin Sais) as Little Beaver (Don Kay Reynolds/aka Little Brown Jug) and Red Ryder (Jim Bannon) look on happily.

Eddie Dean and Emmett (Uncle Ezra) are guiding the wagon caravan in this scene from *Caravan Trail* (1946). It looks as if Eddie is about to sing the hit song from the film, "Wagon Wheels."

Richard "Chito" Martin—sidekick, Latin lover, and mangler of the English language.

RICHARD "CHITO" MARTIN

Richard "Chito" Martin was a cowboy sidekick in over thirty Western films and, it's safe to say, never once fell into a horse trough—an avoidance few comic saddle pards could lay claim to in those halcyon years of the budget Westerns. Chito, who rode alongside Robert Mitchum, James Warren, and Tim Holt in some thirty-two RKO Westerns in the 1940s and early '50s, was among the most subdued of the comic sidekicks, but certainly one of the most engaging and enjoyable with whom to share an hour or so.

Tim Holt was Chito's main film partner, the two of them performing together in twenty-nine Westerns. Most of the comedy of Chito's character in the series evolved out of his malapropos Mexican/English and his extraordinary zeal to dally with beautiful, second-string Western damsels. Tim, when he showed any interest at all in the heroines, was usually contemplating the merits of settling down on a ranch and raising cattle and kids. Chito, however, was more interested in the chase—not for the outlaws, but for the cute little senoritas who usually sang and danced in the cantinas. Chito's thoughts regarding settling down were more likely in terms of a one-night stand. Forget the ranch, cattle, and kids; he was after the romance!

To be fair, however, Chito *did* fall head-over-saddle-horn in love with his inamoratas. It was just that he usually recovered fairly quickly, remounted (his horse), and rode off into the sunset looking for more cantinas with other beautiful senoritas. The worst that he suffered was a scolding from the stalwart and steadfast Tim Holt.

Tim was usually reserved in his portrayal of the Western hero and could seem somewhat aloof at times. His appeal was more to the no-nonsense Western action fans who liked their heroes to shoot straight, hit squarely, and not wear any of those sissy, fringe-ladened shirts. Consequently, Tim's films appealed to adult Western fans as much or more than they did to the Saturday matinee kiddie crowd. And, it should be hastily pointed out, Tim's Western hero portrayal was developed very calculatedly and was in no way a reflection on his acting ability. He had firmly established his acting credentials in such prestigious major films as Orson Welles' *The Magnificent Ambersons* and John Huston's *The Treasure of Sierra Madre* during the same years he was earning his spurs as a Western film cowboy hero.

An unusual aspect of Richard Martin's Chito sidekick character was that he was better looking than his Western hero pal—whether that pal was Mitchum, Warren, or Tim Holt. In the case of Tim, Chito was also taller and generally cut a more dashing figure on the screen, even if he did seem to lack somewhat in the gray matter department. But, of course, it was Tim's job to figure out how to capture the outlaws; Chito was supposed to be fun-loving, a rascal with the ladies, and in a constant tangle with the English language. Unlike most sidekicks, however, Chito could be counted on to hold his own in a shoot-out or a fight. Chito explained his varied abilities in *The Arizona Ranger* (1948):

> **Cowhand:** *Say, Chito, you were pretty good with your dukes in that fight today.*
> **Chito:** *Oh, that was easy; that's the Irish in me.*
> **Tim Holt:** *Don't let him fool you. He's pretty good with the girls, too.*
> **Chito:** *Oh, that's easy, too. That's the Spanish in me.*
> **Cowhand:** *Hey, now wait a minute. Are you an Irishman or a Mexican?*
> **Chito:** *I'm both—Chito Jose Gonzales Bustamonte Rafferty.*

Unlike the physical comedy of the majority of the cowboy sidekicks, Chito's humor was usually verbal. In *Road Agents* (1952) with Tim Holt, Chito's

Tim Holt played a reserved, no-nonsense Western hero in his film series of the late 1940s and early '50s.

difficulties with the language were well represented.

Chito: (Speaking to an outlaw who recently had the drop on him and Tim) How do you like it, senor, when the foot is on the other shoe?

Chito: (Remarking that he and Tim are a team) With everyone of us there is always two.

Chito: (When Tim suggests they become Western Robin Hoods) Oh, with the left hand we rob Brant (the outlaw), with the right hand we give the cattlemen the money they need, and with the third hand they give it back to the banditos who stole it. Magnifico! That makes everybody honest—even me!

Chito: (On his frustration with women) If I ever get married, it will never be with women. They're always blaming somebody else for something they didn't do.

Richard Martin, who has no accent at all in real life, was born in Spokane, Washington, on December 12, 1917. When he was just a youngster, his family moved to Los Angeles. After high school he attended California University where he nurtured his growing desire to become an actor. By the early 1940s his knocking on studio doors had paid off with a contract at Howard Hughes' studio, RKO.

The Chito character, surprisingly, did not originate in a Western picture. As Richard recalled in a recent interview, "The part of Chito started out in a picture called **Bombardier** (1943) with Pat O'Brien and Randolph Scott. It was a war picture designed to recruit bombardiers for World War Two. There was a character called Chito in the picture that Jack Wagner wrote as he went along; Jack was a friend of mine. I was under contract as a stock player at that time, as were Bob Ryan, Walter Reed, and Eddie Albert. We were all in the picture and all trying to get ahead in pictures. Barton MacLane was supposed to be the comic of the film, but Jack kept writing some pretty funny things for Chito to say. The result was that I kept saying them and the part kept getting better as the picture went along. Everyone liked the character of Chito so much that they put him into the Zane Grey films with Bob Mitchum for two pictures and one with Jim Warren. Then when I asked for a twenty-five dollar a week raise, they fired me."

Bounced from RKO, Richard opened a restaurant just around the corner from the studio which soon became a hangout for RKO actors, technical peo-

ple, and directors. Martin was constantly pressed by actor friends and casting directors to return to pictures, but he countered that he could make more money at the cash register than from casting offices. For close to two years Martin resisted most urgings to forsake the role of restaurateur for that of poseur again.

In 1946 he attained the dubious honor of starring in the final Universal Pictures serial, **The Mysterious Mr. M,** an almost totally forgotten serial—and perhaps for good reason. (Even Martin could not remember the title when asked about the serial in 1981.) In early 1947 he agreed to co-star with Frances Rafferty in a Comet/United Artists film entitled **The Adventures of Don Coyote.** The picture's only distinguishing characteristics were that it was filmed in Cinecolor and produced by Buddy Rogers, the actor/husband of Mary Pickford.

Tim Holt was finally mustered out of the Army Air Corps after World War Two and returned to RKO for a series of Westerns. When Tim and his producer Herman Schlom started thinking about a sidekick for the series, someone at RKO remembered Chito Jose Gonzales Bustamonte Rafferty. Richard Martin liked the idea of returning to the role and of working with Tim Holt, a highly respected actor in Hollywood. And so they rode together on the screen in twenty-nine films over the next five years.

The Tim Holt series was one of the best-produced Western series of the post-war era. The scripts generally had more character development; the direction was tighter and stressed a high quota of well-executed action; the photography and music scores were up to the standards of the regular RKO releases. Supporting actors and actresses for the Holt series were drawn mostly from the RKO roster of contract players and included such fine supporting performers as Steve Brodie, Robert Bray (later the forest ranger in the "Lassie" TV series), Jason Robards, Sr., Noah Beery, Jr., Joe Sawyer, Barbara Britton, Robert Livingston, Reed Hadley, Douglas Fowley, Dorothy Malone, Gail "Annie Oakley" Davis, and Elaine Riley (who became Mrs. Richard Martin).

The budgets on the Tim Holt pictures were somewhat higher than for most B Western series being produced during this time. In an interview with writer Paul Dellinger, Richard Martin remembered the budgets as being in the $200,000 to $250,000 range—a rather exaggerated range, one might suspect, since Tim in a 1970 interview with Joe Martelle stated that "when it (the budget) went over $70,000, the producer fainted." Regardless, even at $70,000 the budgets were probably a little higher than all but the Gene Autry and Roy Rogers films of that era and genre.

Tim and Chito are on the move to Western action in this publicity photo from about 1950.

188

When the Tim Holt series ended in 1952, Richard Martin found that he was hopelessly type-cast as Chito, a limitation that killed whatever hopes he might have had for a continued acting career. There was some thought of transferring the Tim Holt series to television, but by the time they were ready to go, television was saturated with Westerns and the plans fell through.

And now, with the speed of a typewriter indenting for a paragraph, we leap from the 1950s to July of 1981 and the Charlotte Western Film Fair where Richard Martin, now in his mid-sixties, was one of the guest Western performers. The dark hair of the past was now salt and pepper, with a dash or two more of salt than pepper; otherwise, Richard Martin had retained his handsome appearance. He now looked like what he had become: a successful insurance man.

Richard confessed to a sense of dismay that so many Western fans still existed, still wanted to see his films, and were still interested in what had become of him since 1952 when he hung up his guns and Chito accent. In a soft-spoken, somewhat bemused manner he answered questions of the fans who had come to see him.

Richard Martin on the Chito accent: When I was a little boy I lived in West Hollywood. West Hollywood is between Hollywood and Beverly Hills. When I was there as a little kid of about five years old, I lived with Mexican kids. During the Depression I lived near the Pacific Electric Railroad yards. The railroad cars were maintained by Mexican people. I went to grammar school with their kids. I used to make fun of them, and they used to make fun of me. They couldn't speak English

Richard "Chito" Martin was a popular guest star at the 1981 Charlotte Western Film Fair.

and I couldn't speak Spanish, but over time I learned some Spanish and they learned English. It was just one of those things I picked up; I held onto it from my childhood. The comedy lines for Chito were all written into the scripts. I did not ad lib very well.

On Robert Mitchum: I still see Bob Mitchum occasionally. When I first met him, I looked at him and said, "You surprised me; I didn't expect you to become a leading man; I expected you to be a character actor." He didn't look to me like what a leading man was supposed to look like in those days. When Bob and I made those two Zane Grey pictures together, Bob was making one hundred and fifty dollars a week, and I was making seventy-five. We used to hide behind the rocks and hope that they picked up our options. We were concerned about it; both of us wanted to stay alive.

I think that anybody who worked with Bob Mitchum and knew him, liked him. He was a great guy. I got along with him; every one of us did, but he was controversial. If you **didn't** like Bob Mitchum, you just didn't like him. He wasn't going to change himself in any way to fit what anybody else might expect of him, and he's still the same today.

The last time I saw him he ran into the back of my car on purpose. It cost me a hundred and fifty dollars. I was at a stop signal on Wilshire Boulevard when it happened. I looked into my rearview mirror and there was Bob. He yelled, "Hi, Chito, how are you?" I hadn't seen him in about five years. I said, "I'm about a hundred and fifty dollars in trouble right now." He said, "Oh, I just wanted to say hello." That's the way Bob Mitchum is; he's just a crazy guy. Sometimes he'd rather go out the window than through the front door.

On Howard Hughes: Tim and I used to call him the phantom. He never came around the studio too much. We met him around two o'clock in the morning one time. Tim and I had the same agent, and we figured out a plan where we could get our options lifted so that Tim would take a raise one year and I'd take one the next year. So we met with Hughes at two o'clock in the

morning. He had his hearing aid on, but we obviously didn't get through to him because we didn't get our raises that year.

Howard Hughes rarely came on the studio lot, but he did select our leading ladies in the latter group of Westerns we made. This was always pretty interesting because we never knew who we were going to meet, and the leading lady wasn't quite sure what she was doing there. Most of these gals had gone directly to dramatic school and from there they came over to the studio to get some experience in the Westerns.

On the ending of the Tim Holt series: Hughes really didn't take to our Westerns too much. He finally decided to eliminate all B pictures at RKO, and we fell into that category. Tim and I found out about it when we came off the road from a personal appearance tour. We were going to go into television, but that didn't work out so Tim said, "I'll see you; I'm going rodeoing." He elected to go rodeoing, so I stayed home. That's where we sort of broke up.

On what Richard's been doing since his acting days: I've been in insurance for twenty-eight years. I enjoy it; I have a lot of people in show business as my clients. I went back and got all of my old friends.

To some of the Western fans at the Charlotte Film Fair it seemed odd that Tim and Chito had not remained close over the years after their Western series concluded, but Richard dismissed that thought. At a later time when Tim's actress sister, Jennifer Holt, was asked if Richard and Tim were friends off screen, she remarked, "I believe so. I've only met Dick Martin once myself. I think Tim's closest friend, though, was Davy Sharpe (the super stuntman and occasional actor), but he and Chito liked each other very much."

In 1970 Cincinnati radio personality Joe Martelle interviewed Tim on his all-night program for WLW (later reported in **The Big Reel**). When asked about his former sidekick, Tim rather vaguely responded, "He's in California, and I understand he's in the insurance business. That's all I know." Tim Holt died of cancer in early 1973.

Hollywood, of course, is like anywhere else; way leads on to way and people scatter to wherever life takes them. Life took Richard Martin out of the show business game, and it seems that he has no regrets or illusions about his screen career. It was fun while it lasted, but when it was over he moved on.

★   ★   ★

RICHARD MARTIN FILMOGRAPHY

ZANE GREY series with Robert Mitchum: (RKO)

Nevada (12/44) Fellow sidekicks Guinn "Big Boy" Williams and Emmett Lynn have featured roles in the film.

West of the Pecos (6/45)

ZANE GREY series with James Warren: (RKO)

Wanderer of the Wasteland (10/45)

ZANE GREY series with Tim Holt: (RKO)

Thunder Mountain (6/47)

Under the Tonto Rim (8/47)

Wild Horse Mesa (11/47)

TIM HOLT series: (RKO)

Western Heritage (2/48) Emmett Lynn is in the cast.

Guns of Hate (5/48)

Arizona Ranger (5/48) Monte Hale's future sidekick, Paul Hurst, is in the cast.

Tim and Chito are shooting it out with the bad guys in this scene from *Dynamite Pass* (1950).

Chito shows great concern over the sad plight of leading lady Joan Dixon in this scene from *Pistol Harvest* **(1951).**

Indian Agent (12/48) Lee "Lasses" White, one of Tim's former sidekicks, is in the cast.

Gun Smugglers (12/48) Paul Hurst joins the cast again.

Brothers in the Saddle (2/49)

Rustlers (2/49)

Stagecoach Kid (6/49)

Masked Raiders (8/49) How fitting it is that Clayton Moore has a featured role in this picture. After completing the film, he started his long-running career as The Lone Ranger.

Mysterious Desperado (9/49)

Riders of the Range (2/50)

Dynamite Pass (3/50)

Storm over Wyoming (4/50)

Rider from Tucson (6/50) Elaine Riley (Mrs. Richard Martin) is the leading lady in this film.

Border Treasure (9/50)

Rio Grande Patrol (10/50)

Law of the Badlands (2/51)

Saddle Legion (4/51)

Gunplay (6/51)

Chito may have a slightly nervous smile on his face, but Tim is his usual steadfast, stalwart self in this scene from *Trail Guide* (1952).

Cannonball Taylor is ready for action in this publicity photo from the Bill Elliott Western series.

DUB "CANNONBALL" TAYLOR

Dub "Cannonball" Taylor had a long career as a cowboy sidekick, working with six Western stars between 1939 and 1950. His broad, slapstick antics and hillbilly rube approach to Western film comedy were considered insufferable by many film critics and some Western fans (this writer included). Nevertheless, Dub kept falling into horse troughs, stumbling into mudholes, having pails of water drop on his head, and generally cavorting in an imbecilic manner throughout a long list of screen credits. Somebody in those darkened theaters must have liked this southern bullyboy and his pugnacious shenanigans or he wouldn't have lasted so long. My interviews with his co-workers certainly made it clear that they loved the fellow.

Charles Starrett: *Following Cliff Edwards, Dub was a different kind of comedian for me. Later, Smiley Burnette was valuable to us, but ol' Dub was wonderful! I just loved working with Dub. He did slapstick, but he knew his comedy and his timing was really good. He not only was a good comic; he was a good actor. We've seen him ripen through the years into a fine actor in character roles.*

Leon McAuliffe: *He was great then and he's great now. I still see him occasionally on television. Dub Taylor was the sidekick for Russell Hayden in the Columbia series we did in 1942 with Bob Wills and His Texas Playboys. I was a member of the band. We spent about six months making those pictures. We went right from one picture to the next. Dub was the kind of guy who would go out with all of us musicians and jam and party and have a good time when the day's shooting was over.*

Jim Bannon: *Oh, I loved Dub Taylor. He was a funny guy, ol' Cannonball. I first worked with him when I was announcing for Chase & Sanborn in radio. He came on as a guest. It was an hour show, and they had a dramatic spot, which Don Ameche did, and a comedy spot. Dub came on as the comedy guest. It was the first time I had ever met him. He played the xylophone and did a comedy routine with Edgar Bergen and Charlie McCarthy. He was known at that time primarily for his vaudeville act. That's where he made his lick—as a xylophone player.*

Dub always drove a station wagon with a boat on top of it. If he passed a stream where he thought there were fish, he'd stop and fish. Occasionally, I'd do a role in the "Casey Jones" TV series which Alan Hale, Jr. starred in and in which Dub was the fireman. Dub was just a funny guy, still is. He thinks funny.

Eddie Dean: *I used to go hunting with Dub. He was great on calling. He could call crows in or coyotes, ducks, or geese. He was one of the greatest at that I ever saw. He was also an excellent shot.*

*Dub and I did a few shows together over the years. He'd play the xylophone and do his comedy routine. He's a great entertainer and a great talent. To me he is just about the same as he appears on the stage—very outgoing and extroverted. Dub was always serious about his hunting and serious about his work, but he enjoyed **everything** to the point where you had fun with him.*

Oliver Drake: *Dub Taylor was a sweetheart to work with. He was a good*

Charles Starrett reminisced about his career at the 1982 Memphis Film Festival.

actor, but now he's doing better pictures, so he won't let anybody call him Cannonball anymore.

Jimmy Wakely, for whom Dub did his final cowboy sidekick work, was the only dissenting voice I heard.

Jimmy Wakely: *I was not as pleased with the type of comedy Dub provided in my pictures. There was a little bit too much slapstick. I just had a feeling that the comedy wasn't there. It seemed like we were making fun of the picture instead of making fun for the audience.*

Born Walter Taylor in Richmond, Virginia, Dub had moved to Augusta, Georgia; Greenville, South Carolina; and Oklahoma City by the time he was a teen-ager. The first instrument he remembers playing was his grandfather's drum when he was about four years old. It was while Dub was attending Classen High School in Oklahoma City that he realized his show business potential as a xylophone and harmonica player. Adding a country bumpkin comedy bent to his musical talents, Dub developed

an "act."

When popular vaudevillian Larry Rich saw the youthful musical-comic, he asked him to join his troupe on the vaudeville circuit. Eventually, Dub ended up in New York where he met and married Florence Dean of the well-known vaudeville act, the Dean Twins. They were blessed with two children—a daughter named Fay and a son named Buck. Buck later became an actor and was featured as Newly O'Brien on the "Gunsmoke" television series with James Arness from 1969 to 1975.

Dub's first movie was to become one of his most famous—***You Can't Take It With You*** (1938) starring James Stewart and Jean Arthur. The film was produced and directed by Frank Capra. Dub, in a rare interview in 1983 with Herb Swilling for ***Favorite Westerns,*** stated that "Mr. Capra is the finest director I have worked for and is really a fine gentleman."

Dub Taylor's first Western series was with Bill Elliott for Columbia Pictures (the same studio which produced ***You Can't Take It With You.***). He and Elliott made twelve pictures together between 1939 and 1941. Dub was called Cannonball in all of the pictures and the name stuck with him through succeeding series. In 1941 Tex Ritter joined the series, but Dub moved over to the new Russell Hayden Columbia series after the first film of the Elliott-Ritter series.

The Russell Hayden films featured Dub as comic sidekick along with the popular musical group, Bob Wills and His Texas Playboys. The nine films of the series were filmed in a six-month period in 1942, but were released gradually through July of 1944.

From 1943 through 1945 Dub continued under contract to Columbia in the popular Charles Starrett Western series, which evolved into Starrett's Durango Kid series during Dub's tenure. When Smiley Burnette was contracted by Columbia for the Starrett series, Dub left Columbia for the Jimmy Wakely singing cowboy series at Monogram Pictures. Between 1947 and 1949 Jimmy and Dub rode together for fifteen films.

Dub, always looking a little like a rustic Pillsbury Doughboy, played his Cannonball character in a consistantly broad, slapstick manner throughout the series in which he appeared. The physical nature of his comedy was exemplified by a tendency to be constantly tripping or getting entangled in something. In Bill Elliott's ***Prairie Schooners*** (1940), for example, Dub gets hopelessly enmeshed in the ranch house curtains as he rushes in to deliver a message to the heroine. In the ensuing struggle to get free, he stumbles and writhes furiously in an exaggerated attempt to extricate himself. In ***Son of Davy Crockett*** (1941), which also stars Elliott, Dub

Dub Taylor took dead aim on seven Columbia Pictures' series during the years he was under contract to the studio.

gets his foot and saddle stirrup caught in a bag of supplies as he is dismounting from his horse. Again, the comic action is overblown as he attempts to free himself.

These two bits of business were typical and appropriate comic routines for cowboy sidekicks. The problem was in the way Dub approached the gags. There was seldom anything subtle in his work; he always seemed to reach for the broadest, most outlandish strategy to present his humor. These same bits done by a comic craftsman like Andy Clyde would have been hilarious. Through Dub's overplaying they became ludicrous to many aisle-sitters.

Dub's hillbilly accent was also overdone (at least for this writer's taste). His thick-as-molasses southern accent and occasionally mangled words were to his Western films what Leo Gorcey's Brooklyn accent and fractured English were to the Bowery Boys films. It is possible that they both could have cut back by half on their verbal abuses and still have come close to the border of excess.

In each of Dub's Western films there would usually be several opportunities for him to play the xylophone and concertina and to sing some comic hillbilly ditties. Occasionally, he also played the harmonica. It was in these scenes that Dub's strongest talent and carefree demeanor were most appealing.

When I interviewed Jimmy Wakely, he found it difficult to talk about his association with Dub. He liked Dub very much as a person, but he was not happy with him as a sidekick in his films.

*Jimmy Wakely: Dub was kind of a rube comic, you know. He was funny in the right situation. He was funny in **You Can't Take It With You** because he's the kind of guy that could walk up to a xylophone,* look silly, and play the xylophone barefooted. But he wasn't a comic character actor at that time like Walter Brennan, Gabby Hayes, Lasses White, or some of the other Western character actors. Dub was more the falling-in-the-water-trough type of comic, and I didn't feel that kind of comedy worked well in my pictures.

Off camera Dub was beautiful; we got along fine. He made one personal appearance tour with me to Canada and then to New Mexico. He drank too much on the road, although he didn't drink when we were making the pictures.

I've told this story a few times, and I don't imagine he'd mind me telling it again now. We were playing New Mexico. I'd just played a date in Santa Fe, and

he'd missed it. Some friends of his brought him in from Las Vegas, New Mexico, but he'd been drinking and wasn't able to go on the stage that night, so we worked the show without him. The next day we went to Tucumcari. Well, we got to Tucumcari and were scheduled to play a matinee at two o'clock. There was a bar next door to the theater and Dub said, "Can I have a drink, Jimmy? I've got to have it; I just need it so bad." I said, "go have **one.**"

The kids were lined up for a block leading into the theater. Dub went through that line of kids into that damned bar and had a drink—and it hit him the wrong way. He walked out onto the sidewalk and upchucked right in front of those kids. I was **so** embarrassed. He

A tight-lipped Charles Starrett has just gotten some important news. You can be sure the ever-faithful Cannonball is ready to do his cowboy hero's bidding.

Cannonball is about to get wet again in this scene from the Jimmy Wakely film, *Partners of the Sunset* (1948).

couldn't help it; he was embarrassed, too. But that was no way to go. I was working my tail off, and I wasn't about to create a bad image. You know, the singing cowboys have always been careful of their image. Even if they were drinkers, they didn't let the public see it too much. Eddie Dean and I were just talking about that—about how the cowboy stars tried to live up to the image they created on the screen. I'm not meaning to bad mouth Dub Taylor; we got along fine, but he was a drinker and I couldn't afford to take him on the road.

Dub and the director would work out the comedy bits for the pictures. I never said anything to them, but I had the feeling that some of it was way overdone. He had done so well with Wild Bill Elliott,

though, that I thought he would be good for our pictures. Pretty soon a little bit of flack started coming in from the distributors, and I wondered what to do. Well, we didn't do anything; we just sort of drew the line on the comedy.

Oliver Drake talked with me about Dub Taylor from the viewpoint of director on the Jimmy Wakely series.

Oliver Drake: *I had never worked with Dub until I made the Wakely films at Monogram, and then we got into a hassle with Scotty Dunlap, an executive at the studio, and I left. They brought in a couple of other producers and directors and the thing they did was take the songs out of the Wakely pictures. Jimmy, who was a*

199

very wonderful guy, said, "Well, I can't act; if they take the songs out of my picture, I'm dead."

He went to the front office and kept losing battles with Scotty Dunlap. Finally, Jimmy went to the front office and said, "Listen, I want Ollie Drake to come back and direct my pictures or there will be no more pictures. You are not going to take my songs out."

A very good friend of mine, Lou Gray, was producing Jimmy's pictures at that time. So I went back to direct the last Jimmy Wakely pictures which had Dub Taylor as the comic sidekick.

Dub was fine to work with. I had no qualms about working with him. Jimmy may have felt that Cannonball was too much on the slapstick side because he had been paired with the more subtle Lasses White in so many pictures. Jimmy and Lasses clicked together. Not only did they click, but they were close friends. Dub Taylor was not one who socialized with Jimmy; he hardly socialized with anybody, in fact. I never had any trouble with Dub. But I think that Jimmy, having been so long with Lasses—and they were a team that enjoyed each other— probably felt that Dub didn't enjoy working in this type of picture the way Lasses did—and he may have been right.

I think, basically, that Dub Taylor resented being a Western comic. He doesn't want to be called Cannonball anymore; today he wants to be called Dub Taylor. I just think he didn't want to be a Western comic.

By the time the Wakely series ended in 1949, the B Westerns were struggling against the onslaught of television. Dub moved from series Western into character parts in a long list of films and took roles in two television series. In 1957 he played fireman Willie Sims in the twenty-six television episodes of "Casey Jones," which starred Alan Hale, Jr. and featured fellow cowboy sidekick, Eddy Waller. The situation comedy, "Please Don't Eat the Daisies," featured Dub in the role of Ed Hewley during the 1965-1966 season. Over the years Dub has appeared in just about every major series in character roles of varying size and importance.

Dub's later feature films have included **The Bounty Hunter** (1954) with Randolph Scott, **The Hallelujah Trail** starring Burt Lancaster, **Bonnie and Clyde** (1967) with Warren Beatty, **Bandolero** (1968) starring James Stewart and Dean Martin, **A Man Called Horse** (1970) with Richard Harris, and **Support Your Local Gunfighter** (1971) with James Garner.

Dub has also found the field of television commercials very lucrative. His Hubba-Bubba Bubblegum and Ryder Truck commercials are particularly well-produced and pleasant to view.

Dub recently told writer Herb Swilling that he has no intention of retiring. "I can't afford to," he stated. "I got too many hobbies to pay for."

In my comments on Dub Taylor's cowboy sidekick career I have been rather harsh in my appraisal. I must not close this profile without mentioning that Dub's work as a character actor in later years has been excellent and highly praised. His characterizations have shown subtle shadings and a diversity of emotions that were impossible to foresee in his early B Westerns. Dub is undoubtedly correct in wanting to divest himself of the early Cannonball image. Cannonball is a faint shadow of the accomplished, multi-dimensional actor Dub has become in his later career.

★   ★   ★

DUB "CANNONBALL" TAYLOR FILMOGRAPHY

WILD BILL SAUNDERS series (Bill Elliott): (Columbia Pictures)

Taming of the West (12/39)

Pioneers of the Frontier (2/40)

The Man from Tumbleweeds (5/40)

The Return of Wild Bill (6/40)

WILD BILL HICKOK series (Bill Elliott): (Columbia Pictures)

Prairie Schooners (9/40)

Beyond the Sacramento (11/40)

Wildcat of Tucson (12/40)

Across the Sierras (2/41)

North from the Lone Star (3/41)

Hands Across the Rockies (6/41)

The cast of "Casey Jones" seems to be enjoying itself in this publicity still. Eddy Waller is lower left; Dub is wearing the fireman's hat; and Alan Hale is standing at the right of the picture.

BILL ELLIOTT series: (Columbia Pictures)

The Return of Daniel Boone (5/41)

The Son of Davy Crockett (7/41)

BILL ELLIOTT-TEX RITTER series: (Columbia Pictures)

King of Dodge City (8/41) Elliott reverted to his Wild Bill Hickok role in the series with Tex Ritter.

RUSSELL HAYDEN series: (Columbia Pictures)

The Lone Prairie (10/42)

Pardon My Gun (12/42)

A Tornado in the Saddle (12/42)

Riders of the Northwest Mounted (2/43)

Saddle and Sagebrush (4/43)

Silver City Raiders (11/43)

The Vigilantes Ride (2/44)

Wyoming Hurricane (4/44)

The Last Horseman (6/44)

CHARLES STARRETT series: (Columbia Pictures)

Cowboy in the Clouds (12/43)

Cowboy from Lonesome River (9/44)

Cyclone Prairie Rangers (11/44)

Jimmy Wakely restrains Sheriff Kenne Duncan from badly bruising Cannonball in this scene from *Gun Runner* **(1949).**

Saddle Leather Law (12/44)

Rough Ridin' Justice (3/45)

DURANGO KID series (Charles Starrett): (Columbia Pictures)

Both Barrels Blazing (5/45)

Rustlers of the Badlands (8/45)

Blazing the Western Trail (9/45)

Outlaws of the Rockies (9/45)

Lawless Empire (11/45)

Texas Panhandle (12/45)

Frontier Gunlaw (1/46)

JIMMY WAKELY series: (Monogram Pictures)

Ridin' Down the Trail (10/47)

Song of the Drifter (1/48)

Oklahoma Blues (3/48)

Rangers Ride (4/48)

Cowboy Cavalier (7/48)

Partners of the Sunset (8/48)

Silver Trails (8/48)

Outlaw Brand (10/48)

Courtin' Trouble (11/48)

Gun Runner (1/49)

Gun Law Justice (3/49)

Across the Rio Grande (5/49)

Brand of Fear (7/49)

Roaring Westward (9/49)

Lawless Code (12/49)

★   ★   ★

Max Terhune and his dummy Elmer Sneezewood.

MAX "LULLABY" TERHUNE

Sammy McKim (Child actor who appeared in many Westerns): Gene Autry and John Wayne were both good guys, but Autry didn't seem to warm-up to kids and was rather cool in his off-camera relationship. Wayne was good natured. The original Three Mesquiteers, Bob Livingston, Ray "Crash" Corrigan, and Max Terhune were the friendliest—always a warm relationship. (Interview with Bob Murphy for **The Big Reel**.)

Tracy Terhune (Grandson of Max): One thing I can say for certain, Max Terhune was the same, fun-loving, understanding person as he often portrayed in his film roles. He was quick to pull a gag, even on members of his own family. The three children would often become unruly. Max would be quick to pipe up in the sweetest of tones, "Who wants it first?" Believing it was some candy or a special treat being offered, all three would chirp, "Me first daddy, me first!" Max proceeded to...spank the one who so eagerly requested it first, finishing the other two in order. (**Nostalgia Monthly,** September, 1978).

Gene Autry (Discussing his film, **Ride, Ranger, Ride**): A footnote to this film was the debut of Max Terhune, who became one of the best liked, off the screen, of all Western actors. As late as 1974, a "Max Terhune Appreciation Society" still flourished. Once a ventriloquist, Max got his start, as I did, at WLS radio in Chicago. He went on to fame as one of "The Three Mesquiteers," whose ranks later included John Wayne.

Robert Max Terhune was a multi-gifted performer—ventriloquist, animal and bird imitator, whistler, magician, card trickster, and actor—who impressed Gene Autry enough while they were both entainers at the "National Barn Dance" in Chicago that Autry talked him into journeying out to Hollywood to work in films, which he did quite successfully from 1936 into the mid-1950s.

Max's round-faced, all-American country boy countenance was fitting for a person who had been born in a log cabin on Lincoln's birthday. That occurred in Franklin, Indiana, back in 1891. Max was the last of five sons who were born to Asa and Nancy Jane Terhune. Max's father died of pneumonia in 1898, after which the family packed up and moved to Lebanon, Indiana, where Max completed grammar school.

By the time he was four years old, Max had displayed a flair for his future calling. He found he had a natural ability to imitate the farm animals and birds that were his daily childhood companions. A mid-West country boy of the turn of the century, Max tended to turn inward for his amusements, practicing by the hour his self-taught whistling, magic and card tricks, imitations, and ventriloquism. His soft-spoken drawl and natural humor complemented his other talents, and soon he was in demand as an unpaid entertainer at various social gatherings in the area.

By 1907 Max's brothers had left home, and it was up to Max to support his mother, which he did until her death in 1921. For a time he worked as a blacksmith's helper on the New York Central Railroad with his cousin Jeptha Leet. Jeptha happened to be an accomplished left-handed fiddle player who enjoyed nothing more than the competition of a good fiddle contest—a popular diversion during this era. Max would demonstrate his talent for whistling in the whistling contest which generally accompanied the fiddle competition.

Max was also quite a baseball player and for a

while had visions of making a career as a professional ball player. When he was twenty, he signed as a pitcher for Indianapolis, a team in the American Association. A wrist injury cut short his dream of a baseball career, although he continued to play for class D minor teams for several years. At one time he pitched against Kermit Maynard (Ken's brother), who would later ride the Hollywood range in dozens of films.

Show business, though, remained Max's main ambition, and by the early 1920s he was touring around the country with such groups as Ezra Buzzington's Rustic Revellers, The Hoosier Hot Shots, and Brownlee's Hickville Follies. In 1931 he was invited to join The Weaver Brothers and Elviry for twenty-five weeks on the Orpheum Circuit. Max was being seen and was making a name for himself in vaudeville as a down-home, versatile funmaker.

As busy as he had been getting his career into gear, Max had found time for a personal life, too. At a New Year's party in 1919 a friend of Max asked him to intercede on his behalf in the courting of a charming young lady named Maude Cassidy. When Max attempted to tell Maude about the many fine qualities of his friend, she surprised him by indicating she preferred Max to the friend. One thing led to another, as they say, and after a lengthy courtship, Max and Maude were married on December 15, 1922.

In 1932 Max was approached by a representative of the "National Barn Dance" radio program which emanated from Chicago. They wanted Max for the program. In the 1930s the "National Barn Dance" was for country/Western performers what the Palace Theatre in New York was for urban entertainers. At that time it was even ranked above the "Grand Ole Opry" in Nashville. This was, indeed, the big time, and Max was ready.

It was on the "National Barn Dance" that Max first got to know Gene Autry, the biggest star of the "Barn Dance" at that time. Smiley Burnette, Little Georgie Gobel, Lulubelle and Scotty, Pat Buttram, and other future stars established their show business credentials on the popular "National Barn Dance" broadcasts. Max Terhune earned his place with them during his tenure on the program.

Life was going well for Max on the home front, too. Between 1923 and 1930 Maude had borne him three children: Doris Maxine, Robert Max, Jr., and Donald Roltaire. Max took his family responsibilities very seriously and tried not to let his blossoming show business career interfere with the business of raising a brood of children. Often he would turn down social events in order to stay home with Maude and the children.

In 1934 Gene Autry got a movie contract with Mascot Pictures and took his pal Smiley Burnette with him to Hollywood. As everyone knows, Autry and Burnette were an immediate hit in films and within a year they were starring in a Western series for Republic Pictures, the new company name following several mergers.

Autry remembered Max and his many talents and felt that he could be an asset in his pictures (which must have caused some fretting on the part of Smiley). When Gene's call came, Max was uneasy about making such a giant move to the uncertainty of film making in Hollywood. After all, he was doing just fine where he was; the work was good and so was his salary. Ultimately, however, Autry's persistence prevailed and Max headed West into a new career as a cowboy sidekick.

Max's first film assignment, as mentioned earlier, was *Ride, Ranger, Ride* (1936) with Gene and Smiley. Max played a buckskin-clad Indian scout for the cavalry. His performance was vigorous, very appealing, and completely overshadowed Smiley's somewhat limited role in the picture. Smiley's main contribution to the film was a running gag with Chief Thundercloud who was trying to scalp him. Max had a funnier running bit in the film. Every time he would wave a speck of snuff around and then stuff it up his nose, the people around him would sneeze uncontrollably, but never Max. Each time Max did the bit it got funnier. The picture was an auspicious beginning for Max and did not go unnoticed by studio officials.

Just eight days before the release of *Ride, Ranger, Ride,* the first episode of a new Western series produced by Republic Pictures, *The Three Mesquiteers,* was released. Robert Livingston, Ray "Crash" Corrigan, and Syd Saylor were the threesome of the title. As conceived for the screen from the novels by William Colt MacDonald, Livingston (Stony Brooke) was the lover, Corrigan (Tucson Smith) was the muscle with occasional lapses into romance, and Saylor (Lullaby Joslin) was the comic relief.

Studio executives liked the series' concept, but they were unhappy with Saylor's performance as Lullaby. The chemistry between Livingston and Corrigan was on the mark, but Saylor, with his bobbing Adam's apple and rather broad playing style was deemed wrong for the part and out of sync with the other performers. It was felt that a more subdued, steadying character was needed to complement the sometimes stormy relationship between Stony and Tucson. (Reportedly, Livingston and Corrigan's personal relationship on the set was stormier than anything that was ever seen on the screen.) The scripts frequently called for Stony and Tucson to get into scraps over plot situations and the affections of the local schoolmarm, rancher's daughter, or whatever guise the feminine lead role happened to be in the episode. It was wisely felt that the easygoing, country cousin appeal of Max Terhune, plus the variety of bucolic talents he had tucked under his hat, would provide a Lullaby characterization perfect for Republic's screen needs—even if he was a far cry from the Lullaby of the original novels.

Max was cast as Lullaby in the second series entry, **Ghost Town Gold** (1936), and was surprised to discover that he had a screen home for what looked like an indefinite run. He signed a contract with Republic calling for a reported $100 per week, with yearly studio options and raises built in. In this first outing as Lullaby, the scriptwriters introduced his dummy, Elmer Sneezewood, by having Max win him in a card game. (During the years Max had toured on the Orpheum Circuit, the dummy had been called Skully Null.)

Max was always justifiably proud of the Mesquiteers films. In a letter to author David Zinman he summed up the appeal of the series as he saw it: "For the girls, it had a running gag of rivalry between Stony and Tucson for the girl in each story. It had plenty of action and fights, and the boys liked that. I like to believe the kids liked Elmer, too. And the adults, I think, liked the variety of plots and the scenery and beautiful horses."

Max was ultimately to make twenty-one films in the Mesquiteers series: fourteen with the original cast of Livingston and Corrigan, one with Ralph Byrd (taking a break from his Dick Tracy serial role) playing Tucson's brother while Robert Livingston recovered from an injury he had sustained, and six with John Wayne who replaced Livingston as Stony Brooke. Three years passed, and Republic, always

Max is demonstrating a little card trickery for his original co-stars in *The Three Mesquiteers* series: Robert Livingston (left) and Ray "Crash" Corrigan (right).

207

Max made six *Three Mesquiteers* films with John Wayne in the role of Stony Brooke. Although the Wayne Mesquiteers films were very popular, it is widely felt that the Livingston/Corrigan team was better because Wayne and Corrigan played their roles so similarly.

cost-conscious, reportedly decided they were paying Max more than was necessary for comic relief. His contract option was not renewed and Raymond Hatton was introduced as Rusty Joslin, a relative of Lullaby. Max was briefly "at liberty."

Max didn't have long to wait, though, for his next screen series. Producer George W. Weeks over at Monogram Pictures was developing a competitive trio Western series called The Range Busters. He wanted and got Max for the cast. Since Weeks was blatantly copying the successful format of the popular Mesquiteers series, he had no compunctions about also luring the, by now, restless Ray Corrigan away from Republic. John "Dusty" King was hired to complete the trio. King had a fairly pleasant baritone voice and sang occasionally in the series—after all, this was the heyday of the singing cowboys as well as the trio Westerns, so George W.

Weeks was shrewdly trying to cover his investment in every way possible.

Max was signed to play a character called Alibi—which sounded a whole lot like Lullaby if you didn't listen too carefully. Max, happy to oblige his new producer, played the role—Elmer and all—exactly as he had played Lullaby over at Republic.

The first entry in the series was appropriately entitled *The Range Busters* (1940) and opened, as all the episodes would, to the strains of "Home on the Range." Don Miller in his book, *Hollywood Corral*, describes the Frank Sanucci musical score for the series as sounding as if it were being performed by "a sextet of kazoos." The Sanucci "kazoo" sound was to permeate all of the Monogram Westerns and, as a member of the audience, you either slowly succumbed into a numbed appreciation or you ran screaming from the theatre.

Sad to say, the other production departments at Monogram were no better. Author Miller also states it well when he describes the sound of the Monogram pictures as "tin-can telephone quality." The scripts were even more predictable than most B Westerns and generally less actionful. Sets were skimpy and the camera work often awkward.

To be fair, an occasional good Range Busters picture would make it into the film can, and when that did happen, the main ingredient for success was the appealing cast. Corrigan, Terhune, and King tried mightily to make the series work, and sometimes they succeeded. The original trio made sixteen episodes in the series between 1940 and 1942. With the film *Texas to Bataan* (1942) Ray Corrigan left the series and was replaced by ace stuntman Dave Sharpe. Sharpe remained in the series for three-and-a-half episodes. During the filming of *Haunted Ranch* in 1943, Sharpe was called to serve in World War Two, and Rex Lease was recruited to complete the picture amid some hasty rewriting by the screenwriters.

For the next film in the series, *Land of the Hunted Men* (1943), Corrigan returned and John King was replaced by Dennis Moore. Moore stayed on for three films, including the last one in the series, but King returned for the next-to-last episode, *Black Market Rustlers* (1943) (The Terhune filmography should clear up this casting game of musical chairs.) Max Terhune was the only fixture in the cast, and he must have needed a program to keep track of his co-stars. The Range Busters busted up upon the completion of *Bullets and Saddles* (1943), the twenty-fourth picture in the series.

For the next three years the picture pickings were pretty lean for Max, so he hit the road, touring the country. In 1944 he tied in with Tex Ritter, Slim Andrews, and Cannonball Taylor. The next year he toured by himself and, for a while, with Wally Fowler and his Georgia Clodhoppers. In 1946 he joined Ron Ormond on the T.D. Kemp circuit. In 1947 Max briefly returned to Republic Studios for a featured role in Monte Hale's *Along the Oregon Trail.*

In early 1948 Max got a call from Monogram Pictures and an invitation to join the Johnny Mack Brown series as a regular. Raymond Hatton, who had been Johnny Mack's sidekick for several years, had three more pictures on his contract and then he was taking his leave. Rumor had it that Hatton's agent convinced him he could get more money freelancing—an error in judgment that Hatton would later regret.

Max joined the highly regarded Johnny Mack Brown series and remained for eight films. Unfor-tunately, 1948-49 turned out to be a period of trans-ition for the Johnny Mack series, and the eight films in which Max appeared were not among his best. Max was given his old Range Busters name of Alibi, but he wasn't given a whole lot to do in the series. It was as if nobody quite knew why he was there or what he was to do. Mostly, he mosied around through the scripts, occasionally offering a few moments of chuckles with his dummy Elmer. It wasn't like the Mesquiteers or Range Busters films where his character was clearly defined for the audience. With the completion of *West of Eldorado* in 1949, Max ended his series Western career.

It was back to the road for Max with only brief returns to Hollywood for supporting roles in films such as *Rawhide* (1951) with Tyrone Power and *Jim Thorpe, All American* (1951) starring Burt Lancaster.

In 1952 Max moved into television as the star of his own local kids' show called "Alibi's Tent Show," which was sponsored by Dad's Root Beer on KNX-TV in Hollywood. From time to time he got roles in such popular television series as "The Lone Ranger," "I Love Lucy," "Ramar of the Jungle," and "Annie Oakley." In 1956 he joined some other oldtimers for a small part in George Stevens' near classic film, *Giant.* His hands were employed for some fancy card footage in Clark Gable's *King and Four Queens* (1956), but the sequence ended up on the cutting room floor. His last movie work was as a "card technician" in *Gunfight at the O.K. Corral* in 1957.

When viewing Max Terhune's films today—The Three Mesquiteers and Range Busters films, primarily—some of his many talents may be clouded by the public's current taste in entertain-ment. The entertainment and entertainers of his time were vastly different from the current crop that lights our movie and television screens. Ventrilo-quists, in particular, are somewhat rare these days and if they do show up on a program, they damned well better not show a quivering lip. Animal and bird imitators find little exposure today even on such bucolic shows as "Hee Haw."

Max Terhune's primary source of comedy in his Western films was ventriloquism with his dummy Elmer. He was not a very good ventriloquist; his lips were a study in Parkinson-like movement, but Max was fortunate to be doing what he was doing at the time he was doing it. In the 1930s and '40s the American public was highly amused each week on radio by the antics of ventriloquist Edgar Bergen and dummy Charlie McCarthy. (The thought of a *radio* ventriloquist today seems an absurd *non sequitar*.) Max and his Elmer provided a visual counterpart to Bergen's radio work with which film audiences could be intrigued and entertained.

To many people ventriloquism bordered on magic, and there was a widespread naive notion among many people that a ventriloquist actually somehow **threw** his voice. More than one mike boom operator had to be stopped from turning the microphone to the dummy whenever its lines were delivered by the ventriloquist. In quite a number of Terhune's films the outlaws would be "tricked" by a voice supposedly emanating from behind them or out of the mouth of a person standing dumbly across the room—all of this vocal chicanery adding to the public confusion and fascination with ventriloquism.

Unlike the superb writing on the Bergen-McCarthy radio show and the rapier wit of an Edgar Bergen, Max received little or no help from the Western screenwriters, and his own predilection was generally for gentle, humorous banter coming from his wooden-headed friend. Seldom was Max given a sufficient interlude to really develop a comedy routine with Elmer in the films. Thus, in the final analysis, Elmer was usually a brief comic diversion between action scenes in the pictures.

The point of all this is that Max Terhune was a gentle soul with a satchel full of varied talents that suited his time and place. If he were starting his career today, he might find little call for his particular services. But we are fortunate that his greatest screen asset shines through as clearly today as when the films were first run through projectors: the warm and gentle nature of his witty, yet folksy, personality—almost a Will Rogers quality—that enhanced and complemented the performances of the actors with whom he worked. In his typically modest way, Max is quoted as saying, "I loved every minute of it and have many wonderful memories. I have had the opportunity of working with some of the most talented people on earth."

Max was badly shaken in 1958 when his younger son, Donald Roltaire, was fatally injured in a car accident. By this time his daughter Doris had married a ranch manager, and his other son, Robert, was active as a film stuntman and occasional actor.

In 1966 Max was devastated by the death of his wife Maude. His grandson Tracy recalled going to the family home upon hearing the news of Maude's death:

> When we arrived I can remember the total silence of the entire house, and we knew that she had, indeed, passed on. I went to the back room on this hot day, August 10, 1966, to see Max sitting on the edge of his bed, crying, and as I entered,

> he looked up at me with tears in his eyes, and said, "Where's Maude? Where did she go?" I left the room startled, having never seen this man, who had made thousands laugh throughout his entire life, crying. A letter written shortly after her death, by Max, to his grandson Gary, who was in the army at the time, said, "I really loved her....and I know I'll never be the same."

Two years later the family moved to Cottonwood, Arizona. At first Max didn't want to make the move because all of his friends were in California and he didn't like big moves—his only other one had been the move from Chicago back in 1936. Apparently he didn't count touring the entire country during his career.

By 1973 Max's health had deteriorated considerably. He suffered from nose bleeds caused by high blood pressure. He also had a mild heart condition and other physical discomfitures typical of a man his age. When he initially survived a heart attack, the family held hope that he would recover. A week later, though, his condition was complicated by a stroke—still he held on. But it was only to be a short reprieve. On June 5, 1973, Max Terhune passed on. His death was mourned by his many friends and fans alike. As Autry had said, "Max Terhune was one of the best liked of all Western actors."

Oh, yes. When last reported, Elmer was residing with Max's son Robert.

★   ★   ★

MAX "LULLABY" TERHUNE FILMOGRAPHY

GENE AUTRY series: (Republic Pictures)

Ride, Ranger, Ride (9/36)

The Big Show (11/36) Max was one of a number of guest performers in this Autry extravaganza built around the Texas Centennial.

THREE MESQUITEERS series (Livingston and Corrigan): (Republic Pictures)

Ghost Town Gold (10/36)

Roarin' Lead (12/36)

Riders of Whistling Skull (1/37)

Max and Elmer are seen here with Smiley Burnette and Gene Autry in a scene which does not appear in the edited-for-television version of *The Big Show*.

Hit the Saddle (3/37) Rita Cansino (Hayworth) is the leading lady in this episode.

Gunsmoke Ranch (5/37)

Come on, Cowboys (5/37) *Tex Ritter's occasional sidekick, Horace Murphy, has a featured role in this film.*

Range Defenders (6/37)

Heart of the Rockies (9/37)

The Trigger Trio (10/37) Ralph Byrd subs for Livingston in this episode.

Wild Horse Rodeo (12/37) Dick Weston (Roy Rogers) has a small role in this one.

The Purple Vigilantes (1/38)

Call the Mesquiteers (3/38) Allan "Rocky" Lane's future sidekick, Eddy Waller is featured in the cast.

Outlaws of Sonora (4/38)

Riders of the Black Hills (6/38) Eddie Dean's future sidekick, Roscoe Ates, is listed fifth in the cast.

Heroes of the Hills (8/38)

THREE MESQUITEERS series (Wayne and Corrigan): (Republic Pictures)

Pals of the Saddle (8/38)

Overland Stage Raiders (9/38)

Santa Fe Stampede (11/38)

Red River Range (12/38) Kirby "Sky King" Grant has a featured role in the cast.

The Night Riders (4/39)

Three Texas Steers (5/38) Roscoe Ates again has a role.

RANGE BUSTERS series (Corrigan and King): (Monogram Pictures)

The Range Busters (8/40) Sidekick Horace Murphy has a small role in the cast.

Trailing Double Trouble (10/40) Future singing cowboy star Jimmy Wakely and His Rough Riders provide some music for this episode.

West of Pinto Basin (11/40)

Trail of the Silver Spurs (1/41) Future singing cowboy star Eddie Dean is featured in the cast.

The Kid's Last Ride (2/41)

Tumbledown Ranch in Arizona (4/41)

Wrangler's Roost (6/41)

Fugitive Valley (7/41)

Saddle Mountain Roundup (8/41)

Tonto Basin Outlaws (10/41)

Underground Rustlers (11/41)

Thunder River Feud (1/42)

Rock River Renegades (2/42)

Boot Hill Bandits (4/42)

Texas Troubleshooters (6/42)

Arizona Stagecoach (9/42) Eddie Dean has a bit part in the cast.

RANGE BUSTERS series (King and Dave Sharpe): (Monogram Pictures)

Texas to Bataan (10/42)

Trail Riders (12/42)

Two Fisted Justice (1/43)

Haunted Ranch (2/43) Dave Sharpe entered the service during the filming of this picture and was replaced by Rex Lease.

RANGE BUSTERS series (Corrigan and Dennis Moore): (Monogram Pictures)

Land of Hunted Men (3/43)

Cowboy Commandos (6/43)

Black Market Rustlers (8/43) John King replaces Moore in this next-to-the-last episode.

Bullets and Saddles (10/43) Dennis Moore returns to end the series with Corrigan and Max Terhune.

JOHNNY MACK BROWN series: (Monogram Pictures)

Range Justice (8/48)

Sheriff of Medicine Bow (10/48) Raymond Hatton is in the cast.

Gunning for Justice (11/48) Ray Hatton is featured.

Hidden Danger (12/48) Hatton completed his Monogram contract with this film.

Law of the West (2/49)

Trail's End (4/49)

West of Eldorado (6/49)

Western Renegades (10/49)

★   ★   ★

Max looks concerned; Johnny Mack, stalwart as Jack Ingram explains his problem in this scene from *Law of the West* **(1949).**

Lee "Lasses" White and singing cowboy Jimmy Wakely are ready for action in this scene from their 1947 feature, *Six Gun Serenade.*

LEE "LASSES" WHITE

Oliver Drake: *Lasses White was a sweetheart. He was originally a minstrel man. Did you ever see the picture* **Lonesome Trail** *that I did with Jimmy Wakely and Lasses? Well, I did a whole minstrel show in it just like they used to do in the old days.*

Dan White: *(Western film character actor): Lasses and singer Ray Whitley were in some of the Tim Holt pictures for RKO in the early 1940s. I don't believe Lasses ever had an evil thought about anyone in his life.*

Eddie Dean: *Lasses was Glenn Strange's cousin. You remember, Glenn played Sam the bartender on "Gunsmoke" for years. They were first cousins and two wonderful friends of mine.*

Jimmy Wakely: *Lasses' voice was very unusual. It sounded almost as if it was intended for minstrel shows—southern milk and honey, but yet with a corn whiskey whine. He got his name Lasses while he was doing an act on WSM in Nashville for the "Grand Ole Opry." It was called Lasses and Honey. They were Lasses White and Honey Childs; it was a blackface comedy routine. This was in the early days of the "Grand Ole Opry."*

Terry Frost: *(Western film bad guy): You had to have a sense of humor working in pictures back in those days. We were always playing practical jokes on each other. You know, one time the script called for me to tie up Lasses White. This occurred just before they called lunch on the set, and I put practical knots on the*

rope. We all went to lunch and left Lasses tied to the post. We played hard and we worked hard in those days, and I had a ball every minute I was with Lasses White.

No doubt about it, Lee "Lasses" White was a popular performer with co-workers and film fans for the nine years he worked in Hollywood, the closing chapter on his long career in show business. Born in Willis Point, Texas, in 1885, Lee White had been performing—year after year—from the turn of the century in minstrel, tent, vaudeville, and radio shows when Hollywood films finally beckoned.

Between 1940 and 1949, when he died, Lasses White made more than thirty movies covering just about every film genre. He is probably best remembered, however, for co-starring as a sidekick with two cowboy stars: Tim Holt and singing cowboy Jimmy Wakely. In the Tim Holt RKO series (1941-1942) he took over the role of Whopper from Emmett Lynn. Lynn had earlier acquired the Whopper character from Chill Wills who had originated it in the George O'Brien RKO series of the 1930s. In 1944 Lasses joined Jimmy Wakely for a series of twelve pictures for Monogram. In the Wakely series his role was called Lasses and, basically, he played the minstrel character he had been honing for over four decades—only now he didn't use blackface to play it.

Lasses White's on-screen trademarks were a "corn whiskey whine" voice (as Jimmy Wakely so aptly described it to me) and his walk. Quoting Wakely again: "He walked like he was walking on rocking chair rockers. You know, up and down, up and down. It was a burlesque of the Black man's walk—which was not true—but it was overdone and considered very funny in those days. Well, Lasses carried it over into Westerns and added rolling eyes like the end men would do in the minstrel shows."

And Lasses certainly had had plenty of

In Jan, 1945 Jimmy Wakely and sidekick Lee "Lasses"
White started a long tour of Texas and Oklahoma
to introduce the first starring movie for Jimmy
SONG OF THE RANGE.

The first theatre they played was in Brownwood,
Texas.

This was strictly a "two act" no musicians
Just the Wakely guitar.

The picture would play... Then Wakely
would be introduced... sing a few songs,
introduce White and play guitar for hi[m]
All for 100.00 (one hundred dollars[)]
a day which they split.

BROWNWOOD BULLETIN

ES TODAY

BROWNWOOD, TEXAS, SATURDAY, JANUARY 6, 1945

VOL. 45.

HUGE OVATION GIVEN
TWO MOVIE STARS

Jimmy would
often give his
pictures away
to the kids after
the show.

One day White, who was
older and much wiser,
asked Jimmy to let the
theatre sell his pictures.
Wakely agreed... The results
were fantastic... The pictures
sold by hundreds per day... The
Hundred a day became secondary.

By the time they reached Dallas for the
official premier of the picture, the crowds
told Monogram that they had a new star on
their hands.

This newspaper clipping and accompanying typed notes are from Jimmy Wakely's personal scrapbook
of memorabilia.

experience in minstrel shows and most other forms of show business. In January of 1945 the Brownwood, Texas, newspaper, the **Brownwood Bulletin,** succinctly covered Lasses' earlier career in their feature story on him and Jimmy Wakely. The two stars had journeyed there to make a personal appearance touting their first picture together, *Song of the Range.* In a column captioned "Thousands Greet Jimmie (sic) Wakely, 'Lasses' White" the paper noted:

Lee White was born on a Texas ranch operated by his father. Attracted by a traveling minstrel show, he joined up to start a career of 28 years in blackface during the era when minstrels were at their peak. For several years he was featured in Al G. Fields Minstrels, later understudying Honey Boy Evans. It was the death of Evans which elevated White to minstrel stardom.

For almost 10 years, White headed the "Lasses" White All-Star Minstrels, continuing to tour the nation after other large units had been replaced by vaudeville. Finally he saw the handwriting on the wall, and became a blackface vaudeville star. When that form of entertainment lost public support, White turned to radio.

He spent six years broadcasting from a station at Nashville, Tenn., including four years with the Grand Ole Opry program, then pulled up stakes and went to Hollywood, from which point he appeared in many nationwide radio programs.

Completing the cycle of the entertainment field, he learned the technique of motion picture acting. For a year he played the Whopper character in the Tim Holt series, and the role of Ed Potts in the Scattergood Baines series based on Clarence Budington Kelland's great stories. He also attracted attention for character roles in "Mark Twain," "Sergeant York," "The Belle of the Yukon," "Talk of the Town," and "Something to Shout About."

His work in Monogram's "Alaska" and "When Strangers Marry" was so outstanding that the studio decided to cast White with Jimmy Wakely and Dennis Moore in the new Jimmy Wakely series. A Texas war bond tour in which Wakely and White appeared brought them to the attention of Phil Isley, owner of the local

theatres and father of Jennifer Jones. Mr. Isley's influence in Monogram's decision to star the two players is widely recognized.

IN PERSON on our STAGE
NEW SINGING COWBOY STAR

JIMMY WAKELY   LEE "LASSES" WHITE

JIMMY WAKELY
DALLAS' OWN **LEE "LASSES" WHITE**
CAPITOL THEATRE
STARTING JAN. 12 - 4 BIG DAYS 4
On our Screen In Their First Starring Feature Picture
"Song Of The Range"
Please Attend The Early Shows

This newspaper clipping is from Jimmy Wakely's personal scrapbook. The Capitol Theatre was in Dallas, Texas.

Jimmy Wakely filled in the details when I interviewed him in August of 1982, just shortly before his death.

Jimmy Wakely: We were in Texas on a band tour with various artists—Wild Bill Elliott, Johnny Mack Brown, Huntz Hall, Big Boy Williams, and Gail Storm—just to name a few. We all went on this bond tour and then we separated into smaller groups and toured Texas selling bonds. This was in 1944.

Lasses was on the trip, too. We were friends already, but we had never worked together. While we were on this Texas bond tour we talked with Phil Isley who had been asked by Monogram Pictures to find a cowboy star for a series they were planning. Phil recommended me for the starring role, and he recommended Lasses for the comedian. So, it was as

A NEW STAR ROARS
OUT OF THE WEST!

His songs have made him a
sensation on records and radio
..his fighting will make him
your action favorite!

JIMMY WAKELY
in

SONG OF THE RANGE

A MONOGRAM PICTURE

with **DENNIS MOORE**
LEE "Lasses" WHITE

JOHNNY BOND and His RED RIVER VALLEY BOYS

10c —— | CHEROKEE | —— 35c

The above newspaper advertisement is another clipping from Jimmy Wakely's personal scrapbook. The Cherokee Theatre played *Song of the Range* early in 1945.

easy as that. Lasses got the comedy sidekick spot, and it worked out very fine.

With Lasses White's comedy you didn't have the falling in the horse trough bit as you did with Smiley Burnette in his pictures. Lasses didn't imitate Smiley or any other comics on anything. He also didn't have to do the pie-in-the-face slapstick. He was another Gabby Hayes. He worked as a character actor and he loved it. He loved the West; he loved Western books and films, and he just lived them on the screen.

When Lasses and I first went out on tour, I didn't have a band. We toured Phil Isley's theatres in Texas and some interstate theatres down there. It was just Lasses and me. Well, it was a tough tour. The theatre managers would show our first picture, **Song of the Range,** and then they'd introduce me. I'd go out in the center of the stage with my guitar and sing a few songs. After I finished, I'd introduce Lasses. He'd come out and do a comedy routine which was always very funny. The comedy would be an outgrowth of his background in minstrels. He'd tell some farm and country jokes that they'd really buy in those small rural towns. After he finished his comedy, I'd come out again and play the guitar for him while he sang. Then the two of us would end it up by singing a song together, something up-tempo. I think we did "Seven Come Eleven, Baby Needs New Shoes."

I found myself working damned hard; I'd practically do the whole show. I'd either be working for me or for Lasses. I discouraged that in the future because Lasses was getting up in age and it was very tough on him, too.

We played some theatres that were so hot that we just about died; they had no air conditioning. Many times they would light the stage with the projector light; you know, that kind of flickers. I would stand there in that light and have it just about put my eyes out. The sweat would just be running off me. Lasses would be so hot that I'd wonder when he was going to keel over.

Lasses was popular in my pictures, but eventually some of the distributors and theatre managers around the country thought we ought to drop Lasses and get Dub Taylor because he was available and might appeal more to the kids. They kept on about this, and, eventually, I thought it was probably a pretty good idea, too, because I was afraid Lasses was going to get hurt in some of the horse and action scenes. You see, the studio wouldn't double Lasses very much.

Monogram was a very cheap company, and they tried to hold down on the

Singing cowboy star Jimmy Wakely and sidekick Lee "Lasses" White appeared in twelve Monogram Westerns together between 1944 and 1947.

expenses. They often had Lasses riding in scenes where I thought they should have use a stuntman. I felt that he was taking a big risk on horseback at his age. One day he and Dennis Moore and I were standing side-by-side on our horses when the horses suddenly bolted. Dennis' spur in some way got caught in Lasses' saddle stirrup and damned near ripped the saddle right off the horse.

Dennis and I were both young, and we were agile on horses, but Lasses was an old man. Don't get me wrong, Lasses was a good rider, but I kept worrying about him getting dumped on his head and maybe getting killed. I was very concerned. I just loved Lasses; he was a great man. He always came through the scenes okay, but I was afraid that one time he wouldn't. Lasses was very well-off financially, and he didn't need the job. As I said before, he just knew everything about the West and riding horses was part of it.

Finally, though, I had to ask Lasses to resign, and I recommended Dub Taylor to the studio. My pictures were making money, so they let me do whatever I wanted to do. It turned out to be a mistake because Dub wasn't as strong in my pictures as Lasses. Dub had been pretty good doing slapstick comedy in the Wild Bill Elliott pictures, but Lasses was a damned good character actor. He could do serious things, which Dub couldn't do. On the very first picture I had Lasses lean against a wagon wheel and sing "I'm Casting My Lasso to the Sky" in a very serious way. It really paid off; people loved it. He was like Gabby Hayes; he could get away with the serious material as well as the comedy.

As I said, Lasses was well-off; he didn't have to work—no way! He had a wife named Norma, and she used to tell him what to eat and what not to eat because he had a touchy stomach. She was very protective of Lasses; she loved him very much.

He had been a drinker. He once told me, "I used to drink, but I wouldn't walk up and hit Jack Dempsey; he'd knock me on my backside. Whiskey is also able to knock me down. Anything that can knock me down, I can't take." So he didn't drink.

He'd quit drinking years before I met him. Unfortunately, Dub wasn't smart enough to do that, you know. He was not the same character as Lasses. Lasses and I always got along just fine. We never had a single quarrel, ever. We never had a single misunderstanding.

Lasses was a Shriner and he lived it to the hilt. He had friends all over. I tell you, when we went down to Texas to play that first tour, they came in from miles around to see ol' Lasses White, the minstrel man they knew from years past. I was new and it was my film series, but the point is, they loved Lasses first because they knew him.

In evaluating the cowboy sidekick career of Lasses White one must look to the stars of the series in which he performed and the overall quality of the productions. Unlike some of the cowboy sidekicks who became almost as popular as their cowboy star companions, Lasses' screen character was not as dominant or dynamic as most.

At RKO where the production values and scripts were of a higher quality and the leading man, Tim Holt, was developing into a forceful action star, Lasses provided solid support and got an appropriate share of chuckles playing his Whopper character. In the less auspicious Wakely series, Lasses had listless scripts, mediocre production values, and a lackluster leading man. Jimmy Wakely was a fine singing cowboy, but as even he acknowledged, he was not an action performer or much of an actor. As a result, Lasses was not as impressive in this Western series, and his minstrel man characteristics seemed dated and/or out of sync with the cowboy sidekick antics that Western audiences (heavily juvenile) had become accustomed to in other Western series of the mid to late 1940s.

After Lasses left the Wakely series, he played featured roles in a variety of films over the next two years before his death. He joined Abbott and Costello in **The Wistful Widow of Wagon Gap** (1947), Eddie Albert in **The Dude Goes West** (1948), and Duncan Renaldo in a Cisco Kid feature entitled **The Valiant Hombre** (1948). Back in 1945, while he was with Jimmy Wakely, Lasses had appeared in an earlier Duncan Renaldo Cisco Kid feature, **In Old Mexico.** Lasses was reunited briefly with Tim Holt for a small role in **Indian Agent** in 1948. Two films— **Red Rock Outlaw** with someone named Bob Gilbert and **The Texan Meets Calamity Jane** with Evelyn Ankers and James Ellison—were released in 1950

It looks as if Lasses is all duded-out for a buggy ride in this scene from *Song of the Sierras* (1946). Jimmy and an unidentified saddle pal are looking pretty spiffy, too.

after Lasses' death.

Oliver Drake, who produced and directed the majority of the Jimmy Wakely/Lasses White films, was close to both Lasses and his wife until they died.

> **Oliver Drake:** *Jimmy had made one or two pictures at Monogram when he got me over there to make them with him. Lasses was already in the series. During the whole bunch of pictures we became good friends. I had a ranch up in the mountains and he and his wife Norma would come up there to visit. Lasses, as far as I was concerned, was the salt of the earth. His wife Norma was a very nice gal. When Lasses died in 1949, he left her pretty well fixed. He had a lot of insurance, and he hadn't been a spendthrift. They had lived*

nice, but he had saved his money. So, as I said, she was pretty well fixed. Some months after Lasses died, she married a guy who took her for everything she had, I guess, and then walked away from her. Not long afterward, she died.

★   ★   ★

LEE "LASSES" WHITE FILMOGRAPHY

TIM HOLT series: (RKO)

Cyclone on Horseback (6/41) Singer Ray Whitley appeared in all of the Tim Holt films with Lasses White.

Six Gun Gold (8/41)

Jimmy Wakely and Lasses are about to make their escape in this scene from their last picture together, *Song of the Wasteland* (1947).

The situation looks grim for Lasses and Jimmy in this scene from *Trail To Mexico* (1946). The dude outlaw (left) wearing the hat is popular Western heavy, Terry Frost.

222

Tim Holt and Lasses White rode together for eight RKO Westerns. These pictures and six more with Cliff Edwards as sidekick were hurriedly filmed so that Tim could enlist for World War II. He served in the Army Air Corps.

Bandit Trail (10/41)

Dude Cowboy (12/41)

Riding the Wind (2/42)

Land of the Open Range (4/42)

Come on, Danger (6/42)

Thundering Hoofs (7/42)

JIMMY WAKELY series: (Monogram Pictures)

Song of the Range (12/44)

Springtime in Texas (6/45) Tex Ritter's old sidekick, Horace Murphy, is in the cast.

Saddle Serenade (8/45)

Riders of the Dawn (9/45) Horace Murphy is on hand again.

Lonesome Trail (12/45) Horace Murphy, too.

Moon Over Montana (2/46)

West of the Alamo (4/46) Ray Whitley does some singing in this one.

Trail to Mexico (7/46)

Song of the Sierras (11/46)

Rainbow Over the Rockies (2/47)

Six Gun Serenade (4/47)

Song of the Wasteland (5/47)

★   ★   ★

I'm Just a Cowpoke Pokin' Along:

Roundin' Up the Strays

1223-86

226

PAT BRADY

Charles Starrett: *Pat was a member of the Sons of the Pioneers when they were in my series during the late 1930s. I loved Pat's happy-go-lucky good humor. I wish I could have kept that group. Boy, they left a big hole in my pictures when they went over to Republic to join Roy Rogers in his series.*

Rand Brooks: *Pat was a good guy and most easy to work with. I did some of the TV episodes with Roy and Pat. He drove that jeep Nellybelle in the series. I felt Pat had a lot of talent that was not exposed in the Rogers TV series. You don't get a lot of chance to show off your ability in a secondary role in a TV series because they make them so fast. You have to be a damned good actor, though, to work in those quickies because they want it NOW!*

When one thinks of Pat Brady, it is practically impossible not to think of his almost equally well-known jeep Nellybelle. For one hundred half-hour television episodes in the 1950s, Pat and Nellybelle provided the comedy on "The Roy Rogers Show." The popularity of the television series has probably clouded much of the remembrance of Pat's earlier career in films and as a member of the Sons of the Pioneers.

Pat was born on December 31, 1914, in Toledo, Ohio. His real name was Robert Ellsworth Patrick Aloysious O'Brady. He was the only child of John and Lucille O'Brady, who were vaudeville performers. Their act consisted of music, dancing, and comedy. Pat's father was a Toby clown and served as an inspiration for Pat years later when he became a comic sidekick in Western films.

Traveling constantly around the country and watching his parents and other vaudeville acts per-

form every day, young Bob (as he was known then) soon acquired a love for show business that propelled him onto the stage. At the tender age of four he performed in "Mrs. Wiggs of the Cabbage Patch." From then on he was hooked for life on show business.

When Bob was twelve years old, his parents separated and he went to live in California with his father. During his teen years he became a proficient bass player and was drawn to pop and jazz music. By 1935 he and his father were playing in a quartet in a small club in Sunset Beach, California.

One night a fellow in a hunting outfit came in for a drink and listened to their music. He later identified himself as Len Slye and told Bob that he was a member of the Sons of the Pioneers, a Western musical group that was beginning to make a reputation for itself. Bob's father suggested that Len bring the Pioneers to the club, which he did a few weeks later.

Then fate took over. In 1937 Len Slye received a contract from Republic Pictures to star (under the name of Roy Rogers) in a singing cowboy film series. Roy, who was under contract to Columbia Pictures at the time as a member of the Sons of the Pioneers, needed a replacement so that he could accept the Republic contract. He remembered Bob Brady and felt that Bob would fit into the Pioneers group very well. Bob agreed, and a new Pioneer was born. It was at this point in time that Bob Brady became Pat Brady. One Bob—Bob Nolan—was felt to be enough in the musical group. Pat Brady became a member of the Sons of the Pioneers on October 16, 1937, and remained with them for much of his show business career.

From 1937 until 1941, the Pioneers were regular cast members of the Charles Starrett Columbia Pictures series. This aspect of Pat's work with the Pioneers was particularly appealing to him, since he had always had a desire to get into motion pictures. Pat's first film in the Starrett series was *Outlaws of*

227

The Sons of the Pioneers of the early 1940s. From left to right: Bob Nolan, Tim Spencer, Lloyd Perryman, Karl Farr, Pat Brady, and Hugh Farr.

the Prairie, which was released in December of 1937. Because of his natural comic bent, Pat was soon providing comedy bits in the Starrett pictures. He was not a sidekick, as such, but within the confines of the Pioneers' contribution to the films, he was able to establish himself as the comical character. The Starrett films proved to be an excellent training ground for Pat's later emergence as a cowboy sidekick for Roy Rogers.

In 1941 Republic Pictures was able to lure the Sons of the Pioneers away from Columbia so that they could join Roy Rogers in his series. It was a good move for everyone except Charles Starrett. The Pioneers remained with Roy through forty-one pictures, starting with **Red River Valley** in 1941 and concluding with **Night Time in Nevada** in 1948.

Pat left the Pioneers and Roy for three years during World War II. He served much of his tour of duty in Patton's Third Army in France and won cita-

tions for valor and two Purple Hearts. Shug Fisher, bull fiddle player and comic, took Pat's place in the Pioneers and the films during the war.

When sidekick Andy Devine left the Roy Rogers series in 1948, Roy asked his old pal Pat Brady to take over. Pat played the part of Sparrow Biffle starting with **Down Dakota Way** in 1949 and continued in the role through five excellent episodes in the popular series.

His character name of Sparrow Biffle was well-chosen because it suggested the frenetic, birdlike, physical activity that Pat brought to his role. He was always on the move, hopping about excitedly and mugging broadly in his frantic, comic attempts to help Roy. Because of his well-known association with the Sons of the Pioneers, he was often given a novelty song to perform in the features. In a couple of the films Sparrow was the reluctant recipient of the amorous attentions of Mexican chili pepper

Estelita Rodriguez. In **The Golden Stallion** (1949) the concept of the jeep—Nellybelle, the jeep with a mind of its own—was introduced as Pat's means of transportation. Roy liked the idea so much that he revived it for his television series two years later.

Roy commented on the use of the jeep in a 1978 interview with Earl Blair for **Nostalgia Monthly.**

> **Roy Rogers:** *Right after the war, jeeps became very popular. If you had a jeep and would pass a bunch of kids on the corner, they would always point at you. You could see their reaction. I also thought it would give Pat something different, rather than to just get on a horse like all the other sidekicks, if he used a jeep. I rigged the jeep myself. It was my jeep. All my kids learned to drive on that jeep out at the ranch. I cut those doors*

> *on Nellybelle out of airplane aluminum. I had to cut them with an electric hacksaw to make them the shape I wanted them—and it was tough. I rigged a place for a hidden driver, so Nellybelle could run away from Pat or back away and do things in the pictures.*

When the Roy Rogers television series wound down in 1957, Pat knocked around for a while making personal appearances. In 1959 Shug Fisher decided to retire from the Sons of the Pioneers and Pat was asked to return, which he did. He remained with the Pioneers until 1967.

Pat, like Bob Nolan and a few other Pioneers over the years, was known to enjoy a drink or two—or three. As Pat grew older, his drinking became a cause of some concern. An acquaintance of mine commented on the change in Pat's appearance

Roy Rogers and his sidekick Pat Brady pose for this publicity photo from *Bells of Coronado* (1950).

during a Pioneers USO performance in Okinawa around 1965. He related to me that Pat was heavier, "with a red face and nose characteristic of a heavy drinker." Photos that I have seen of Pat during the mid 1960s verify the comment.

In 1967 Pat left the Pioneers and moved from Northridge, California, to Colorado Springs, Colorado, where he became the manager of the Pine Cone Ranch, a guest ranch in the Black Forest area.

Later Pat was associated with the Furniture Ranch, described to me as "a typical cheap furniture store with many sales promotions." Pat made radio commercials for the store and, during at least one promotion, gave rides to children in his jeep Nellybelle from the front of the Furniture Ranch. During this period of the late 1960s, Pat also formed a musical group which played small clubs in the Colorado Springs area. Pat's final employment was with the local Ford dealer.

Pat died on February 27, 1972, in The Ark, a rehabilitation center for alcoholics in Green Mountain Falls. He had admitted himself the day before.

The cause of death was reported to be a heart attack.

At Pat's funeral on March 1, 1972, Hugh Farr and Lloyd Perryman of the Sons of the Pioneers played "Tumbling Tumbleweeds" and "At the Rainbow's End." The minister in his remarks made reference to Pat's drinking problem and gave him credit for admitting himself for rehabilitation. Pat was buried at the Evergreen Cemetery with full military honors. His wife Carol and their son, Pat, Jr., are his survivors.

★　　　★　　　★

PAT BRADY FILMOGRAPHY

ROY ROGERS series: (Republic Pictures)

Down Dakota Way (9/49)

The Golden Stallion (11/49)

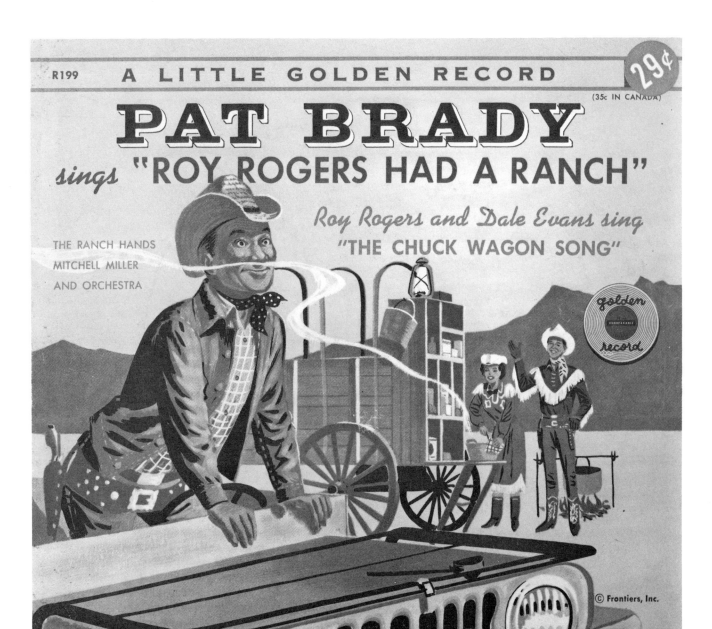

During the popularity of the Roy Rogers television show, Little Golden Records put out this record by Pat.

Bells of Coronado (1/50)

Twilight in the Sierras (3/50)

Trigger, Jr. (6/50)

★   ★   ★

Leo Carrillo has been *the* Pancho to several generations of Cisco Kid fans.

LEO CARRILLO
and
The Other Cisco Kid Sidekicks

Writer William Sydney Porter, better known as O. Henry, created the character of the Cisco Kid in 1907 when he wrote the short story, "The Caballero's Way." Hollywood discovered the character in 1929 and a number of well-known actors portrayed the "Robin Hood of the Plains" through the mid-1950s.

Duncan Renaldo played the Cisco Kid in eight feature films and 176 half-hour television programs.

The first Cisco, Warner Baxter, won an Academy Award for his portrayal in the first sound Western, *In Old Arizona* (1929). Baxter made three Cisco films before he rode off into the sunset and later became the Crime Doctor in a 1940s Columbia series. Baxter was followed in the Cisco Kid series by Cesar Romero, who starred in six episodes; Gilbert Roland, who made another six; and Duncan Renaldo, who made the last eight episodes in the series. Renaldo, of course, went on to become the television Cisco and, consequently, blurred the memories of most members of the audience for the previous Ciscos.

All of the Cisco Kids had sidekicks (of one name or another), who were played by fine character actors such as Chris-Pin Martin, Martin Garralaga, Frank Yaconelli, and Leo Carrillo. Just as Duncan Renaldo finally became the best-known Cisco, Leo Carrillo became the definitive sidekick of the Cisco Kid, the English-fracturing Pancho.

Duncan Renaldo commented on his movie and television sidekick in a 1973 interview.

> *Duncan Renaldo: Leo was reluctant to play Pancho at first because he thought the character would be a buffoon. But I convinced him that it wasn't so and he took it on and started a new career. Do you know that he was seventy-five years old when we were chasing through those rocks? Leo used to say we were nothing more than babysitters for the whole country, but the films had a lot of action and gimmicks and people liked them.*

In an interview with writer Jon Tuska for his book, *The Filming of the West*, Duncan gave a few more details regarding Leo's playing of Pancho:

233

"I wanted Leo Carrillo to play Pancho," Duncan recalled, chuckling. *"Leo refused. 'The part, amigo, is that of a buffoon,' he said. 'I am a serious actor, not a buffoon.' I explained to Leo that he wasn't to play it as a buffoon, but rather as a tragic and humane Sancho Panza. Leo said, 'All right. I do eet. But only once!' We did five features for United Artists and then a hundred seventy-six half-hour episodes for television, many in color so that they are still playing around the country."*

"For all that," I [Tuska] demurred, *"Leo played Pancho as a buffoon."*

"I know," Duncan said, shrugging his shoulders. *"He overdid it, but everyone liked him. His accent was so exaggerated that when we finished a picture no one in the cast or crew could talk normal English anymore."*

Leo Carrillo was born in Los Angeles in 1880. His great-grandfather, Carlos Antonio Carrillo, served as the first governor of California in 1837. Before undertaking a show business career, Leo got his degree from St. Vincent of Loyola. His career then branched in many directions before the role of Pancho was handed to him in the 1940s. He started as a newspaper cartoonist, became a vaudeville dialect comic, and made it to Broadway as an actor by 1915.

Leo made his film debut in **Mr. Antonio** in 1929 and continued in a variety of films such as **Viva Villa** (1934) with Wallace Beery, **The Gay Desperado** (1934) with Ida Lupino, **History Is Made at Night** (1937) starring Charles Boyer, and **Horror Island** (1941) with Dick Foran. Finally, in 1949 Duncan Renaldo and the Cisco Kid came along. Much to Leo's surprise his long previous career was quickly forgotten as he **became** Pancho forevermore.

Oliver Drake was a good friend of Leo Carrillo and happily reminisced with me about some of the private times he spent with Leo during the actor's later years.

Oliver Drake: *I worked with Leo Carrillo in a lot of pictures. In fact, I was more or less Leo Carrillo's father confessor for years. When Leo had problems or things would happen to him, he'd come and cry on my shoulder.*

He had a ranch at Escondido, a beautiful hacienda down there. He had a caretaker who watched over the place while he was away. Leo got his Pancho accent from this old guy who worked for him. You see, Leo spoke English as well as anyone, but he listened to the old Mexican talk, and he picked up the accent from this guy who lived on his ranch until he died. Leo gave him a house to live in, and he stayed there all his life.

Leo and I would go down there occasionally. I played a mandolin, so I'd take my mandolin and we'd get this old guy to play the guitar and sing in Spanish. I knew a lot of Mexican songs. We'd have a ball down at his place.

I would go hunting on Leo's property. He had three or four lakes and in the morning the ducks would fly in. I'd shoot a duck at one of the lakes and then Leo would cook it—I'd clean it and Leo would cook it, just the two of us. Then we'd go and have a ball with this old guy again.

Leo had relatives all over the place and, occasionally, we'd go visit them. They had the darnedest names. Some of them were Mexican and some were Italians. Leo was really a remarkable person and much older that I thought. When he died and they gave his right age, I had no idea he was that old. When he died, he was in his eighties.

In fact, Leo Carrillo was eighty-one when he died of cancer on September 10, 1961.

★   ★   ★

Chris-Pin Martin appeared in **The Cisco Kid** (1931) and **The Return of the Cisco Kid** (1939) with Warner Baxter as Cisco. When Cesar Romero took over as Cisco, Chris-Pin was his sidekick for the six-episode run from 1939 through 1941. In 1947, when Gilbert Roland was riding as Cisco, Chris-Pin returned for two final episodes.

The roly-poly, slow-talking character actor was born in Tucson, Arizona, in 1893 with the name Ysabel Poinciana Chris-Pin Martin Piaz. (Imagine that on a marquee!) His film career ranged far beyond the Cisco Kid films, including roles with many of the top Hollywood stars. Most often his roles were small, but the bear of a man was seldom unnoticed. His film credits include **The Mark of Zorro** (1940) starring Tyrone Power, **The Ox-Bow Incident** (1943) with Henry Fonda, **San Antonio** (1945) starring Errol Flynn, and **Along Came Jones** (1945) with Gary Cooper.

Chris-Pin Martin died of a sudden heart attack on June 27, 1953, while speaking to a Moose Lodge meeting in Los Angeles.

During the radio and television years of "The Cisco Kid" series, it was sponsored by a number of different bread companies, much as "The Lone Ranger" series was. These publicity photos were used to advertise the show and the product during the 1950s. Duncan Renaldo and Leo Carrillo did not play the roles on radio.

Cisco's horse was named Diablo; Pancho's palomino was called Loco. Notice that Cisco's pinto horse here is different from the one pictured previously. Duncan used the two horses interchangeably throughout the series.

Above: Cisco reads some love poetry as his perplexed sidekick, Chris-Pin Martin, looks on in this scene from *Robin Hood of Monterey* (1947).

Right: Martin Garralaga

★   ★   ★

Martin Garralaga was another popular character actor who played a multitude of film roles before and after the Cisco Kid series. He had small roles in such major films as **Message to Garcia** (1936) with Wallace Beery, **For Whom the Bell Tolls** (1943) starring Gary Cooper, and **Ride the Pink Horse** (1947) with Robert Montgomery. To these notable films could be added the titles of dozens of B pictures in which he played similar roles of Spanish or Italian extraction.

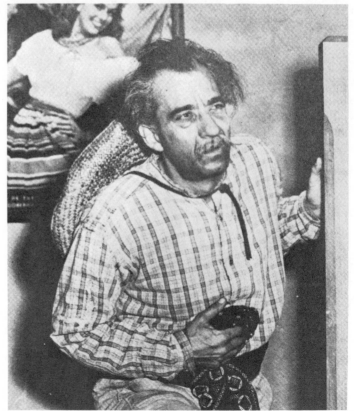

Duncan Renaldo told author Jon Tuska, "Martin was perfect as Pancho. His comedy was very, very human. But he just couldn't stand horses. He was allergic to them." It was for this reason that he quickly left the role of sidekick Pancho and portrayed a variety of roles in seven Cisco Kid films during 1945 and 1946.

★　　　★　　　★

Frank Yaconelli, who was not allergic to horses, was the next sidekick to ride with Gilbert Roland as the Cisco Kid. The diminutive Yaconelli was a master at dialect humor and had practiced his broken English briefly in the late 1930s and early 1940s as a sidekick with two lesser-known Monogram Pictures' cowboys, Jack Randall (Robert Livingston's brother) and Tom Keene. Yaconelli's tenure with Cisco was brief—just three films—and

then he was off to other film roles, most notably *September Affair* (1950) with Joseph Cotton, *Abbott and Costello Meet Captain Kidd* (1953), and his final movie, *Serenade* (1956) with Mario Lanza. Frank Yaconelli died of lung cancer on November 19, 1965.

★　　　★　　　★

THE CISCO KID SIDEKICKS FILMOGRAPHY

CHRIS-PIN MARTIN

CISCO KID series (Warner Baxter): (Fox Film Corp.)

The Cisco Kid (11/31)

The Return of the Cisco Kid (4/39) Cesar Romero and Eddy Waller have roles in the film.

Frank Yaconelli (right) only appeared as Cisco's sidekick in three films. He is seen here with the dashing Gilbert Roland and supporting actor George J. Lewis. The scene is from *South of Monterey* (1946).

Pancho tries out the old egg trick on this youngster with the knowing smile in *The Daring Caballero* (1949). Leo was already wearing his television attire in this feature film.

CISCO KID series (Cesar Romero): *(20th Century-Fox)*

The Cisco Kid and the Lady (1/40)

Viva Cisco Kid (4/40)

Lucky Cisco Kid (6/40)

The Gay Caballero (6/40)

Romance of the Rio Grande (1/41)

Ride On, Vaquero (4/41)

CISCO KID series (Gilbert Roland): *(Monogram Pictures)*

Robin Hood of Monterey (9/47)

King of the Bandits (11/47)

MARTIN GARRALAGA

CISCO KID series (Duncan Renaldo): *(Monogram Pictures)*

The Cisco Kid Returns (2/45)

The Cisco Kid in Old New Mexico (5/45)

South of the Rio Grande (9/45)

CISCO KID series (Gilbert Roland): *(Monogram Pictures)*

The Gay Cavalier (3/46)

South of Monterey (7/46) Frank Yaconelli is also in the cast.

Beauty and the Bandit (11/46) Frank Yaconelli again joins the cast of the film.

Riding the California Trail (1/47) Frank Yaconelli is riding here, too.

FRANK YACONELLI

CISCO KID series (Gilbert Roland): (Monogram Pictures)

South of Monterey (7/46) Martin Garralaga is also in the cast of the film.

Beauty and the Bandit (11/46) Martin Garralaga is again on hand in the picture.

Riding the California Trail (1/47) This is Martin Garralaga's last appearance in a Cisco Kid film.

LEO CARILLO

CISCO KID series (Duncan Renaldo): (United Artists)

The Valiant Hombre (12/48) Lee "Lasses" White has a small role in the picture.

The Gay Amigo (5/49)

The Daring Caballero (6/49)

Satan's Cradle (10/49)

The Girl from San Lorenzo (2/50)

★   ★   ★

Philip N. Krasne presents
The CISCO KID In
"THE GIRL FROM SAN LORENZO"
starring
DUNCAN RENALDO as CISCO
LEO CARRILLO as PANCHO

Original Screenplay by FORD BEEBE   Directed by DERWIN ABRAHAMS
Produced by PHILIP N. KRASNE   Released thru United Artists

Rufe Davis is exuding some of his country bumpkin, tongue-in-cheek humor in this publicity still from 1949.

RUFE DAVIS

When Rufe Davis toured the nation with Gene Autry in 1949, he was billed as "The One-Man Barnyard Symphony," a classy title which signified his extraordinary ability to imitate just about every barnyard critter you might find down on the farm. Down on his family's farm in Mangum, Oklahoma, was where Rufe first displayed his proclivity for this unusual ability. According to his father, Rufe was only five years old when he first started imitating cats, dogs, cows, donkeys, horses, and fowl. Nobody ever taught him how to do it, but his folks used to claim that he could make a noise like an angry rooster that would fool even the hens.

It wasn't until his teen years that Rufe thought about making money with his animal noises and funny songs which he had added to his repertoire. It was during this time that some high school friends urged him to enter an amateur night contest put on by a touring show which had come to Mangum. Much to Rufe's surprise, his imitations and silly songs won first prize—five dollars.

The husky country boy was so astounded that anyone would pay five dollars for his sort of entertainment that he got the notion he should try show business. Rufe felt it certainly had more appeal than working on the farm. With two dollars and fifty cents in his pocket—that was the money his father could spare—he went off to seek his fortune in show business.

Rufe was a shrewd and resourceful young fellow who quickly learned that you had to be seen by the right people if you expected to succeed in show business. The right people in his case were "The Weaver Brothers and Elviry," a highly successful vaudeville act. They signed him to a three-year contract to perform with them in all the top vaudeville theaters in the country, including the Palace Theater in New York.

In 1937 Hollywood beckoned and Rufe heeded the call, eventually making over fifty movies during the next twenty years. He appeared in such popular pictures as *The Big Broadcast of 1938* with Bing Crosby, *Cocoanut Grove* (1938) starring Fred Mac-Murray and Harriet Hilliard, and *Dr. Rhythm*, again with Bing Crosby and another future cowboy sidekick, Andy Devine.

Rufe is probably best remembered for his role of Lullaby in the Three Mesquiteers series. He played the role in fourteen films between 1940 and 1942, succeeding Raymond Hatton as the comic sidekick to the other Mesquiteers. Rufe was the fourth actor to play the part of Lullaby, Guinn "Big Boy" Williams, Syd Saylor, and Max Terhune having earlier dibs on the role. When Rufe first assumed the role, his Mesquiteer pals were Robert Livingston (Stony) and Bob Steele (Tucson). After seven pictures, Tom Tyler took over for Robert Livingston as Stony.

Rufe played the role of Lullaby much in the manner of a young Max Terhune—there was even a physical resemblance. Like Terhune, Rufe's humor was gentle and his occasional songs and barnyard impressions added a welcome light touch to the series. It would probably be stretching a point to say that Rufe Davis had "star quality," but he was a likable actor and entertainer with whom audiences felt comfortable. He was a sidekick who did his job, but one who didn't intrude too much into the star's turf—whether it was in films or personal appearances.

After his stint in the Three Mesquiteers series, Rufe appeared in other films occasionally, but his main work was on radio, television, and personal appearance tours. In 1963 he joined the "Petticoat Junction" television series in the role of Floyd Smoot, a train engineer. Another Gene Autry pal, Smiley Burnette, worked alongside Rufe in the series. Rufe continued in the series through 1968.

Rufe Davis died at the age of sixty-five on December 13, 1974. He was survived by his wife, two sons, and two daughters. A lot of people miss his barnyard symphony.

★　　　★　　　★

RUFE DAVIS FILMOGRAPHY

THREE MESQUITEERS *series (Livingston and Steele):* *(Republic Pictures)*

Under Texas Skies (9/40)

The Trail Blazers (11/40)

Lone Star Raiders (12/40)

Prairie Pioneers (2/41)

Pals of the Pecos (4/41)

Saddlemates (5/41)

Gangs of Sonora (7/41)

THREE MESQUITEERS *series (Steele and Tyler):* *(Republic Pictures)*

Outlaws of the Cherokee Trail (9/41)

Gauchos of Eldorado (10/41)

West of Cimarron (12/41)

Code of the Outlaw (1/42)

Raiders of the Range (3/42)

Westward Ho (4/42) Emmett Lynn has a small role in this film.

The Phantom Plainsman (6/42)

★　　　★　　　★

242

Jimmie Dodd was the last comic sidekick in Republic's Three Mesquiteers series.

Pictured here is the last Three Mesquiteers cast: Tom Tyler, Jimmie Dodd, and Bob Steele.

JIMMIE DODD

From Mesquiteer to Mouseketeer

Jimmie Dodd had an extremely brief career as a cowboy sidekick, appearing in only the last six episodes of the Three Mesquiteers series as Lullaby Joslin. Jimmie, a Cincinnati, Ohio, boy, was the fifth and final actor to assume the role in the long series. His Mesquiteer buddies in these final episodes were Bob Steele (Tucson) and Tom Tyler (Stony).

Much of the steam had gone out of the series by the time Jimmie joined the threesome—forty-six episodes had already been made by Republic Pictures—nevertheless, he did his best to provide a few chuckles and sing some original songs (which he had written himself) as diversion to the action provided by his co-stars. Jimmie had a winsome quality on the screen which audiences found appealing if not overly exciting. He also had the distinction of being one of the youngest sidekicks ever utilized in a Western series, a contrast which probably went unnoticed at the time.

Jimmie appeared in a few pictures before and after the Mesquiteers series, most notably *Flying Tigers* (1942) with John Wayne, *Buck Privates Come Home* (1947) with Abbott and Costello, *Singing Guns* (1950, Jimmie had a bit as a stagecoach driver) starring singer Vaughn Monroe, and *The Winning Team* (1952) with Ronald Reagan. It was Jimmie's last film.

Jimmie Dodd's greatest fame came when he was signed by Walt Disney to be the top Mouseketeer on "The Mickey Mouse Club" television series, a role he played for over 300 daily episodes starting on October 3, 1955. "The Mickey Mouse Club" is generally conceded to be a landmark children's television series, and Jimmie was proud of his association with the Disney organization. When the series concluded, however, he found it difficult to move into new show business areas; he was forever typed as a Mouseketeer.

When the work dried up in Hollywood, Jimmie moved to Hawaii where he had received an offer to do a "Jimmie Dodd Show" on a Honolulu television station. Before the series could get under way, Jimmie died of a sudden heart attack on November 10, 1964. He was only fifty-one years old.

★　　　　★　　　　★

JIMMIE DODD FILMOGRAPHY

***THREE MESQUITEERS* series (Steele and Tyler):**
(Republic Pictures)

Shadows of the Sage (9/42)

Valley of Hunted Men (11/42)

Thundering Trails (1/43)

The Blocked Trail (3/43)

Santa Fe Scouts (4/43)

Riders of the Rio Grande (5/43)

★　　　　★　　　　★

Buddy Ebsen (as Muscles Benton) seems to be losing the battle with a recalitrant mule in this scene from the Rex Allen film, *Rodeo King and the Senorita* (1951).

BUDDY EBSEN

Born in 1908 with the moniker Christian Rudolf Ebsen, young Buddy (as he was called) learned to dance with his sister Vilma at his father's dancing school in Florida. Their terpsichorean talent was considerable, but Buddy felt that dancing was too sissified and quit. His real desire was to study medicine and eventually become a doctor. Family financial problems, however, put a crimp in these plans and forced him to put on his dancing shoes again and take to the stage with his talented sister.

Together Buddy and Vilma Ebsen eventually danced their way to Broadway, appearing in **Whoopee** with Eddie Cantor in 1928. In 1932 they were a sensation in the musical revue **Flying Colors** with Clifton Webb and Imogene Coca. Their big number in the show was "A Shine on Your Shoes." For many years their comedy-dance act was featured in the famous **Ziegfeld Follies.** Vilma eventually tired of the strenuous life of a Broadway dancer and retired.

When Hollywood started producing lavish musicals in the 1930s, Buddy headed West. He was featured in such productions as **Broadway Melody of 1936** with Jack Benny and Eleanor Powell, **Captain January** (1936) with Shirley Temple, **Banjo On My Knee** (1937) with Barbara Stanwyck and Joel McCrea, and **My Lucky Star** (1939) with Sonja Henie.

The 1940s proved to be a fairly dry period for Buddy in Hollywood, so he headed back to Broadway, appearing in a revival of the musical **Show Boat** in 1946. With his career going in no particular direction, Buddy must have been pleased when the opportunity to play Rex Allen's cowboy sidekick came along in 1950.

Buddy only made five pictures with Rex, the Arizona singing cowboy, but his countryfied, loose-jointed, laid-back performances made him very appealing to audiences. He could handle a silly, slapstick scene when he had to, but generally he played his sidekick role as a warm, friendly uncle type of character who talked softly and had a twinkle in his eye.

Buddy was especially appealing in scenes with children. In **Silver City Bonanza** (1951) he has several comical and tender scenes with a little girl named Suzi. At one point Buddy pretends to be a doctor so that he can treat the little girl's "sick" doll. He has another warm, funny scene in which he plays "pretend baseball" with a young boy. In a birthday party scene he dances humorously with Suzi in a manner which is reminiscent of his famous dance with Shirley Temple in **Captain January.**

Buddy's amiable uncle characteristics were very endearing, but they somewhat diminished his effectiveness in action scenes. He didn't appear too comfortable in the fisticuff scenes and shoot outs. In fact, he sometimes arrived on the scene just a bit too late to participate in the action.

Buddy had a different character name in each episode, although the roles were played about the same. His character names suggested the comical aspect of his roles. He was Homer Oglethorpe in **Under Mexicali Star** (1950), Happy Hooper in **Thunder in God's Country** (1951), and Snooper Trent in **Utah Wagon Train** (1951).

When his stint in the Rex Allen series ended, Buddy dropped from sight until Walt Disney's Davy Crockett television episodes in 1954. Surprisingly, Buddy was considered for the title role until the Disney staff noticed young Fess Parker in the science fiction picture **Them!** (1954). Fess got the Crockett part and Buddy was a sidekick again in the colorful role of George Russel. In his book, **The Disney Films,** Leonard Maltin comments on Buddy's playing of the George Russel role:

> Buddy Ebsen provided a perfect counterpart for Parker's dry, understated manner with his affable and often boisterous performance as Georgie Russel. It is his exuberance, not Parker's, that puts over a scene, such as the one

where the two scouts save some British soldiers from an Indian ambush by giving the appearance of having the redskins "surrounded," purely by verbal tricks.

The tremendous popularity of the three one-hour television episodes of Davy Crockett caught Disney off guard. Walt Disney commented later: "We had no idea what was going to happen to 'Crockett'. Why, by the time the first show finally got on the air, we were already shooting the third one and calmly killing Davy off at the Alamo. It became one of the biggest overnight hits in TV history, and there we were with just three films and a dead hero."

Riding on the crest of the Crockett phenomenon, the Disney studio edited the three television episodes into a theatrical feature called **Davy Crockett, King of the Wild Frontier** (1955). Two more television episodes were also edited into a feature and released to theaters in 1956 under the title **Davy Crockett and the River Pirates.** The two films were extremely successful in movie theaters even after the television exposure ("Thrill to Davy Crockett on the giant movie screen") and added millions to the Disney coffers.

In April of 1983 the Associated Press reported that at a dinner for Queen Elizabeth II at 20th Century-Fox Studios, two old friends met after several years apart: Fess Parker and Buddy Ebsen. The AP stated:

> *The two lanky actors were sidekicks in one of early television's most sensational programs, the Davy Crockett series on the Walt Disney show in 1954. Parker played Crockett, the man who created a craze for coonskin hats, and Ebsen was George Russel.*
>
> *After a happy reunion, Ebsen said, "When I was working with Fess I never had to worry about a double chin. Fess was one actor I always looked up to."*
> *Ebsen is 6-foot-3, but Parker is 6-foot-5.*

After the success of the Crockett films, Buddy concentrated primarily on television for the remainder of his career. He worked for Walt Disney again when he played Sheriff Matt Brady in the "Corky and White Shadow" serial that was featured on the "Mickey Mouse Club" television series. "Northwest Passage" was a one-year series (1958-1959) about the search for an inland waterway to enable boats to cross the breadth of America. Buddy played an Indian fighter friend of Major Robert Rogers, played by Keith Larsen in the series.

In 1962 Buddy struck oil in the hit television series "The Beverly Hillbillies." The series ran for nine years and was at the top or in the top ten of the ratings for most of its run. Ebsen played Jed Clampett, the widower patriarch of the Clampett clan—a good-hearted group of backhills rustics who adjust to their new Beverly Hills abode with more aplomb than their pseudo-sophisticated neighbors adjust to them.

When the "Beverly Hillbillies" series retired to rerun heaven, Buddy segued into an entirely different image in the television series "Barnaby Jones." Buddy played an elderly, retired private detective who returns to active duty when his son is murdered. After capturing his son's killer, Barnaby decides to remain active in the pursuit of wrongdoers. Utilizing his home crime laboratory and super powers of deduction which would rival Sherlock Holmes', Barnaby Jones remained a popular television private eye from 1973 until the late '70s.

Buddy Ebsen's career has spanned over fifty years and is still going as of this writing. In early 1984 he made a guest star appearance in a multi-episode story on "The Yellow Rose" television series. From young hoofer to cowboy sidekick to Beverly Hillbilly to private eye, Buddy Ebsen has retained his homespun, Uncle Buddy, comfortable-as-an-old-shoe ambience that has always been his trademark as a performer. It has brought him millions of fans and made him a millionaire.

★   ★   ★

BUDDY EBSEN FILMOGRAPHY

REX ALLEN series: *(Republic Pictures)*

Under Mexicali Stars (11/50)

Silver City Bonanza (3/51)

Thunder in God's Country (4/51)

Rodeo King and the Senorita (6/51)

Utah Wagon Train (10/51)

DAVY CROCKETT series (Fess Parker): *(Buena Vista)*

Davy Crockett, King of the Wild Frontier (6/55)

Davy Crockett and the River Pirates (7/56)

With nary an outlaw in sight, the rodeo king and his senorita can relax for a few moments. Pictured (left to right) are Buddy Ebsen, Bonnie DeSimone, Mary Ellen Kay, and Rex Allen.

Gene is attempting to reassure crippled jockey John Duncan that he will be able to ride again. William Henry and Sterling "Droopy Sterns" Holloway lend moral support to Gene's efforts in this scene from *Trail to San Antone* (1947)

"Well, let's see. They might have gone that way, but, then again, they might have gone this way," Pokey seems to be drawling as the impatient Gene Autry and the Cass County Boys stand in frustration. The scene is from *Twilight on the Rio Grande* (1947).

STERLING HOLLOWAY

Sterling Holloway's cowboy sidekick screen presence was that of a woebegone, foggy-voiced wimp in Gene Autry's last five pictures for Republic Studios. Holloway was, in fact, not really a sidekick in the pictures; he was just assigned the task of the comic relief between the songs and action. Saddled with such character names as Pokey, Droopy, and Nelson "Nelly" Bly, he was hard-pressed to create a character unlike the screen presence described above. Sterling's frail features also mitigated against the likelihood of his grabbing a six-gun and

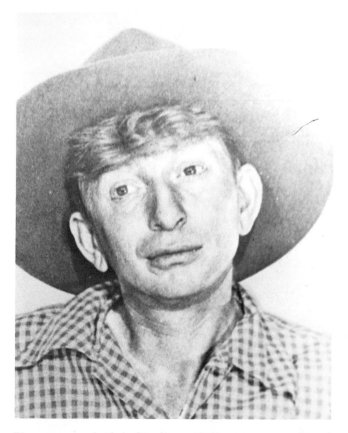

The wan, wistful Sterling Holloway meandered through five Gene Autry features in the the mid-1940s.

participating in a high-noon shoot out. Neither was he likely to lead the way into a barroom brawl. He might, however, be found under a table during such goings on. Unfortunately, it can also be said that few performers have looked more ridiculous astride a horse. As one can gather from these comments, Sterling Holloway looked totally out of place in Westerns—as, indeed, he was.

Born in 1905 in Cedartown, Georgia, Sterling went to New York while still a teen-ager and studied acting at Sargent's Dramatic School. In the mid 1920s he worked alongside such future giants of the theatre as Sanford Meisner and Lee Strasburg in several successful productions of the **Garrick Gaieties.** These musical-comedy revues were very popular and helped Sterling to gain a quick reputation as a top performer. Two musical standards by Lorenz Hart—"Manhattan" and "Mountain Greenery"—were first introduced by Sterling when he was barely in his twenties.

A long career in Hollywood followed, both in silent and sound pictures. He quickly became typed in films as either a bumpkin or eccentric. Then, too, the characters he was given to play usually possessed either a frenetic or lethargic demeanor within their mundane sameness. Sterling once commented, "I delivered so many telegrams and jerked so many sodas I got tired of it." Fed up with Hollywood, he returned to live theatre in California, performing regularly at the Pasadena Playhouse and the Los Angeles Civic Light Opera.

Sterling Holloway's voice is probably more recognized than his face due to his frequent work with the Walt Disney Studio. His distinctive, foggy voice was noticed by the Disney organization in the early 1940s and was subsequently used often in their animated productions. Sterling's voice emanated from the stork which delivered the baby elephant in **Dumbo** (1941); he served as the narrator in **The Three Caballeros** (1945) and "A Fairy Tale with Music" in **Make Mine Music** (1946); his voicing of the coy Cheshire Cat in *Alice in Wonderland* (1951) and his singing of "Jabberwocky" were particular delights with film audiences; and his Ben the mouse saved many of Ben Franklin's inventions in the featurette, *Ben and Me* (1954). In *The Jungle Book* (1967) he hissed the voice of Kaa the hypnotic snake. In addition to the Disney voices, Sterling provided the voice-overs for a multitude of television commercials through the years.

Sterling Holloway has been semi-retired now for many years. At last report he was living in South Laguna, California, amid a valuable collection of paintings that he acquired throughout his career. For Sterling his paintings are a love, hobby, and investment.

Sterling never married. He explained to Richard Lamparski, tracer of lost celebrities, "that he never married because he does not feel lacking in anything and doesn't wish to disturb his pattern of life." Sterling hasn't expressed a desire to make any more Westerns either.

★   ★   ★

STERLING HOLLOWAY FILMOGRAPHY

GENE AUTRY series: (Republic Pictures)

Sioux City Sue (11/46)

Trail to San Antone (1/47)

Twilight On the Rio Grande (4/47)

Saddle Pals (7/47)

Robin Hood of Texas (7/47)

Gene doesn't appear to be taking Droopy's extended-finger-warning too seriously in this scene from *Robin Hood of Texas* (1947).

PAUL HURST

You're safe, Paul. Two-gun Monte Hale won't let anything happen to his sidekick.

Paul Hurst was a true Westerner, born and raised on the Miller and Lux Ranch in Tulare County, California, in 1888. He got his theatrical start painting scenery as part of a backstage crew. Eventually, he forsook scenery paint for grease paint and started "trodding the boards" as an actor.

Never the leading man type in appearance or demeanor, Paul was always cast in character parts even as a young man. He had a face which could register sinisterness and humor with equal aplomb, and so his roles varied greatly over the years.

By 1911 he was active in silent films as an actor, writer, and director. Preferring to free lance, he found work at most of the movie studios during the silent era and built a solid reputation for his work

in front of the camera as well as behind it.

As sound films came on the scene in the 1930s, Hurst gradually restricted his movie work to acting. He had a small but impressive screen moment as a Yankee looter who encounters a ferocious Scarlett O'Hara in *Gone With the Wind* (1939). In 1943 his hangman's role in *The Ox-Bow Incident* was a chillingly memorable characterization amid a plethora of outstanding roles by such stellar actors as Henry Fonda, Dana Andrews, and Anthony Quinn. In John Wayne's *Angel and the Badman* (1947) Hurst played a crotchety old rancher who refuses to give the Quakers of the story any water, although he has plenty for himself. Gunfighter Wayne causes him to see the error of his ways in a series of scenes which

253

run a wide range of emotions and ultimately touch the heartstrings. Hurst was rightfully proud of his work in this popular film. It was shortly after Republic's **Angel and the Badman** that Hurst was asked by the studio to join the Monte Hale Western series as a comic sidekick.

Hurst's sidekick portrayal bore a similarity to those of Raymond Hatton and Eddy Waller, although he didn't have the flair and flamboyance that either of these other sidekick practitioners would often display. Like Waller and Hatton (in his later films) Paul Hurst did not usually go for belly laughs in his sidekick roles; he appeared to be content with chuckles. It might be added that the scripts did little to help him in the comedy department, and he seemed to be only occasionally inspired to improvise on his own. He chose the character actor approach to his roles rather than the buffoonish slapstick technique (which was to his credit), but in the process he lost character definition.

He was also hampered in making a strong impression because he played a different character in each Monte Hale film. Hatton and Waller—to continue the comparison a little further—became known to fans as Sandy Hopkins and Nugget Clark through their role names, even though their character's responsibilities would generally change with each film. Hurst was never able to establish name identification with the film audience. Sad to say, Paul Hurst, a very competent character actor, might well qualify as the least remembered of the cowboy sidekicks who were around for a number of years.

After the Monte Hale series ran its course, Hurst continued in pictures, playing a variety of small character parts. His last film was John Ford's **The Sun Shines Bright** in 1953. Paul Hurst died in Hollywood on February 27, 1953. His death was ruled a suicide by the police who conducted an investigation.

★   ★   ★

PAUL HURST FILMOGRAPHY

MONTE HALE series: (Republic Pictures)

Under Colorado Skies (12/47)

California Firebrand (4/48)

Son of God's Country (9/48)

Prince of the Plains (4/49)

Law of the Golden West (5/49)

Outcasts of the Trail (6/49)

South of Rio (7/49)

San Antone Ambush (10/49)

Ranger of the Cherokee Strip (11/49)

Pioneer Marshal (11/49)

Vanishing Westerner (3/50)

The Old Frontier (7/50)

The Missourians (11/50)

★   ★   ★

A disgruntled Paul Hurst is obviously not looking forward to the gunfight that Monte Hale is preparing for in this scene from *California Firebrand* (1948).

GORDON JONES

Gordon Jones entered the cowboy sidekick ranks rather late in the genre's existence. His first opportunity was as I.Q. Barton in Rex Allen's first film, **The Arizona Cowboy** (1950). After that picture Gordon went to the Roy Rogers series for six films in 1950 and 1951. Then it was all over. Television's emergence caused the field of B Western films to thin out rather drastically, reducing the opportunities for sidekicks, and Gordon Jones moved on to other types of roles.

Gordon Jones made a successful career out of playing simple-minded oafs.

Jones played the character of Splinters McGonigle in the Rogers films, and he acted the role in the same manner as he had played most of his film roles—as a big, dumb oaf. This appraisal of his stock character is not meant to be a put-down. Gordon had mastered his blustery, befuddled, hulk-of-a-man character until he had the role down pat. His round Irish face was a study in total, incomprehensible blankness, as if he didn't understand what was happening (a not uncommon situation), or it was beaming brightly from ear to ear in a silly-ass, goofy grin. He was lovable, though, in a manner similar to a big, floppy-eared puppy dog. He was also delightful performing with children because he was like a big, overgrown child himself.

What worked against Gordon's character in the Roy Rogers series was that he was too simple-minded. It was inconceivable that a smart cowboy like Roy Rogers (with important jobs such as Indian agent, federal marshal, and government spy smasher) would pal around with and give considerable responsibility to a guy who obviously had a few screws missing or at least loose. Granted the B Western scripts were not to be taken too seriously, but even the youngest buckaroos in the audience could see the disasters which lay ahead for Roy when he sent Splinters out to complete a task.

Gordon Jones was fortunate that he joined the Roy Rogers series during the time when the films were well-budgeted, in color, and were directed by action ace, William Witney. As a result, several of the films are probably among the most fondly remembered by Roy's fans. **Trigger, Jr., North of the Great Divide,** and **Trail of Robin Hood** certainly fall into this category.

Born in 1911 in Alden, Iowa, Gordon Jones was a football player (as one would suspect) while attending UCLA. Prior to entering films he sold radio advertising and did sports announcing. Among his early films were **Out West with the Hardys** (1938) in which he played a handsome cowboy-hero type with no oafishness; the popular serial, *The Green Hornet* (1940), in which he played Britt Reid, the title character; and an early PRC drama entitled *I Take This Oath* (1940). He had supporting roles in such major productions as *My Sister Eileen* (1942) with Rosalind Russell, and *Flying Tigers* (1942) starring John Wayne. Upon his return from service in World War II, he played featured roles in *The Wistful Widow of Wagon Gap* (1947) with Abbott and Costello, *Foreign Affair* (1948) with Jean Arthur and Marlene Dietrich, and many other films.

After the Roy Rogers films, Gordon had supporting roles in several television series. He played a dumb cop in "The Abbott and Costello Show" (1952); he was Professor Ray McNulty's none-too-bright friend on "The Ray Milland Show" (1953-1954); he played Mitzi Green's stuntman boy friend, Hubie Dodd, in the short-lived "So This Is Hollywood" (1955); and he was Butch during the 1959-1960 season of "The Adventures of Ozzie and Harriet."

Gordon Jones died in 1963. He had a long career in show business even if his range of characterizations was, with few exceptions, rather narrow. His very brief cowboy sidekick experience will likely be remembered only as a footnote to his many other roles.

★   ★   ★

GORDON JONES FILMOGRAPHY

REX ALLEN series: *(Republic Pictures)*

The Arizona Cowboy (4/50)

ROY ROGERS series: *(Republic Pictures)*

Trigger, Jr. (6/50) Pat Brady is also in the cast.

Sunset in the West (9/50)

North of the Great Divide (11/50)

Trail of Robin Hood (12/50)

Spoilers of the Plains (2/51)

Heart of the Rockies (3/51)

Below: Roy seems a little concerned that Penny Edwards is paying too much attention to Splinters in this scene from *Sunset in the West* (1950).

PINKY LEE

Pinky Lee was Roy Rogers' final feature film sidekick, appearing in Roy's last three episodes for Republic Pictures in 1951. It might be added that Pinky Lee was not only the last, but probably the least of Roy's sidekicks. When compared with such greats as Gabby Hayes, Smiley Burnette, and Andy Devine, Pinky's frantic antics, uncontrolled mugging, and slushy, lisping voice—straight from his vaudeville/burlesque/kiddie TV background— seem almost totally incongruous.

Even if one grants that Roy's sidekicks were not as good after Andy Devine left the series in 1948, Pinky makes those successors, Pat Brady and Gordon Jones, look very good by comparison. Pinky just looked and acted out of place in a Western film— much in the way Wally Vernon and Frank Mitchell did. All three of these tenderfeet looked uncomfortable in the wide open spaces and seemed to be craving the noisy familiarity of a New York street corner—with a hotdog vendor close by.

It should be quickly noted, however, that it wasn't Pinky's fault that he was not very successful as a cowboy sidekick. After all, he was only doing the type of zany comedy that he had been doing successfully for decades. Republic Pictures knew what it was getting when he was hired.

Pinky was born Pinkus Leff in 1916. The trademark Pinky Lee lisp was inherited, according to Lee. All of his cousins for generations has the lisp. When Pinky was only five years old, he started taking singing, dancing, and xylophone lessons. By the time he was thirteen he was in Gus Edwards' "School Days," a famous vaudeville act which toured the country for years. During the 1930s Pinky was in Harold Minsky's burlesque shows, the top spot at Earl Carroll's famous Hollywood theatre-restaurant, and he appeared in the 1945 movie, *Earl Carroll's Vanities.* Although Pinky only made a few films, *Lady of Burlesque* (1943) with Barbara Stanwyck would probably be ranked his best. He played a top banana comic in the picture.

When television came along in the late 1940s, Pinky quickly jumped on board. He performed his vaudeville/burlesque routines on "Hollywood Premiere," a short-lived TV show on NBC in Hollywood in 1949. In April of 1950 NBC starred him in "The Pinky Lee Show," a loosely structured situation comedy set in a vaudeville theatre. Again he was able to do his old routines within the framework of the show. The program was done live in Hollywood and kinescoped for the rest of the country. The success of "The Pinky Lee Show" resulted in the offer to do the Roy Rogers films. It must have seemed like a good idea at the time.

After his three films with Roy in 1951—*In Old Amarillo, South of Caliente,* and *Pals of the Golden West*—Pinky went on to continued popularity in television. From 1951 through 1953 Pinky co-starred in NBC's "Those Two," an entertaining fifteen-minute situation comedy with music each Monday, Wednesday, and Friday from 7:30 to 7:45 p.m. Vivian Blaine and Martha Stewart each served a year as the female half of "Those Two."

Starting in 1954 Pinky devoted his TV efforts almost exclusively to an afternoon and Saturday morning children's show. Loved by kids and hated by parents and critics, the program was almost totally non-stop mayhem with Pinky leading the way at a madman's pace. As writer Gary Grossman comments in his book, *Saturday Morning TV:*

> From the moment he would burst a balloon and sing the lyric, "Yoo Hoo, It's me," he'd be on the move. First he'd dance, then he'd romp through the audience. He seemed to pause for breath only when Molly Bee or Jymmey Shore sang a song or Barbara Luke or Jimmy Brown performed an act. Whether he was supervising "Game Show" or performing in a skit, Lee was in motion. He was loud and physical.

In 1955 Pinky collapsed on the air as a result of a bad sinus condition and had to quit the show. Pinky told writer Grossman, "I was being poisoned from a nasal drip." After a year or so in the dry air of Arizona, Pinky returned to Los Angeles and, he hoped, his television career. Such was not to be the case. He found that his old show was cancelled for good, and that there were no new offers forthcoming. His own idea for a new show, "The Perils of Pinky," never got off the ground with network executives. He did a few guest appearances and was a temporary host replacement on a kids' show, but that was about it.

Then in 1965 ABC thought there might be some mileage in Pinky's old format and decided to put him on at 7:30 in the morning on weekdays. The air time was wrong and the show did not work. Neither Pinky nor the network was happy, and soon the show was gone from the air.

While Pinky still works occasionally these days, he is mostly living in retirement in California. He and his wife Bebe have two children and a grandson. None of the offspring, fortunately, has inherited the Lee lisp.

★   ★   ★

PINKY LEE FILMOGRAPHY

ROY ROGERS series: (Republic Pictures)

In Old Amarillo (5/51) Pat Brady has small roles in these three films with Pinky Lee. He also sings as a member of the Roy Rogers musical group.

South of Caliente (10/51)

Pals of the Golden West (12/51)

In Old Amarillo (1951) was the first of three films in which Pinky Lee was Roy Rogers' sidekick.

TOM LONDON

Sunset Carson: I had the pleasure of working with Tom London. I killed him a few times and then he turned out to be my comedian. He was a terrific, terrific comedian and a wonderful person to work with.

*Pat Buttram: He was a great actor. Tom was a lot better than the parts he had. They'd have him doing a storekeeper and things like that. We were doing a picture—about the second or third one I did with Gene Autry—and there was a great part in it with a big death scene. Tom played this part in **Riders in the Sky,** and he was really the star of that picture. I think it was the best acting he did in his whole career because they gave him a part he could act in.*

Jock Mahoney: I had the privilege of calling Tom my friend. He was gentle, kind, and considerate. I loved him.

Tom London hardly qualifies as a cowboy sidekick, since he appeared as one so rarely. In literally dozens of Westerns he usually played the honest town sheriff who welcomed the assistance of the cowboy hero and his sidekick in cleaning up the outlaw gang that was terrorizing his town.

Once in a while, though, Tom took out his store-bought teeth, grew some chin whiskers, and played the comical "oldtimer" sidekick—most notably in a few of the Sunset Carson films for Republic Pictures in the mid-1940s. In fact, Tom was in practically all of the Republic Sunset Carson films, but his roles varied from outlaw to sheriff to sidekick; you never knew until the picture started what type of role Tom London might be playing this time. He and heroine Peggy Stewart (who was also in most of Sunset's pictures) are also credited with

Peggy Stewart is still a beautiful heroine today. This photo was taken by the author at the 1982 Memphis Film Festival.

helping the untrained Sunset to speak his lines in as convincing a manner as possible. They, as viewers of Sunset's films know, had only limited success at this task. Sunset, though, through sheer physical presence and his ability to handle action scenes, managed to become a popular Western star.

Tom London was born in Louisville, Kentucky, on

259

Tom London doesn't look too happy about the parrot on his shoulder in this scene from *Red River Renegades* (1946). That young fellow with the boyish grin spread all over his face is, of course, the star of the picture, Sunset Carson.

August 24, 1889. His real name was Leonard Clapham, which he used professionally from the time he began his picture career in 1917 until the mid-1920s. During the silent film era and on through sound pictures of the '30s, '40s, and '50s, Tom worked regularly in many features and serials. He appeared in featured and small roles with just about every cowboy star who roamed the celluloid range from 1917 to the end of the B Western era in the mid-1950s.

Tom played such humorous codgers as Utah in *The Cherokee Flash* (1945), Bandy McCabe in *Days of Buffalo Bill* (1946), Dakota in *Alias Billy the Kid* (1946), and Old Pop Underwood in *Red River Renegades* (1946)—never repeating a role, but they could all be interchangeable. The films listed all starred Sunset Carson. Peggy Stewart was the heroine in all of these films with the exception of *The Cherokee Flash,* which had popular Linda

Sterling for the feminine lure.

When much of the movie work started to dry up in the 1950s, Tom continued acting in many television series. He remained fairly active in occasional television and movie roles until just a few years before his death in 1963. One of his last films was *The Saga of Hemp Brown* (1958) starring Rory Calhoun.

In "An Interview with Peggy Stewart" by Minard Coons (which appeared in *Western Corral,* number one) Peggy reminisced briefly about her friends and co-stars, Tom London and Sunset Carson.

Peggy Stewart: Sunset I just adored....Tom London and I were very close to Sunny and had many experiences teaching him [to act]....It was just like papa and daughter. Tommy only lived about eight blocks from me with his

sister, Anita. I used to go down there and pick the plums from the trees and, of course, I don't care too much for cooking, but Anita used to jelly them and jam them (or whatever you do with them) and give me some of them. Tommy and I were forever off to local rodeo grounds or local theatres in town on Saturdays when they had matinees and [we were] doing personal appearances together. We loved each other, so I guess it reeked from both of us. I guess people liked to see us together. In fact, there were a couple of times that people thought that Tom and I were father and daughter. We helped, as I said, with Sunset. He was like our adopted child.

★　　　★　　　★

TOM LONDON FILMOGRAPHY

Since Tom London appeared infrequently as a comic sidekick throughout his long career, it is practically impossible to separate those few roles from his dozens of others. Therefore, only the sidekick roles in the Sunset Carson films are included in the filmography.

SUNSET CARSON series: *(Republic Pictures)*

The Cherokee Flash (12/45)

Days of Buffalo Bill (2/46)

Alias Billy the Kid (4/46)

Red River Renegades (8/46)

Old Tom is sidekicking with Monte Hale in this tense scene from *Last Frontier Uprising* (1947).

7/83
To David.
Best Wishes.
Frank Mitchell

Frank Mitchell played the role of Cannonball in seven Bill Elliott-Tex Ritter Westerns.

FRANK MITCHELL

Frank Mitchell was a comic sidekick in only one Western series, the Bill Elliott-Tex Ritter series made at Columbia Pictures during 1941-'42. I had the opportunity to meet and talk with Frank at the 1983 Western Film Fair in Charlotte, North Carolina. I'll let him speak for himself about his career.

Frank Mitchell: I was born in New York City on May 13, 1905. I learned to be an acrobat at the YMCA on the East Side of New York. About 1916 when I was only eleven years old, I started entering Charlie Chaplin imitation contests, which were popular then in all the theaters. I would dress up as Charlie the Tramp and do an imitation of him, using a lot of slapstick and acrobatic bits that I created.

An acrobat who had a big Arabian acrobatic troup saw me at one of these Chaplin contests and asked if I would like to be in an acrobatic act in vaudeville; he said that he'd train me for the act. I told him that I'd love it, and that's how I got started in show business.

*We toured all over the country doing a comedy acrobatic act. I was only twelve years old when we started. I continued doing vaudeville for many years, by myself and with various partners. When I was twenty-one, I got a fellow by the name of Jack Durant as a partner. We became Broadway favorites in such shows as George White's **Scandals** and Earl Carroll's **Vanities**. We also had a lot of success at the Palladium Theater in London.*

*We made several pictures together such as **The Singing Kid** with Al Jolson and **Stand Up and Cheer** with Shirley Temple. In 1935 Durant and I split up and went*

our separate ways.

In late 1941 an agent friend of mine, Mitch Hamilburg, called and told me that Dub Taylor was going to leave the Bill Elliott-Tex Ritter series at Columbia. Mitch knew that I had created the act of Mitchell and Durant which featured a lot of slapstick comedy and falls— knockabout things like that. He also figured that the fact that I was about the same height as Dub Taylor and because of my background, I'd be a good replacement for him. Mitch submitted my name to Columbia and when they heard my name, they bought me. It wasn't anything that I had to audition for because I was so well-known.

*In my first Elliott-Ritter picture, **Roaring Frontier,** I didn't do any comedy. It was a straight character part of a miner. Towards the end of the picture, you may have noticed, Bill called me Cannonball. That was just to establish that I was the character of Cannonball for the next pictures that I was going to do for them.*

I know there are stories that Bill and Tex weren't too happy to be co-starring in that series, that they both wanted their own starring series. I never heard them say anything to that effect, ever. All I know is that we got along fine, and they didn't mind how much comedy I did in the pictures. They didn't care about how much dialogue I had or how many laughs I got. They figured I wouldn't hurt the pictures and would only help them.

Most of my comic acrobatic bits in the films were improvised on the set. They would ask me if I could do a slip or a fall or come off the horse in a funny way. The comedy bits were developed extempo-

raneously by me. I just made it up as I went along. The producer and director didn't care because they knew I had done all kinds of slapstick and falls. I always created my own slapstick comedy, same as with my act in vaudeville. I had a double that did my fast riding, although I could ride just as good as any stuntman. They never wanted me to do it because they were afraid that I might get hurt and that could stop production on the pictures.

I didn't really observe the other comic sidekicks who were working then in Westerns. I didn't know many of them personally, but they were good comics. I knew Dub Taylor because we were under contract at the same studio, Columbia.

Bill Elliott was a wonderful fellow. Tex was an easygoing person with a slow Texas drawl. He would draw out his dialogue. He'd lengthen his words out and say, "W-e-l-l, h-o-w a-r-e y-o-u t-o-d-a-y, F-r-a-n-k?" When I talked, I talked fast. Somebody in the cutting room told me that I had a little bit of a New York accent. I said, "Naturally, I was born in New York City." Finally, I started to pace myself. I started to imitate Tex, and that's how I got into the character of Cannonball. By imitating Tex, I didn't sound so New Yorkish.

After I finished the Westerns, I did quite a few pictures around Universal and MGM. I did **Neptune's Daughter** with Esther Williams and Red Skelton. Later on I went to work with Skelton in about a dozen of his shows for CBS Television.

Frank Mitchell and author David Rothel pose for the camera at the 1983 Charlotte Western Film Fair.

This looks like a pretty tense moment between Tex Ritter and Cannonball. They are probably vying to see who gets to play the guitar. The scene is from *Bullets for Bandits* (1942).

I was in Scaramouche with Stewart Granger and Advance to the Rear with Glenn Ford. I did many parts over the years at many different studios, working as a free-lance actor.

I finally left show business and went into real estate in Palm Springs, California. When my wife passed away a few years ago, I retired and moved to North Hollywood, where I now live. My two daughters live near me. I sure do enjoy coming to these film festivals.

★   ★   ★

FRANK MITCHELL FILMOGRAPHY

BILL ELLIOTT-TEX RITTER series: (Columbia Pictures)

Roaring Frontier (10/41)

The Lone Star Vigilantes (1/42)

Bullets for Bandits (2/42)

North of the Rockies (4/42)

The Devil's Trail (5/42)

Prairie Gunsmoke (7/42)

Vengeance of the West (8/42)

Horace Murphy and Snub Pollard worked as a sidekick team in a string of Tex Ritter films during the late 1930s.

HORACE MURPHY and SNUB POLLARD

Horace Murphy, joined occasionally by former silent screen comic Snub Pollard, played Tex Ritter's sidekick from 1937 through 1939. Prior to and during his tenure with Tex, Horace rode with Bob Steele, Rex Bell, and Johnny Mack Brown in their Westerns, but only occasionally as a sidekick. Often he would be a sheriff, rancher, or town businessman. You could never be sure what type of character role he would be playing until the picture began—much as in the case of Tom London, another busy character actor. Even in the early Tex Ritter pictures like *Sing, Cowboy, Sing* (1937), Murphy showed up as the town marshal.

After playing sidekick characters with such names as Lucky and Doc, Horace was finally assigned the name of Stubby in the film *The Mystery of the Hooded Horsemen* (1937) and kept that moniker for three films. When *Rollin' Plains* (1938) came along, Horace was given the character name of Ananias for most of the balance of his Tex Ritter pictures. (In some of these early series Westerns there seems to have been little thought given to the recognition value of the character's name.)

Writer John A. Rutherford in his article for *Under Western Skies* entitled "The Pards of Tex Ritter," catches the essence of Horace Murphy's sidekick characterization when he describes Murphy as a "portly, pompous windbag." Murphy was certainly that! A frequent accompaniment to the comic windbag routine was to have Tex give sidekick Horace extraordinary credit for helping in the fights and shoot outs, with Horace eagerly acknowledging his vast importance and then continuing endlessly with a self-serving, exaggerated version of the fracas for any and all bystanders. Murphy certainly never ranked very high among cowboy sidekicks, but he did manage to squeeze a few chuckles out of most film audiences with his whiskey-whining voice and exaggerated self-importance.

Working with Murphy and Tex in many of these films was Snub Pollard of the droopy mustache and

Tex Ritter was one of the most popular singing cowboys of the late 1930s and early 1940s.

hangdog face. Snub, called Pee Wee in most of the Ritter films in which he sidekicked with Murphy, always had the sad facial countenance of a little boy who had just wet his pants and knew he would be scolded. Snub rarely said much; if he did try to utter something, he was usually interrupted by the verbose Murphy. As a result, Snub's performances consisted primarily of pantomine bits and woebegone looks into the camera as Murphy expounded ad nauseam. It is doubtful that the Murphy-Pollard

Horace Murphy is seen here in an early Johnny Mack Brown feature made for Republic Pictures in 1937.

sidekick teaming was missed much when they were dropped from the Tex Ritter films in 1939.

Murphy was born on May 3, 1880, in Finley, Tennessee. He got his show business baptism as a juvenile actor on Mississippi riverboats. Later, when he was grown up, he bought a part-interest in the famous Cottonblossom showboat and was "Captain" for two seasons. After selling out his portion, Murphy started a series of tent shows that toured the South and West. Ending up in Los Angeles, he again sold out and built two hardtop theaters.

By this time (1936) the poverty row movie companies were seeking character actors who would work cheap. Murphy was their man—appearing in a multitude of films for such companies as Colony, Supreme, Principal, and Grand National. While he was Tex's sidekick, he continued acting for these various other studios.

After the Ritter series, he continued in bit and featured roles until the late 1940s. He died on

January 20, 1975, at the age of ninety-four. The venerable old actor may not have been able to look back on a memorable screen career, but he was a cowboy sidekick for a few years, and he could be seen thereafter in the background or over at the corner of the giant screen while the camera focused on the star in the center.

Snub Pollard was an Australian who found his way from Melbourne (where he was born in 1886) to the Hollywood of silent films in 1914. Hal Roach selected him to be one of the original Keystone Cops in 1915, and he supported Harold Lloyd in some of his early "Lonesome Luke" comedy shorts. He later estimated that he made over 250 shorts for Hal Roach and others during the silent film years.

With the coming of sound in 1929, Snub found the going rough in Tinsel Town. He was reduced to bit and small parts throughout the rest of his film career—a career which continued plugging along until his death on January 19, 1962. His last movie role was in **A Pocketful of Miracles** in 1961.

In 1959 Snub appeared with several other oldtimers in a "Cimarron City" television episode. In an interview on the set, he made some observations about his long career.

> *Snub Pollard: I guess I was better at slinging pies than lead. In one role I was to stick up a guy, and I charged in with my gun drawn. The director nearly had a fit. Guess I wasn't holding the shooting iron right.*
>
> *The kids are the best audiences. You can't fool them, but they're your most loyal fans. They'll go anywhere to see you.*

★   ★   ★

HORACE MURPHY FILMOGRAPHY

Horace Murphy appeared in several Western series in a variety of roles. The filmography includes all of the major series in which he appeared, whether as a sidekick or other character.

JOHNNY MACK BROWN series: *(Republic Pictures)*

Undercover Man (9/36)

Gambling Terror (2/37)

Trail of Vengeance (3/37)

Lawless Land (4/37)

Bar Z Bad Men (4/37)

Veteran comedians Hank Mann, Snub Pollard, and Matthew McCue surround Audrey Totter in this scene from a 1959 "Cimarron City" television episode.

It looks as if the whole posse is ready for action in this scene from an early Bob Steele Western. Horace, Steve Clark, and Bob Steele are in the first row.

Boothill Brigade (8/37)

BOB STEELE series: (Republic Pictures)

Sundown Saunders (12/36) This picture was released by Supreme Pictures.

Lightnin' Crandall (3/37)

Gun Lords of Stirrup Basin (5/37)

Doomed at Sundown (7/37)

The Red Rope (7/37)

Colorado Kid (12/37)

Paroled to Die (1/38)

Thunder in the Desert (3/38)

Durango Valley Raiders (8/38)

TEX RITTER series: (Grand National Pictures)

Arizona Days (1/37)

Trouble in Texas (3/37)

Sing, Cowboy, Sing (5/37)

Riders of the Rockies (7/37)

Mystery of the Hooded Horsemen (8/37)

Tex Rides with the Boy Scouts (1/38)

Frontier Town (3/38)

Rollin' Plains (7/38)

Utah Trail (8/38)

TEX RITTER series: (Monogram Pictures)

Starlight Over Texas (9/38)

Where the Buffalo Roam (10/38)

Song of Buckaroo (12/38)

Sundown on the Prairie (2/39)

Rollin' Westward (3/39)

Down the Wyoming Trail (6/39)

★   ★   ★

SNUB POLLARD FILMOGRAPHY

Snub Pollard played bit and sidekick roles in the Tex Ritter series. All of the Ritter films in which Snub appeared are included in the filmography.

TEX RITTER series: (Grand National Pictures)

Headin' for the Rio Grande (12/36)

Arizona Days (1/37)

Hittin' the Trail (4/37)

Sing, Cowboy, Sing (5/37)

Riders of the Rockies (7/37)

Tex Rides with the Boy Scouts (1/38)

Frontier Town (3/38)

Rollin' Plains (7/38)

Utah Trail (8/38)

TEX RITTER series: (Monogram Pictures)

Starlight Over Texas (9/38)

Where the Buffalo Roam (10/38)

Song of the Buckaroo (1/39)

Slim Pickens was a sidekick in the Rex Allen series.

SLIM PICKENS

Roy Rogers: *I thought he was terrific. I would have been proud to have had him as a sidekick. He was funny, and also a good cowboy. He was a heck of a cowboy.*

Rex Allen: *When Slim Pickens was my sidekick in those Republic Westerns, he was actually slim. In fact, we both were.*

Slim Pickens was born in Kingsburg, California, on June 29, 1919. In a 1979 interview with UPI's Vernon Scott, Slim recapped some of the events of his early life.

Slim Pickens: *I got my first horse when I was four years old right here in California's central valley. By fourteen I was riding bareback, saddle broncs, and bulls in the rodeos. My father was against rodeoing and told me he didn't want to see my name on the entry lists ever again. So this old rodeo guy said to use another name. "Why don't you use Slim Pickens, 'cause that's what it's going to be." My real name was Louis Bert Lindley, Jr., and I figured I improved my moniker.*

All that rodeo punishment just conditioned me for what I had to put up with later from movie and TV producers. Hell, I had one side of my body X-rayed after I got throwed one time and it showed I had seventeen broken bones on that side alone. I busted ribs, arms, legs, collarbones, and all the rest. I even broke my back once. But I only had three casts put on them breaks. The rest healed up by theirselves.

Only time I was embarrassed was when a horse kicked me in the head and throwed me into the $2.50 seats at San Francisco's Cow Palace. That rascal kicked me right in the head and they took me to the hospital. The doctor gave me a mirror. I looked at this hole in my head and asked the nurse, "What's that white stuff showing through?" And she said, "That's your skull." Well, hell, I went right into shock. They put thirteen stitches in my head. I told the doc that was unlucky so he put in another one. But I was back in the arena in a clown suit fighting the bulls the next night.

Slim's movie career started in 1945 when he was paid twenty-five dollars to appear in the film **Smoky** starring Fred MacMurray. In the picture Slim rode, as he called it, "a shute-fightin' son-of-a-gun named Sundown." After his brief stint in **Smoky,** he headed back to the rodeo circuit.

It wasn't until 1950 that he got his second chance in films. Director William Keighley saw Slim at a rodeo in Saugus, California, and offered him a screen test. Slim responded by asking, "How much will it cost me?" As he told Vernon Scott:

I couldn't believe it when they said Warner Brothers would pay me for the test. I did the screen test only because I was crippled up from a bull and thought I could make some money while I was healing up.

*They put me in **Rocky Mountain** with Errol Flynn. Spent seven weeks off in Arizona on locations. I couldn't act for damn sure. I felt kinda guilty, like I was stealing their money. I asked myself how long this had been going on. So I got myself an agent and I've been acting ever since. I've been foolin' them now for thirty years and I really mean foolin' 'em.*

In 1951 Slim got a call from Republic Pictures asking if he would take over for Buddy Ebsen as the comic sidekick in Rex Allen's series of Westerns. Slim told Republic he'd be "much obliged to ride with Mr. Allen." For the next two years he toiled on the Republic back lot, turning out eleven features in the popular series.

Slim's sidekick characterization was just an extension of his real life, good-hearted, outgoing, garrulous, gangly, young cowboy self. He essayed his role as none too bright at "book larnin'," but loaded with the knowledge acquired from the school of hard knocks. Slim exaggerated his natural, raspy Western twang and said his dialogue the way he thought Slim Pickens would say it. As Slim put it, "As far as I'm concerned, acting is like a license to steal. I know of no occupation where with less money invested you can make so much money. Hell, an actor will tell you how hard he is working, but you just go and ask him when was the last time he dug ditches or post holes."

After the Rex Allen series shut down, Slim went on to a very successful career as a Western character actor. He worked for the Disney Studio in several pictures: *The Great Locomotive Chase* (1956), *Tonka* (1958), and *Savage Sam* (1963). In *The Big Country* with Gregory Peck, Slim got into an unscheduled fracas with a Brahma bull that knocked his nose out of kilter and required thirty-one stitches. Regarding his battered nose, Slim later commented, "I got it put back in the middle of my face this spring and I figure I'm better looking now. Not much, but every little bit helps."

Slim's most famous role was probably Major King Kong in Stanley Kubrick's satiric *Dr. Strangelove* (1964). Audiences will not soon forget a whooping and hollering Slim riding a nuclear bomb like a bucking bronc as it falls from a B-52 bomber to its target.

PHANTOM Stallion

STARRING
Rex Allen
THE ARIZONA COWBOY
KOKO
THE MIRACLE HORSE
OF THE MOVIES

WITH
SLIM PICKENS · CARLA BALENDA · HARRY SHANNON · DON HAGGERTY

Written by GERALD GERAGHTY
Directed by HARRY KELLER

A REPUBLIC PICTURE

REPUBLIC PICTURES CORPORATION
HERBERT J. YATES, PRESIDENT

"Ride 'em, Cowboy!" If Slim had not been such an excellent rodeo cowboy, you can bet it would be a double on that horse.

Slim commented after the picture was released, "After **Dr. Strangelove,** my salary jumped five times and assistant directors started saying 'Hey, Slim,' instead of 'Hey, you.' "

He had prominent roles in such other popular films as the irreverent Western, **Blazing Saddles** (1974), **White Line Fever** (1975), and **Honeysuckle Rose** (1980)—probably his most tender and moving performance. He co-starred in the picture with Willie Nelson and Dyan Cannon.

Through the years Slim was a guest star on many of the major television series and was a regular in several. He was featured in two action series—"The Outlaws" (1961-1962) and "Custer" (1967). In 1981 he was host of "The Nashville Palace" and became a regular on "Hee Haw" as the comic proprietor of Slim's Bar-B-Que. While working on a short-lived series entitled "Filthy Rich" in 1982, it was discovered that he had a brain tumor.

In August he underwent brain surgery to remove the tumor. According to Slim's daughter, Daryle Ann, "After his recovery from surgery, he went back to work and seemingly was doing great. And all of a sudden he kind of started going downhill." Slim Pickens died on December 8, 1983, at the age of sixty-four. Surviving were his wife, Maggie, two daughters, Daryle Ann and Margaret Lou, and a son, Thom.

The year before his death, Slim was awarded one of the highest honors a cowboy actor can receive. He was inducted into the National Cowboy Hall of Fame in Oklahoma City. The honor was in recognition of his many unforgettable Western film roles and for his true-to-life depiction of the American cowboy in films.

In 1981 Slim commented on the current plight of the Western film: "They're not making many right now, but all it takes is just one good one and they'll come back like 'Gangbusters.' The Western is the closest thing to a fairy tale that we have in this country. It's our heritage. A lot of people still love Westerns."

★   ★   ★

SLIM PICKENS FILMOGRAPHY

REX ALLEN series: (Republic Pictures)

Colorado Sundown (2/52)

The Last Musketeer (3/52)

Border Saddlemates (4/52)

Old Oklahoma Plains (7/52)

South Pacific Trail (10/52)

Old Overland Trail (2/53)

Iron Mountain Trail (5/53)

Down Laredo Way (8/53)

Shadows of Tombstone (9/53)

Red River Shore (12/53)

Phantom Stallion (2/54)

"You'll only find the stolen money over my dead body," said the outlaw chief. It looks as if that's what Syd has done. The scene is from *Thunder Town* (1946).

SYD SAYLOR

Born in the wild West town of Chicago on May 24, 1895, Leo Sailor (as he was known then) never dreamed during his Windy City years that he would eventually make his living riding horses in front of movie cameras. He wanted to be an artist, pursuing his goal at the Chicago Art Institute. After starving as an artist, he thought he might as well see what it would be like starving as an actor.

Syd was never to find out, because success came fairly easily to the young thespian, and after many years of stage work he headed for the silent world of Hollywood in the 1920s. His luck continued and he was hired to make a series of two-reel comedies for Universal. Eventually, Syd was cast in several Westerns during the late 1920s and early 1930s with such stars as Richard Arlen, Gary Cooper, George O'Brien, and Buck Jones. Soon typed as a supporting actor in Westerns, Syd found the work fairly steady and the company pleasant.

Although Syd Saylor was briefly the sidekick for a number of cowboy stars, he will probably be best remembered by Western buffs and be a footnote in Western film histories for the role at which he failed—Lullaby in the first episode of Republic's Three Mesquiteers series. The film, *The Three Mesquiteers* (1936), was a hit with the fans and raked in a lot of coins for Republic, but Saylor's chemistry as a comic relief character was deemed not right in partnership with the lively joshing and jostling of Robert Livingston and Ray Corrigan, the other Mesquiteers. Saylor's bobbing Adam's apple and comic stutter didn't provide the "class" that Republic sought for the series. He was a lightweight comic with little to draw upon other than those two comic gimmicks. As a result, Republic looked elsewhere and found Max Terhune for the Lullaby role, and he was perfect. Max had a bag full of comic tricks to draw upon (see the Max Terhune profile) and, in addition, was able to lend strong acting support to the series—a necessity when sharing the camera lens with such charismatic companions as the handsome Livingston and the flamboyant Corrigan.

After flunking his test as a Mesquiteer, Syd saddled up to ride with Tex Ritter in two of his early Grand National pictures. In his second Ritter film, *Arizona Days* (1937), Syd plays a character called Mr. Hopper. Tex gives him the nickname of Grass. Get it? Clod might have been a more appropriate first moniker, since Syd was given little to do except smile appreciatively as Tex sang and to periodically blow on an old trombone (for no apparent reason other than it was there), scaring animals and probably humans within range of the instrument's blat. There was no comedy written into the script, and Syd seemed little inspired to create any. Syd was a likable character in the film and he did not overplay his limited role; he just was not given much to do.

Syd meandered from one studio to another through the late 1930s and early 1940s, accepting sidekick and smaller roles—whatever came his way. He had small roles in Johnny Mack Brown's *Guns in the Dark* (1937) and *Born to the West* (1937), which also starred Duke Wayne. Singing cowboy Bob Baker also shared the trail with Syd in *Courage of the West* (1937). Syd got third billing with Don Barry in Republic's *Wyoming Wildcat* in 1941.

In 1945 Syd began a four-episode series as the sidekick of Bob Steele. The low-budget series produced by PRC is not well remembered, but it represents Syd Saylor's main stint as a cowboy sidekick. Although he mugged broadly, stuttered, and bobbed his Adam's apple like a jackhammer, Syd did not make a big impression as Steele's pal.

By mid-1946 he was back to small roles in Westerns with such stars as Gene Autry and Charles Starrett. He continued acting in these sometimes minuscule roles in Westerns and other film genres for the rest of his life. Syd Saylor died of a heart attack on December 21, 1962.

★   ★   ★

It is sweet revenge for sidekick Syd as Bob Steele holds the bad guy in this scene from *Thunder Town* (1946).

SYD SAYLOR FILMOGRAPHY

BOB STEELE **series:** *(Producers Releasing Corporation)*

  The Navajo Kid (11/45)

Six Gun Man (2/46)

Ambush Trail (2/46)

Thunder Town (4/46)

Syd rode alongside Buck Jones in *When a Man Sees Red* (1934).

Wally Vernon—the Damon Runyon cowboy sidekick.

WALLY VERNON

Wally Vernon's sidekick career was limited to the series of two cowboy heroes, Don "Red" Barry and Allan Lane, and was divided into two two-year hitches—1943-'44 and 1949-'50. All but two of his Western sidekick films were with Barry, who liked Vernon because he was popular with juvenile audiences and (perhaps even more importantly) because he was shorter than Barry when he wore flat heels.

Vernon looked and sounded totally out of place in Western films. Everything about him bespoke New York, probably Brooklyn. He would have been perfectly at home as one of Damon Runyon's shady, shyster, comic characters in *Guys and Dolls* or any of the other Runyon "Big Apple" stories. When Vernon played a Brooklyn-type tattooed gob in *Sailor's Lady* (1940) with Nancy Kelly, Jon Hall, Joan Davis, and Dana Andrews, he was in his true element. Watching Wally Vernon on the screen, one could detect a slight trace of a less frenetic Curly from The Three Stooges and a smidgen of a less-pugnacious Leo Gorcey from The Bowery Boys.

A former Broadway song and dance man, Vernon reached Hollywood in the mid-1930s and became a popular contract player on the 20th Century-Fox lot, usually appearing in musical comedies. His films included *This Way Please* (1937) with Betty Grable, Buddy Rogers, and Fibber McGee and Molly; *Happy Landing* (1938) with Sonja Henie, Don Ameche, and Ethel Merman; *Kentucky Moonshine* (1938) in which he played Tony Martin's buddy in a feuding hillbillies plot; *Alexander's Ragtime Band* (1938) in which he was a musician in Tyrone Power's ragtime band; and *Sharpshooters* (1938) starring Brian Donlevy and Lynn Bari. This was the first in an intended series depicting the exploits of a newsreel cameraman. Vernon played Donlevy's sidekick in the film.

By the early 1940s Wally Vernon's contract with 20th Century-Fox had been dropped and he was looking for new film work. Through some mysterious, circuitous route he found his way to Republic Studios and the Don "Red" Barry Western series. Their first film together was *Fugitive from Sonora* (1943) in which he played a character called Jackpot Murphy. *Variety* called Vernon's acting "standout."

The second episode, *Black Hills Express* (1943), was probably their best picture together and merits some individual attention. In the film Vernon played a deputy sheriff by the name of Deadeye—an appellation probably pinned on him because of his ineptness with a pistol.

Vernon's sidekick demeanor was variable, depending upon the plot circumstances and the company he was in. With cowboy hero Barry he projected somewhat the aura of a not-too-bright basset hound, tagging around after his master, but ready to come to his defense when needed. With outlaws he would often assume a false bravado and forcefully confront the villains face-to-face—as he does with the despicable Ace (George J. Lewis) in *Black Hills Express* with disastrous results:

> *Ace: (standing at the saloon bar) Hi, Deadeye. Have a drink?*
> *Deadeye: No, thanks. You made a pretty quick trip out of town and back again, didn't you, Ace? Kind of funny the stagecoach happened to be held up just about the same time. (Ace punches Deadeye in the face, sending him across a saloon table to the floor.)*
> *Ace: You shouldn't joke about things like that, Deadeye. You might give someone the wrong impression. I think I'll kick your teeth in for good measure. (Barry enters and comes to Deadeye's rescue, punching Ace into a deuce.)*
> *Deadeye: (acting very officious after Barry's fight) Remember, we'll have no more fighting around here. All right, break it up, break it up!*

A part of Vernon's comedy technique was to get words tangled or to talk at length and make no sense at all. At one point in **Black Hills Express** he malaprops the following speech:

> **Deadeye:** *A bunch of those outlaws jumped us, but I think they found out they bit off a little more than I could chew.*

When an old lady inquires about the safety of riding the stage, Vernon clearly responds:

> **Deadeye:** *Well, yes and then again, yes. You see, the stagecoaches are a little different these days than they were in the days before. Years ago it has been proven that—well, might I say, necessity is the mother of invention that gathers no rolling hand in the stone is worth two bushes in the glass house and freed all the slaves later on, of course. And that is my point. That is why stagecoaches are absolutely safe today.*
> **Old Lady:** *I feel so relieved. Thank you very much.*

I can't resist mentioning an interesting total aside pertaining to the **Black Hills Express** film. In the picture Barry is hired to capture a gang of stage robbers. In a montage sequence wanted posters are superimposed on the screen and crossed out with a black marker as Barry captures the holdup men. Two of the wanted posters contain pictures of Roy Barcroft, Republic's top outlaw actor, and Yakima Canutt, Republic actor, stuntman, and action-director—neither of whom actually appear in the film.

When Don Barry moseyed out of Republic's Western stable for a while, Vernon moved into Allan Lane's new starring series for two episodes: **Silver City Kid** (1944) and **Stagecoach to Monterey** (1944). The sidekick humor remained essentially the same, as did Vernon's costume. The costume worn by Allan Lane was the same as the one worn by Barry during most of his series. Republic was wise in the ways of saving money. By keeping the same costumes, they could use stock footage out of the Barry series.

After the two Lane episodes, Vernon then dropped out of series Westerns until his old buddy, Don Barry, called him back into action for a series he was making for Lippert Pictures in 1949 and '50. The first episode was a musical-variety Western featuring many musical performers and vaudeville-type acts. Such musical-variety talent as Spade Cooley,

Cowboy Copas, The Tumbleweed Tumblers, Max Terhune, and Britt Wood were on hand for the picture. The final four episodes in the series were more traditional B Westerns, with Robert Lowery co-starring with Barry. It was an extremely low-budget series which went almost unnoticed because of the onslaught of television by 1950.

Wally Vernon's tenure as a cowboy sidekick was brief and his suitability for such a role was surely questionable. To his credit, he was a likable actor who could handle the comic demands without becoming ludicrous, and, when given the opportunity, he could play a serious scene with genuine feeling and warmth. He died in 1970 at the age of sixty-five.

★   ★   ★

WALLY VERNON FILMOGRAPHY

DON "RED" BARRY series: (Republic Pictures)

Fugitive from Sonora (7/43)

Black Hills Express (8/43)

Man from the Rio Grande (10/43)

Canyon City (11/43)

California Joe (12/43)

Outlaws of Santa Fe (4/44) Emmett Lynn has a small part in this episode.

ALLAN LANE series: (Republic Pictures)

Silver City Kid (7/44)

Stagecoach to Monterey (9/44)

DON BARRY series: (Lippert Pictures)

Square Dance Jubilee (11/49) Former sidekicks Max Terhune and Britt Wood appear in this picture.

Gunfire (8/50) Robert Lowery co-stars with Don Barry in this and the next three films.

I Shot Billy the Kid (8/50)

Trail to Tombstone (9/50)

Border Rangers (10/50)

Wally Vernon and Allan Lane cautiously step from the mine in this scene from *Silver City Kid* (1944).

Eddy Waller was probably better known by the name Nugget Clark because of his long association with the character in the Allan "Rocky" Lane Western series.

EDDY WALLER

Eddy Waller was born in Wisconsin in 1889. He is the only actor I have ever researched who has managed to keep the activities of his early years out of the record books. Also, very few people I interviewed for this book had any knowledge of Eddy other than his fine work in front of the camera.

In 1936 he found his way to Hollywood and began an extremely active career as a character actor which continued until the late 1950s. His first film was **Rhythm on the Range** (1936), in which he played a judge of horse events. Bing Crosby was the star of the picture. Through the succeeding years Eddy played small character parts in major and minor films, always lending strong support to the leading players.

Eddy was the kind of character actor that stars loved to have in their casts. His acting was always excellent regardless of the size or type of role. Most of his roles called for him to play such mundane characters as a shopkeeper, a small rancher, an old prospector, a post office clerk, the town coroner, a jeweler, or a stage driver—none of which are very stimulating parts for an excellent actor. But Eddy Waller was different; he would take one of these "nothing parts" and make it into an interesting cameo.

In his screen work Eddy exuded the salt-of-the-earth human qualities of warmth, good humor, honesty, loyalty, integrity, and what we sometimes like to call the American pioneer spirit. Other character actors cited in this book had some of these characteristics—Raymond Hatton and Gabby Hayes in particular—but Eddy Waller managed to convey these qualities while playing mostly very small roles, and he rarely ever upstaged the stars while making a strong screen impression—an accomplishment that Ray Hatton and Gabby cannot claim.

One of Eddy's most impressive small roles was in Bill Elliott's 1941 picture entitled **Hands Across the Rockies.** Eddy plays the court judge in the film, a role listed twelfth in the cast. We don't see much of him until the trial scenes begin late in the picture, but from the time court convenes until the final decision is rendered, it is Eddy's picture. He is spellbinding as a judge who will brook no nonsense from anyone, who runs his court like a fine-tuned machine, and who champions law and order in the finest tradition of the old American West. Eddy conveys all of these character traits in a totally convincing manner, and yet he is hilariously funny throughout the scenes. It is a tour de force acting job in an otherwise forgettable film.

Eddy's cowboy sidekick career (except for occasional isolated roles) was confined to the Allan "Rocky" Lane series produced by Republic Pictures from 1947 through 1953. They made thirty-two pictures together during those years. Throughout the series Eddy played an "old coot" (as he was frequently described in the films) by the name of Nugget Clark.

Nugget was not the usual cowboy sidekick in that he frequently did not know Rocky Lane until the script situation introduced them and caused them to work together to right whatever wrong was being perpetrated. In each film Eddy had a different character background, but he was always called Nugget Clark, thus lending a sense of continuity to the role where there really was none.

The Rocky Lane series was well-produced by Republic despite the low budgets and remained popular with the fans until television killed off all the B Western series in the early 1950s. The enduring high respect for the series among Western fans is due mainly to the stringent personal demands for a quality product that were made by Allan Lane (who was grudgingly respected, but not generally liked by management and his co-workers) and the strong support that Eddy Waller provided the series.

After the Rocky Lane series concluded in 1953, Eddy continued his long career in short roles. He

Allan "Rocky" Lane and Eddy Waller pose for a publicity photo to promote their Republic Western series.

appeared in such films as *Man Without a Star* (1955) with Kirk Douglas, *The Far Country* (1955) starring James Stewart, and *Day of the Bad Man* (1958) with Fred MacMurray, Eddy's last film.

In 1955 he co-starred with Douglas Kennedy in the short-lived syndicated television series, "Steve Donovan, Western Marshal." He also played the role of Red Rock, the train conductor, in the 1957 television series entitled "Casey Jones." Alan Hale, Jr. starred and Cannonball Taylor was in the cast of this one-season series.

Eddy Waller lived quietly in retirement for twenty years, much in the way he had conducted his career. Even his death on August 9, 1977, was largely unnoticed by the show business community and the general public. Eddy Waller will be remembered, though, for Nugget Clark and for the other character roles which displayed his abundant talent.

★   ★   ★

EDDY WALLER FILMOGRAPHY

ALLAN "ROCKY" LANE series: (Republic Pictures)

The Wild Frontier (10/47)

Bandits of Dark Canyon (12/47)

Oklahoma Badlands (2/48)

The Bold Frontiersman (4/48)

Carson City Raiders (5/48)

Marshal of Amarillo (7/48)

Desperadoes of Dodge City (9/48)

The Denver Kid (11/48)

Sundown in Santa Fe (11/48)

Renegades of Sonora (11/48)

Sheriff of Wichita (1/49)

Death Valley Gunfighter (3/49)

Frontier Marshal (5/49)

Wyoming Bandit (7/49)

Bandit King of Texas (8/49)

Navajo Trail Raiders (10/49)

Powder River Rustlers (11/49)

Gunmen of Abilene (2/50)

Code of the Silver Sage (3/50)

Salt Lake Raiders (5/50)

Covered Wagon Raid (6/50)

Vigilante Hideout (8/50)

Frisco Tornado (10/50)

Rustlers on Horseback (10/50)

Leadville Gunslinger (3/52)

Black Hills Ambush (5/52)

Thundering Caravans (7/52)

Desperadoes' Outpost (10/52)

The graveyard seems to have Nugget spooked in this scene from *Bandits of Dark Canyon* (1947).

Rocky and Nugget shoot it out with the outlaws in their last series episode for Republic, *El Paso Stampede* (1953).

Marshal of Cedar Rock (5/53)

Savage Frontier (5/53)

Bandits of the West (8/53)

El Paso Stampede (9/53)

GUY WILKERSON

Guy Wilkerson played Panhandle Perkins in the very low budget PRC trio series called The Texas Rangers! Wilkerson was born in 1901 near Katy, Texas. His background, like so many of the other sidekicks, was in tent shows, minstrels, vaudeville, and burlesque. And like the others he brought his trunkful of comic gimcracks with him into his Western films. He played small roles in many films before and after the Texas Rangers series, but he is best remembered for his Panhandle character and for his role of Tennessee in the classic film, *Sergeant York* (1941).

Wilkerson's two pals for the first fourteen entries in the twenty-two episode series were Dave O'Brien and James Newill. Newill had a trained singing voice and would occasionally stop the action to render a Western ballad or two. For the last eight episodes Tex Ritter took over for Newill, and the musical style changed from James Newill's full-voiced, Broadway stage delivery to Tex's downhome Western twang. The voices were so different that it was a matter of personal preference for the audience as to which was better. Since the series was obviously aimed at a mostly juvenile assemblage, a vote would probably have eliminated the vocalizing altogether.

Guy Wilkerson was a tall string bean of a galoot who generally drawled out his words at a molasses-in-winter tempo unless aroused to reluctant action because of some script consideration. The comedy that he provided was seldom of the slapstick variety and was often just a humorous touch to the proceedings. It was a rarity for comic sequences to be built into the scripts.

Spook Town (1944), one of the last pictures with O'Brien and Newill, did provide Wilkerson with the rare opportunity for broad humor, and he played it to a fare-thee-well. The setting for most of the film was a ghost town. Most of the comic sequences took place at night inside the darkened, deserted buildings. The exaggerated antics included the sudden entrance of a sheet-covered mule which

Panhandle, amid much fear and trembling, assumed was some sort of four-legged ghost. Later, an oil lamp mysteriously brightened and then darkened as the terrified Panhandle—glazed eyes widened to poached-egg size—scrambled out of the premises.

In *Gangsters of the Frontier*, the first episode with Tex Ritter, Wilkerson's comic behavior was more typical of his usual contribution to the series. The film provided him with an occasional funny line here and there, the comic use of his skeletal, gangly body, and a laugh-provoking fight with comic villain Charlie King in which he gets the befuddled King dizzy in a swivel chair just before he knocks him silly.

The Panhandle Perkins character was not too bright when it came to providing strategy for the capture of the outlaws in the various films. In fact, it badly stretched script credulity to believe that the Texas Rangers would even let such a thimble brain into their illustrious ranks. But that's carping, of course. Panhandle may not have had too much going on beneath his curled brim, high-crowned, ten-gallon hat, but he was a likable and comical cuss who did the job that was expected of him in the scripts; he added a touch of humor to the sagebrush proceedings.

Oliver Drake smiled warmly when I mentioned Guy Wilkerson to him.

> **Oliver Drake:** Guy Wilkerson, bless his heart. I wrote four or five of the Texas Rangers films and directed them. These were with Dave O'Brien and Jimmy Newill. They were all really pros, and Guy Wilkerson was a very funny guy—funnier than most gave him credit for. He was a nice guy to work with, too.
>
> I remember we did one picture where they put him in jail with an outlaw to try to find out where the outlaw had hidden a treasure. The outlaw, Charlie King,

It looks as if Mary McLaren has eyes for the lady-shy Panhandle in this scene from *Fighting Valley* (1943). Dave O'Brien, Patti McCarthy, and Jim Newill seem to enjoy Panhandle's predicament.

draws the map to the treasure on the bottom of Guy's foot while he's asleep. A little later they escape together. Wilkerson, not knowing anything about the map, takes off his socks and throws them away and washes his feet. Well, the map ends up on the bottom of the socks, and, fortunately, the socks are retrieved and the treasure is eventually found. It was a funny bit in the picture. Wilkerson was a good comedian and a funny man. He was a tall drink of water!

Guy was a very quiet person off camera. He wasn't at all in person like he was on the screen. Most comedians are very serious people. Fuzzy Knight was serious, for example. Wilkerson was not funny at all off screen, but he became funny when you saw him in a picture.

There wasn't much improvisation in the Texas Rangers series as far as Wilkerson's comedy was concerned; they pretty much stuck to the script. It wasn't like a Fuzzy Knight who would ad lib a lot of things. Wilkerson played more of a serious part. All three stars in the Texas Rangers series were pretty much equal. It was patterned after The Three Mesquiteers, and Wilkerson's character was fairly serious like Max Terhune in that series.

While the Texas Rangers series was a far cry from the highly respected and well-remembered Three Mesquiteers films made by Republic Pictures, it, nevertheless, was fairly popular in its time. The popularity that it did have was primarily due to the on-screen rapport of its stars, and much of that can be placed at the large feet of Guy Wilkerson.

Guy Wilkerson died on July 15, 1971, at the age of seventy.

★   ★   ★

GUY WILKERSON FILMOGRAPHY

THE TEXAS RANGERS series (O'Brien and Newill):
(PRC Pictures)

The Rangers Take Over (12/42)

Bad Men of Thunder Gap (3/43)

West of Texas (5/43)

Border Buckaroos (6/43)

Fighting Valley (8/43)

Trail of Terror (9/43)

Return of the Rangers (10/43) Emmett Lynn has a small part in this episode.

Boss of Rawhide (11/43)

Gunsmoke Mesa (1/44)

Outlaw Roundup (2/44)

Guns of the Law (3/44)

The Pinto Bandit (4/44)

Spook Town (6/44)

A lot of the Saturday matinee kids are probably headed for the popcorn machine about now, but Tex Ritter fans are enjoying his rendering of another Western ballad. Guy Wilkerson, Lorraine Miller, and two unidentified cowhands certainly seem to be happy to have this little musical interlude.

Guy Wilkerson and outlaw John Cason both seem startled to be suddenly face-to-face in this comic shoot out from *Spook Town* (1944).

Brand of the Devil (7/44)

THE TEXAS RANGERS series (O'Brien and Tex Ritter): (PRC Pictures)

Gangsters of the Frontier (9/44)

Dead or Alive (11/44)

The Whispering Skull (12/44)

Marked for Murder (2/45)

Enemy of the Law (5/45)

Three in the Saddle (7/45)

Frontier Fugitives (9/45)

Flaming Frontier (10/45)

GUINN "BIG BOY" WILLIAMS

Jock Mahoney: He was one, big beautiful man. As a matter of fact, he was a lawyer, you know, from Texas. He was very intelligent and could drink warm beer; I never could do that. (laugh) When I was a young buck doing a picture, I was always the type of guy who was never pushy in any way. Anyhow, a bunch of the guys who were playing the heavies were, Big Boy said, "taking advantage of me." He said, "You can't let them do that, Jocko." I said, "Oh, no, they're just funning." He said, "No, they're not funning."

So later, during the big scene that we were to do, I was to knock out the guys and he was to pick them up and put them in a big walk-in safe—loading them like cord wood. (laugh) Big Boy Williams was a big, tough man. I mean, he was muscular and he could handle himself. Well, he picked up those guys and threw them into that walk-in safe a little rougher than was necessary according to the script. When the scene was over, he had dented more heads than you can imagine. He said to them, "There, now you be a little bit nicer to Jocko." (laugh) Oh, Big Boy was a good man!

He was a nice, easygoing character, but you didn't want to cross him. He was jovial and outgoing as long as you were "straight arrow" with him, but you didn't want to cross Big Boy. He wasn't easy to anger, but you didn't want to push him into a corner. If you did, he was likely to come out like a big bear.

Victor Jory, a frequent Western film heavy, gave a first-hand account (at the 1979 St. Louis Western Film Fair) of the ferociousness of Big Boy Williams

when his temper was aroused. The incident occurred while they were on location for Errol Flynn's picture, *Dodge City*.

Victor Jory had a slight altercation with Big Boy during the filming of *Dodge City* (1939).

Victor Jory: Ward Bond and Guinn "Big Boy" Williams were very close to Flynn. I think he sicked them on me one at a time. I gave Mr. Bond his broken nose which you notice he carried with him through "Wagon Train," because he couldn't hit me with a handful of confetti. Then Big Boy Williams came up to my

Guinn Williams got his nickname from Will Rogers when they worked together in an early silent film.

room. He yelled, "I'm going to break the door in because you have my girl in there." I had nobody in there. I said, "Big Boy, don't do it because I'm going to break a chair over your head if you do." So he came through the door like it was a paper hoop, and I broke the chair over his head. I hit him several times, driving him out into the hall. I clamped a headlock on him, hoping I'd get him unconscious. I held him until my arm began to go to sleep. When I tried to loosen up, he said, "You'd better not let go!"

I could have killed him outside where I would have had room to move, but I didn't have room to move and finally my arm went to sleep and I stood up. He said, "I'm going to throw you out of the third-story window." I thought that would be fun! I got hold of a fire extinguisher just as the police came up, thank God.

They said, "You're both under arrest for fighting." I said, "We're not fighting; we're just having a little rough and tumble fun." I guess Big Boy liked that. The police said, "Well, go to bed and stop all of this." Big Boy said, "You're all right, Victor." He took hold of my pajamas and when he pulled his hand away, I had no pajamas. He said, "Let's have a drink." I had a quart of gin in my room. We went into my room with no door and he poured me a drink in a small glass and poured the rest into a water pitcher. While I drank the glass, he drank the water pitcher.

Buster Crabbe recalled an incident with Big Boy while they were working on a Western together.

Buster Crabbe: He was a great big husky guy, you know. It was a Randy Scott Western we were working on—can't remember the name. We filmed it just outside of Lake Arrowhead. Timberline, I think, was the name of the place, and Big Boy was supposed to rustle this damned mule, throw it over. He tried to pick up the mule to turn it over, but the mule braced and Big Boy couldn't do anything with the damned thing. At one point Big Boy bent over and the mule kicked him right in the fanny—moved him real quick about three feet. We kept that in; it was in the final cut of the film. Big Boy was a nice guy.

Guinn "Big Boy" Williams, despite the fact that he starred, co-starred, and played featured roles in dozens of major and B Westerns during his long career, hardly qualifies for this book. The only B Western series in which he played a comic sidekick was the Roy Rogers series, and that was for only two films. Big Boy also appeared frequently in a hard-to-categorize musical-Western-comedy series Columbia Pictures made in the mid-1940s starring Ken Curtis and a rotating group of mostly Western musical and variety entertainers. In this mercifully mostly forgotten hodgepodge series, Big Boy played a variety of comic roles, but he would not be classified as a sidekick.

Guinn had two shots at the Three Mesquiteers series, appearing in the Normandy Pictures production of **Law of the 45's** (1935) as Tucson and RKO Radio Pictures' **Powdersmoke Range** (1935) as Lullaby. He was the first actor to play the role of Lullaby Joslin. When Republic Pictures acquired the rights to the Three Mesquiteers stories, they selected an entirely new cast for the series, so Big Boy never appeared in the Three Mesquiteers films when they were a series.

Guinn Williams was an authentic cowboy, born on April 26, 1900, in Decatur, Texas. He studied law at North Texas State College and was a rodeo performer before he headed for Hollywood and silent films. Will Rogers tagged him with the nickname of Big Boy when the overgrown Texan worked as an extra in a 1919 Rogers film. He and Rogers remained friends and polo pals until Rogers' tragic death.

By the mid-1920s Guinn had achieved star status in Westerns and was able to carry his success into sound pictures of the 1930s. During 1934 and '35 he starred in his final series of Westerns which was made by a shoe-string company called Beacon/First Division. Despite his rugged, masculine features, Guinn's facial appearance worked against him in hero roles. Whenever he smiled, his grin was that of a good-hearted simpleton. He was just out of place as a cowboy hero.

Gradually, Big Boy became a popular featured actor in a long string of Westerns and supported most of the Western stars of that period, quite often in major productions. He was with Errol Flynn (a buddy) in **Dodge City** (1939) and **Virginia City** (1940), Robert Taylor in **Billy the Kid** (1941), and Randolph Scott and Glenn Ford in **The Desperados.**

In 1944 he joined Roy Rogers as a sidekick for two films in which he played the role of Teddy Bear. Various reviewers have described his stock-in-trade character as exuding "baffled dumbness," being "dull-witted," or a "happy-go-lucky, perplexed muscular type." All of these descriptions fit Big

Guinn appeared in a variety of roles in the inane Columbia Pictures series of musical-Western-comedies starring Ken Curtis. This publicity photo of Ken spanking Big Boy provides an idea of the foolishness which transpired in this quickie series.

During their first encounter in *Hands Across the Border* (1944) Guinn Williams tries to steal Roy's horse. Roy finds the bumbling attempt so humorous that he nicknames him Teddy Bear because he's like "a big ol' cuddly teddy bear."

Boy's screen persona. His Teddy Bear role with Rogers was typical, but included a gentleness or "cuddly" quality that was often hidden under his rough-hewn, grizzly bear exterior.

Williams continued to appear in a variety of roles during the 1950s and early 1960s with such stars as Dick Powell, Randy Scott, and Gary Cooper. His last role was with John Wayne in *The Comancheros* (1962). Guinn "Big Boy" Williams died of uremic poisoning on June 6, 1962.

★   ★   ★

GUINN "BIG BOY" WILLIAMS FILMOGRAPHY

ROY ROGERS series: (Republic Pictures)

Hands Across the Border (1/44)

The Cowboy and the Senorita (5/44) Fuzzy Knight is also in the cast for a few laughs.

Teddy Bear, Roy, Duncan Renaldo, and the Sons of the Pioneers (background) look to boss lady Ruth Terry for guidance in this tense scene from *Hands Across the Border* (1944).

George O'Brien calms leading lady June Cameron in this scene from *Trouble in Sundown* (1939). Howard Hickman, Ray Whitley, and Chill Wills have nothing to do and are doing it well.

CHILL WILLS

Chill Wills: *I started out singing with my brothers in Texas. My father played a little guitar and taught us how to sing. We went to the Baptist church revivals and sang. The reason we went to the Baptist church was that they were the most tolerant to listen to us. We'd sing for anybody. I've been through all the facets of show business. From medicine shows on up to tent shows to dramatic stock to burlesque to motion pictures. And every morning that I earn the love of the American people I think I get taller and taller and taller. [Then, mocking his own sentimentality] THIS IS CHILL WILLS; THIS IS A RECORDING.*

Eddie Dean: *Chill was a very fine actor. He also played the guitar and sang some. He had a group called the Avalon Boys. Chill did some of the earliest Hoppy pictures with the Avalon Boys. When he became an actor, he didn't need the other.*

There are two versions regarding how Chill Wills acquired his unusual first name. The story that Chill liked to tell was that he was born on the hottest July 18th (1903) ever recorded in the history of his hometown of Seagoville, Texas. Another version of the story is that he was named after the horse and buggy doctor who delivered him—Dr. Chillin. You can take your choice of stories.

What follows regarding Chill's early career is probably a mixture of fact and publicity-release fiction. It is information I have gathered from Chill (who was known to "dress-up" history) and from a release that was issued at the time of his death. Here goes:

Chill Wills began singing as a "falsetto tenor" in church choirs when he was nine years old and was soon earning five dollars per engagement at local parties (a handsome sum for those times). When he was fifteen, he left home and headed for Chicago where his country cousin characterization brought him work in burlesque. Success in burlesque led to vaudeville and eventually New York where he became (reportedly) a six-hundred-dollar-a-week master of ceremonies.

As Chill reached maturity, his voice grew distinctive— deep, gravelly, and expressive. He

*Hello Cousin
Was Just Ruminatin'
'Bout You
Chill Wills*

once claimed his voice degenerated as his salary rose.

Chill's vaudeville success allowed him to climb another step up the show business ladder to high-class dinner clubs. Presently, he found himself at the posh Trocadero in Hollywood where he was spotted by film studio scouts and eventually became a top character actor in motion pictures.

It is a bit disconcerting that the above summary of Chill's early career does not make the link between his work at the posh Trocadero and the reality of "Chill Wills and His Avalon Boys" making their brief screen debut in a 1935 Hopalong Cassidy picture called **Bar 20 Rides Again.** In show business terms the Trocadero and the Bar 20 are "a fur piece away from each other." Nevertheless, Chill did appear with his Avalon Boys in several Hoppy pictures and continued in B Westerns for several years before he was "discovered" by the big studios.

Chill Wills would eventually spend more than sixty years in show business, but only a very short period of that time was as a cowboy sidekick in series Westerns. In fact, his only series was with George O'Brien in 1938 and 1939. He made six pictures with O'Brien and was not a sidekick in all of them.

Oliver Drake was writing the screenplays for the George O'Brien pictures when Chill was brought in as a possible comic sidekick. Ollie told me how it all came about.

> *Oliver Drake: We were looking for someone who might serve as a sidekick for George O'Brien. Ray Whitley brought a guy over one day whom he had met on one of his tours. He said, "This is a very funny guy, and he's been a vaudevillian." Ray also introduced him to Burt Gilroy, who was the producer of the O'Brien pictures. Well, the fellow Ray introduced to us was Chill Wills.*
>
> *Gilroy said to me, "You take Chill Wills for a couple of weeks and see what kind of character you can work out for him. If you come up with an interesting character, we'll use him in the George O'Brien pictures."*
>
> *So Chill and I sat down and talked and yakked. We finally ended up with a character called Whopper, which is the character he eventually played in the O'Brien series. I worked out the character with him and wrote the first stories he was in as Whopper. We were trying to get away from the usual type of sidekick. If*

you started adding up the sidekicks, they all looked and acted pretty much alike. So somewhere in the shuffle—whether I suggested it or he did—we came up with this guy who was always telling tall tales, and we called him Whopper.

Chill summed up his experience in the George O'Brien pictures very succinctly at the 1976 Orlando Western Film Festival.

> *Chill Wills: I did about four or five pictures with George O'Brien. George was all right, but he came up and put his arm around me one day and said, "You're going to do good in these pictures [Westerns], but you ain't goin' to be in no more of mine.*

Chill's big break in films came in 1939 when he was cast with Clark Gable and Spencer Tracy in MGM's **Boom Town.** Eddie Dean remembers the day Chill got his contract for the picture.

> *Eddie Dean: Chill and I both lived in Burbank at the time. We used to get our groceries at the same little store. My wife and I were in there one day when Chill came in and hollered all the way across the store, "I just got a job in **Boom Town** with Clark Gable and Spencer Tracy. I've got the contract." He was the happiest guy I ever saw. The other people in the store looked around as if he was crazy. Chill was not exactly inhibited. He was so proud, you know, and that's the movie that really gave him his break.*

After the success of **Boom Town**, Chill was on his way to a highly successful film career as a character actor in Westerns and most other types of pictures. Over the years his outstanding films included **Honky Tonk** (1941) with Clark Gable and Lana Turner, **Meet Me in St. Louis** (1944) with Judy Garland, **The Yearling** (1946) starring Gregory Peck, **Rio Grande** (1950) with John Wayne, **Giant** (1956) with Rock Hudson and Elizabeth Taylor, **The Alamo** (1960) starring John Wayne, and **McLintock** (1963) again with Wayne. In addition, Chill was the voice of Francis the Talking Mule is seven very popular films made during the 1950s.

Television never treated Chill too kindly. He starred in two brief series: "Frontier Circus" (1961-1962) which co-starred John Derek and Richard Jaeckel; and "The Rounders" (1966-1967), a comedy Western series with Ron Hayes and

That may be a grin on Chill's face, but I'd be careful. This publicity photo reveals another facet from Chill's bag of acting tricks.

Patrick Wayne (John's son) sharing the starring honors with Chill.

At one time during the 1960s, Chill considered running for governor of Texas. He told a reporter at the time, "I'm a professional Texan and proud of it. I could take a sack of rattrap cheese and crackers and walk the length and breadth of that proud land and shoot Connally and Smith (two former governors) out of the saddle at the same time with one shot." His remarks sounded strangely reminiscent of his Whopper character from the old George O'Brien pictures.

Chill Wills was one of the great character actors of motion pictures. He was in a league with such performers as Walter Brennan, George Hayes, Edgar Buchanan, Wallace Beery, and Andy Devine. Chill could be gentle or he could be tough; he could bring a smile to your face one minute and a tear to your eye the next; he could be irascible and then give the shirt off his back. From wheeler-dealer to country cousin, Chill Wills was whatever the director wanted him to be in a film, and he was always excellent.

Chill Wills died of cancer at his Encino, California, home on Friday, December 16, 1978. He had been released from the Motion Picture Home Hospital just a few hours previously so that he could be with his family at home when death came.

We all miss ya, Cousin.

★　　　★　　　★

CHILL WILLS FILMOGRAPHY

GEORGE O'BRIEN series: (RKO Pictures)

Lawless Valley (11/38) Chill plays a deputy sheriff named Speedy McGow in his first episode. Kirby Grant has a small role in the picture.

Arizona Legion (1/39) Chill plays Whopper Hatch for the first time in this film.

Trouble in Sundown (3/39) Chill is called Tombstone in this picture.

Racketeers of the Range (6/39) Chill is Whopper again.

Timber Stampede (6/39) This is Chill's last George O'Brien film and his last appearance as Whopper.

It looks as if the skirmish is just about over as George O'Brien restrains a very youthful and slim Chill Wills. That's Ward Bond thinking about drawing his gun. The scene is from *Trouble in Sundown* (1939).

BRITT WOOD

Britt Wood was practically born in the proverbial theatrical trunk in 1895. While still a young boy, Britt entered vaudeville as a highly-skilled harmonica player. As he matured, he added comedy to his act and eventually reached the pinnacle of vaudeville success by repeatedly playing the famous Palace Theater in New York. When vaudeville went belly up, Britt headed for Hollywood where he found sporadic work between personal appearance gigs. He never made it big in show business after his early vaudeville success, but he was always on the fringes of the uncertain business of show.

Britt Wood's only Western series sidekick role was in five Hopalong Cassidy films made in 1939 and 1940. Britt was brought into the Hoppy pictures when Gabby Hayes left the series for a contract with Republic Pictures.

Producer Harry Sherman and star Bill Boyd tried several comics in their attempt to successfully replace the Windy Halliday character that George Hayes had made so popular in the series. Britt Wood came close to succeeding with his character of Speedy McGinnis, a harmonica-playing, slow-talking, raspy-voiced, pessimistic, droopy-eyed, hound-dog-faced lump of a man.

The Speedy character was rather intriguing for a film or two, but familiarity soon bred discontent, if not contempt. He was an interesting codger to ride to town with once or twice, but you wouldn't want him as a constant trail mate. In short, Speedy didn't wear well. When Hoppy found California Carlson (Andy Clyde), it was all over for Speedy.

Britt continued in films for many years after the Hoppy pictures, playing featured and bit parts in pictures with Charles Starrett, Lash LaRue, Gene Autry, Don Barry, Randy Scott, and many other popular stars. Generally, you had to look quickly or you missed Britt in these films. A good example of the frequent brevity of his roles can be found in the Ronald Reagan remake of the classic Western film, **Law and Order** (1953). In the film Marshal Reagan initiates a new policy of "no guns to be worn in town." Shortly after Reagan posts the notice of the new ordinance, a drunken Britt Wood stumbles out of the saloon bearing two six-guns. In a flash Marshal Reagan relieves the inebriated Britt of his weapons, leaving him standing there on the dusty street with a stunned expression on his hangdog face. That's the last we ever see of Britt in the picture.

Singing cowboy Eddie Dean was one of the few performers I talked with who remembered Britt with any clarity.

> **Eddie Dean:** *I worked a lot of shows with Britt Wood before he became Hoppy's sidekick and also afterwards. We were good friends. I remember he wrote a song called "Titanic" that he sat down at the piano and sang for me around 1950. I wanted him to make a recording of it because soon after that they made a picture called **Titanic**. I think he could have had a big recording on it. He was so great doing the song. It was blues and told the story of the Titanic. He played it on the piano with the old blues licks, you know.*
>
> *Britt passed away years ago [April 16, 1965]. I went to his funeral. In fact, I was supposed to be one of the pallbearers, but I'd just had an appendectomy, so I couldn't do my share.*

★   ★   ★

BRITT WOOD FILMOGRAPHY

HOPALONG CASSIDY series (William Boyd): (Paramount Pictures)

Range War (9/39)

Harmonica-playing Britt Wood is seen here in his role of Speedy McGinnis from the Hopalong Cassidy series.

Santa Fe Marshal (1/40) Britt plays a character called Axel in this episode.

The Showdown (3/40)

Hidden Gold (6/40)

Stagecoach War (7/40)

Britt scratches his head and looks as if he might be about to say, "A funny thing happened to me on my way to a Hollywood career." The scene is from *The Return of the Durango Kid* (1945).

Bibliography

Printed Sources:

Aaronson, Charles S. *1963 International Motion Picture Almanac.* New York: Quigley, 1963.

Adams, Les, and Rainey, Buck. *Shoot-Em-Ups.* New York: Arlington House, 1978.

Autry, Gene, with Mickey Herskowitz. *Back In the Saddle Again.* New York: Doubleday, 1978.

Brooks, Tim and Marsh, Earle. *Complete Directory to Prime Time Network TV Shows.* New York: Ballantine, 1979.

Calio, Jim. "His Horse Is Champion, His Angels Are Not, But Gene Autry Can Dream." *People* (May 26, 1980).

Canutt, Yakima, with Oliver Drake. *Stunt Man.* New York: Walker, 1979.

Carman, Bob, and Scapperotti, Dan. *Rex Allen—The Arizona Cowboy.* (privately published), 1982.

_____. *Roy Rogers, King of the Cowboys, A Film Guide.* (privately published), 1979.

_____. *The Western Films of Sunset Carson.* (privately published), 1981.

Dellinger, Paul. "Chito!" *Under Western Skies.* (No. 21, November, 1982).

_____. "Sunset Carson, The Action Man." *Under Western Skies.* (No. 8, October, 1979).

DeMarco, Mario. *Gallant Defender, The Durango Kid, Charles Starrett.* (privately published).

_____. *Republic's Wild & Wooley Western Heroes, Heroines, Heavies & Side-Kicks.* (privately published).

Dunning, John. *Tune in Yesterday.* New Jersey: Prentice-Hall, 1976.

Everson, William K. *A Pictorial History of the Western Film.* New York: Citadel, 1969.

Fenin, George N. and Everson, William K. *The Western.* New York: Bonanza Books, 1962.

Fernett, Gene. *Hollywood's Poverty Row.* Satellite Beach, Florida: Coral Reef Publications, 1973.

Griffis, Ken. *Hear My Song.* Los Angeles: John Edwards Memorial Foundation, Inc., 1977.

Garfield, Brian. *Western Films.* New York: Rawson Associates, 1982.

Grossman, Gary H. *Saturday Morning TV.* New York: Dell, 1981.

Halliwell, Leslie. *Filmgoer's Companion, The.* New York: Avon, 1971.

Hanley, Loretta, ed. *Series, Serials and Packages.* New York: Broadcast Information Bureau, Inc., Volume 15: Issue 2D, 1974.

Hurst, Richard Maurice. *Republic Studios: Between Poverty Row and the Majors.* New Jersey: Scarecrow Press, 1979.

Lackey, Wayne, and Smith, M.P. "Smiley Burnette's Career." *Western Film Collector* (March, 1973).

Lamparski, Richard. *Whatever Became Of. . . ?* Volumes 1, 2, 3, 4, 5, and 8. New York: Crown, 1967-1982.

_____. *Whatever Became of*. . . *?* New York: Bantam Books, 1976.

Leonard, John W. *Wild Bill Elliott.* (privately published), 1976.

Loppnow, Ray. "Whip Wilson: Hero With a Bullwhip." *Under Western Skies* (No. 5, January, 1979).

Maltin, Leonard. *Disney Films, The.* New York: Crown, 1973.

Martelle, Joe. "Tim Holt Remembered." *The Big Reel* (June, 1983).

McClure, Arthur F., and Jones, Ken D. *Heroes, Heavies and Sagebrush.* South Brunswick and New York: A.S. Barnes, 1972.

Meyer, William R. *Making of the Great Westerns, The*. New York: Arlington House, 1979.

Meyers, Monica. *Crashing Thru—My Life with Whip Wilson.* St. Louis: Robert T. Shockey, 1981.

Michael, Paul, ed. *American Movies Reference Book, The.* New Jersey: Prentice-Hall, 1970.

Miller, Don. *Hollywood Corral.* New York: Popular Library, 1976.

Miller, Lee O. *Great Cowboy Stars of Movies & Television, The.* New York: Arlington House, 1979.

New York Times Film Reviews, 1913-1968, The. New York: The New York Times and Arno Press. 1970.

Parish, James Robert. *Great Movie Series, The.* South Brunswick and New York: A.S. Barnes, 1971.

Parkinson, Michael, and Jeavons, Clyde. *Pictorial History of Westerns, A.* London, Hamlyn, 1972.

Pontes, Bob. "Favorite Westerns Interviews Fred Scott." *Favorite Westerns* (No. 10, April, 1983).

Rainey, Buck. *Fabulous Holts, The.* Nashville: Western Film Collector Press, 1976.

_____. *Saddle Aces of the Cinema.* San Diego: A.S. Barnes, 1980.

_____, assisted by Les Adams. "Lash & Fuzzy Too." *Under Western Skies* (No. 10, May, 1980).

Rogers, Roy, and Evans, Dale, and Stowers, Carlton. *Happy Trails.* Texas: Word Books, 1979.

Roper, William L. *Roy Rogers, King of the Cowboys.* Minneapolis: T.S. Denison, 1971.

Rothel, David. *The Singing Cowboys.* South Brunswick and New York: A.S. Barnes, 1978.

Rutherford, John A. "Better Known as 'Jingles'." *Under Western Skies* (No. 23, May, 1983).

_____. "Cisco's Pals." *Under Western Skies* (No. 15, July, 1981).

_____. "Don't Call Me 'Oldtimer'." *Under Western Skies* (No. 13, March, 1981).

_____. "Fuzzy Q. Jones." *Under Western Skies* (No. 10, May, 1980).

_____. "Gabby." *Under Western Skies* (No. 7, July, 1979).

_____. "Lullaby—The Third Mesquiteer." *Under Western Skies* (No. 16, November, 1981).

_____. " 'Nugget' Clark." *Under Western Skies* (No. 20, July, 1982).

_____. "Pards of Tex Ritter, The." *Under Western Skies* (No. 22, January, 1983).

_____. "Paul Hurst: From Heavy to Sidekick." *Under Western Skies* (No. 21, November, 1982).

_____. "Sidekick with a Burr." *Under Western Skies* (No. 14, May, 1981).

Schiller, Ralph. "Where is the Cisco Kid?" *Under Western Skies* (No. 7, July, 1979).

Scott, Vernon. "Pickings Not Slim for Pickens." *UPI* (September, 1979).

Shelton, Robert, and Goldblatt, Burt. *Country Music Story, The.* New Jersey: Castle Books, 1971.

Smith, III, Richard B. *B Westerns in Perspective.* (privately published), (Issues No. 1 through 12; January, 1983 through February, 1984).

_____. "Those Unforgettable Saddle Pals." *The Big Reel* (August, 1983).

Spivey, O.D. "Smiley (Frog Millhouse) Burnette." *Under Western Skies* (No. 1, January, 1978).

Strauss, David P. and Worth, Fred L. *Hollywood Trivia.* New York: Warner Books, 1981.

Stumpf, Charles K. "Slim Pickens." *Under Western Skies* (No. 23, May, 1983).

Swilling, Herb. "I Talked with Dub 'Cannonball' Taylor." *Favorite Westerns* (No. 15, September, 1983).

Terhune, Tracy. "Max Terhune As I Knew Him." *Nostalgia Monthly* (No. 9, September, 1978)

Tuska, Jon. *Filming of the West, The.* New York: Doubleday, 1976.

Twomey, Alfred E., and McClure, Arthur F. *Versatiles, The.* New York: Castle, 1969.

Variety (Files from 1934 through 1955).

Williams, Nick. "The Western Sidekick." *Western Film Collector* (March, 1973).

_____. "Three Comedians of the Horse Opera." *The Real Stars #2.* New York: Curtis Books, 1973.

Zinman, David. *Saturday Afternoon at the Bijou.* New York: Arlington House, 1973.

Personal interviews:

Rex Allen (7/76)

Slim Andrews (7/83)

Gene Autry (1/77)

Jim Bannon (7/82)

Don Barry (7/79)

Rand Brooks (7/82)

Ewing Brown (7/82)

Yakima Canutt (7/79)

Sunset Carson (3/82)

Buster Crabbe (5/82)

Eddie Dean (6/82)

Oliver Drake (7/82)

Tommy Farrell (7/83)

Carolyn Grant (7/82)

Kirby Grant (7/82)

Clark Hayes (7/82)

Pee Wee King (7/83)

Lash LaRue (8/82)

Gordon MacDonnell (5/82)

Petria MacDonnell (5/82 and 3/84)

Jock Mahoney (6/82)

Frank Mitchell (7/83)

Roy Rogers (1/77)

Charles Starrett (6/82)

Jimmy Wakely (6/82)

Film festivals: (Guest Star Forums)

Florida Mid-Winter Western Film Round-Up (February, 1976)

Nashville Western Film Festival (July, 1976)

HoustonCon '77 (June, 1977)

St. Louis Western Film Fair (July, 1978-1979)

Charlotte Western Film Fair (July, 1980-1983)

Tifton, Georgia, Western Film Festival (March, 1982)

Memphis Film Festival (August, 1982-1983)

Miscellaneous sources:

"John Davidson Show, The." Group W Productions (April 1, 1982).

" 'Happy Trails' with Roy Rogers and Dale Evans." The Disney Channel (November, 1983).

Film Index

General Index